GW01048600

From Fallow Fields to Hallowed Halls

From
Fallow
Fields to
Hallowed
Halls
A Theologian's Journey

John Dillenberger

From Fallow Fields to Hallowed Halls: A Theologian's Journey

Published in 2004 by Polebridge Press, P.O. Box 6144, Santa Rosa, California 95406.

Copyright © 2004 by John Dillenberger

All rights reserved. Printed in the United States of America. No part of this book may be used or reproduced in any manner whatsoever without written permission except in the case of brief quotations embodied in critical articles and reviews. For information address Polebridge Press, P.O. Box 6144, Santa Rosa, California 95406.

ISBN 0-944344-52-6

Library of Congress Cataloging-in-Publication Data

Dillenberger, John.
    From fallow fields to hallowed halls : a theologian's journey / John Dillenberger.
        p. cm.
    Includes bibliographical references.
    ISBN 0-944344-52-6
    1. Dillenberger, John. 2. Theologians--United States--Biography. I. Title.

BX4827.D55A3 2004
230'.092--dc22
[B]

2004048831

This book is dedicated to Jean, whose love, curiosity, and wide-ranging knowledge continue to stretch my horizons.

Table of Contents

THREE/CONTINUING REFLECTIONS

PHOTOS

Preface
A NARRATIVE PROFILE

After I retired in the year 2000, various persons kept asking me, What are you going to do next? Some of them said you have been at interesting places at pivotal times and have participated in forming their futures. In short, your life has been intertwined with developments in the last eight decades of the twentieth century. You should tell us how you became part of them, and what it was like, particularly as you experienced them. When Polebridge Press expressed interest in the project, the last excuse for not doing it fell away.

Still, I was clearer in what I did not want to do than in what shape it should take. I knew I did not want to write a history of my life, though historical aspects have dominated my work. I did not want to write how I experienced things, since I am somewhat uncomfortable with the subjective. I did not want it to be a theological tract, though theological currents have been a central part of my life. I did not want it to be anecdotal, though I know many stories that illumine how I perceived and was perceived and so could not ignore them. So I decided simply to write, and I hoped that letting it flow as I relived it would disclose some things of interest, perhaps of importance, and that ambiguity and humor might be as apparent as the few certainties I disclosed. In retrospect it is clear that historical sequence won out, that doing so made it possible to write mostly in the present tense with backward and forward glances on developing themes.

From early on I was sure I would not stay on the Mississippi Valley farm on which I grew up, though I was not sure what I would do. The business world was one possibility, perhaps as an accountant, like one of my uncles. Another was the Christian ministry, which my parents thought was desirable if I were not going to stay on the farm. I went to Elmhurst College, an institution that could be a feeder to almost any profession. Any tendency toward business was soon side tracked as I was captivated at Elmhurst College by the lectures of Paul Lehmann on religion and theology. After college, I went to Union Theological Seminary in New York City for three years because I had won a scholarship and was interested in the theological stars on its faculty.

After two and a half years as a Navy chaplain, I returned to Union to read for a few months before taking a parish. As a chaplain my commitment to the parish was, if anything, reinforced. Doctoral work was not on the horizon until I was asked to consider it, a kind of imprimatur. In retrospect, it dawns on me that my friendship with the stars of the Union faculty was based on their regard for my academic record, that in fact my work, including research interests, public speaking and early publications, had led to their thinking of me in academic life. That had not occurred to me, though I was somewhat startled by how quickly I moved in that direction. The possibility of ending up in a college or university did not seem strange, since I knew what it involved – teaching, writing, elements of administrative work, and something of a public life.

But I had no thoughts about where I would be teaching or whether there would be an opening somewhere. What happened in a succession of events was that positions came my way, unexpectedly and unplanned, sometimes for good and sometimes not so good reasons: Princeton, Columbia, Harvard, Drew, San Francisco Theological Seminary and the Graduate Theological Union, Hartford Seminary, and GTU again. The range of schools and their order must be bewildering to those who know them. Once, a person who was asked to introduce me as the speaker at a public event, reading from a script prepared for him, glanced up from his text and blurted out, "Looks like you couldn't hold a job." I averred there was some truth in his comment.

But the institutions had one characteristic in common; they were going through rather pronounced transitions. For me, that was not a negative situation, but one full of promise and excitement. Change was what life seemed to be about. Teaching was a way of opening new horizons, including new fields for myself, such as natural science and art history. Administration was a way of bringing about institutional change. So, I enjoyed each of the institutions, different as they were.

I learned about differences in how institutional change came about. At Harvard, for instance, one found an old reason to do something radical and if one succeeded once, it was tradition and would not be challenged again. At Berkeley, on the other hand, one can do anything one wants but everyone reserves the right to tear it up in the future. In such different settings, one learns diverse strategies.

While not officially active as a clergy person in my teaching and administrative life, I was a regular church member and participated in services from my youth until a decade ago. In addition to my being a clergy person in the United Church of Christ, I also became a lay Episcopalian in the sixties, being attracted to liturgical life. But just as I did that, the new liturgical chaos was also overtaking that body. When asked as to what I personally believed, I replied that in addition to being a member of the United Church of Christ and an Episcopalian, I was also a crypto-Catholic. All of these elements are still in my being, but no longer in traditional embodied settings. If anything, elements of religious conviction have become stronger. Mystery has increased as perceptions have become more pronounced. I stand in awe of that development.

Throughout this memoir, I have tried to give an account of things as they presented themselves to me, from the cultural deprivation of the farm to absorbing the wider world almost totally from scratch. In the process I learned to accept the situations in which I found myself, with the impulse to do the best I could. I learned not to hold grudges in adversity that came my way or to be defeated by my own dubious actions. Most of all, it was important to forgive, to be forgiven, and not to be defeated by the absence of forgiveness.

I enjoy most people, can be angry on occasion, but I have an incapacity to hate. Life has been just and unjust, and my wife, Jean, keeps reminding me of the adage, "Who said the world is just?" In the midst of that kind of world, I have been given many gifts. I hope that comes through in what I have written.

As my life unfolds, it will be obvious how many persons influenced it and how much I owe to them. In the writing of this account, I want to acknowledge the contributions of particular individuals. To Robert W. Funk, Jim Wiggins, and Lane McGaughy, who gave two full days to a discussion the four of us had on theological and cultural developments of the last seven decades. Those conversations led to changes and additions, and in the case of Lane particularly, to chapter titles that he proposed. On stylistic matters and clarifications of thought thanks go to Adrianne Bank, Yolanda Adelson, Meredith Higgins Hargrave, Chris Shea, and Tim Nuveen. Doug Adams, as on other occasions, suggested changes that I readily accepted. But for the editing of the whole for publication I am, as on previous occasions, grateful to Susan Carpenter, who without changing my style has enhanced the whole. I also thank Wendy Jackson for editing an early version. Marion Pauck, friend for fifty five years, has been helpful in checking and comparing memories, particularly since she was involved in similar and sometimes identical projects. Given her publishing and writing expertise, she has suggested stylistic improvements. Most of all, she has been a conversation partner on the contents of this volume. At Polebridge Press, I am thankful to Char Matejovsky who with her sure touch steered me though the various processes. I am grateful also to the Nuveen Benevolent Trust for a grant that helped meet out of pocket expenses in preparing the manuscript. Finally, my wife, Jean, who is part of this history, has again helped guide me through calm and turbulent waters.

Given that this volume follows a chronological sequence, I have listed my publications in that order. That makes it possible to see the progression of my thinking. Book reviews I have written or have been written of my works, insofar as I know of them, can be found in the Syracuse University Library Special Collections.

Most of the plates or photographs come from various sources inasmuch as my own copies burned over a decade ago. I thank those who have supplied them or made them available for this project.

ONE
An Expanding World

John Dillenberger dressed up for a high school event

1

ROOTED IN GERMAN-AMERICAN SOIL
"How do I get out of here!"

The Geographical Compass and Early Memories

"How do I get out of here?" is the pervasive memory of my childhood and it persisted until I went to college. Here refers first of all to the farm and its environs in the Mississippi Valley, some thirty-five miles south of East St. Louis, Illinois. Looking west from the farm, the Missouri bluffs emerged directly across the Mississippi River, while toward the east was flat land, from which rose, some two miles away, the stone and tree filled Illinois bluffs, some two to three hundred feet high, with a large cave directly visible from the farm. The flat land between the bluffs was called the American Bottom, known for its rich land and periodic flooding. In the fall, the red maple leaves of the trees on the bluffs brought visitors from afar.

The farmhouse nearest to ours was a half-mile away to the north, while a mile to the south were a few farmhouses. About two miles to the southeast was the small town of Fults, with its grain elevator, blacksmith shop, protestant church, post office, general store, saloon, and railroad station. The country school, at the edge of Fults, was special because it had two rooms instead of the usual one. Except in the most inclement weather I walked a mile and a half to school across the frequently muddy fields. For ordinary supplies we gravitated toward Fults. Today, Fults no longer exists, for it was destroyed in one of the Mississippi River floods two decades ago, and federal agencies forbade its being rebuilt.

As I was growing up I gradually discovered that the wider surrounding area was not without its own interesting history. Less than ten miles away, toward the southeast was the town of Renault, and toward the south,

Prairie du Rocher. In the few times that as a young boy I was in the latter town, one still heard French and saw the iron railing porches so character-istic of the French in the Mississippi Valley, both of which disappeared long ago. The ruins of Fort Chartres, about two miles north of Prairie du Rocher, were a witness to the once French hegemony of the area. But our life was orientated to the north, for the lines between the German and French areas were as clear as if a fence existed between the two.

To the north, just south of East St. Louis, was Cahokia, another fort and town, with its Indian name and an old restored church. Still farther to the north were the Cahokia Indian mounds, now a public park. It was not unusual to see slight mounds in the fields near Fults, and with a little dig-ging, Indian arrows could always be found. It was a matter of great curios-ity to all of us when an expedition from the University of Illinois began digging on a neighbor's farm, finding skeletons and artifacts as well as arrowheads. In those days, all of us had collections of arrowheads.

About six miles to the north of Fults was Maeystown, a little village up a creek bed from the valley, positioned just where the hills and bluffs began. Its stone houses, made from stone quarries nearby, have brought the town landmark status through the work of the late Gloria Maeys Bundy, a descendant of the original founder of the town and a cousin through my mother's side of the family.

Maeystown rather than Fults was the center of our life inasmuch as both my father's and my mother's families were anchored there. At the north end of the town were the Maeys' houses, then just below and across a stone bridge over a creek was the Dillenberger house, adjacent to which was the blacksmith building and the house of Grandpa George Hoffmann. I knew the Hoffmann establishment well, inasmuch as I was fascinated by the glowing fire and hammering of metal. Later, my parents inherited the buildings and had to remove the blacksmith shed and modernize the house. During the early days there were four George Hoffmann families on the one street through town, my grandfather being known as smith George, the others as fat George, laughing George, and corner (where two streets intersected) George. While I do not remember my Grandmother Hoffmann's death, I do remember the death of my grandfathers. Grandpa Dillenberger was brought from the field where he had passed out and was laid on the living room floor, awaiting the doctor. Soon thereafter he died. Grandfather Hoffmann lived with us for the last year of his life. Death was very present in those days, and there was no attempt to hide its presence. Only Grandma Dillenberger lived until my college years.

Here in Maeystown was the Protestant church to which my parents belonged, with all the services in the German language. But language transitions began. First on one Sunday each month the service was in English, then one Sunday each month was in German, then all were in English. A German dialect was the language of the street, and in the county seat, Waterloo, some ten miles to the north of Maeystown, this was also the case. My parents spoke German with each other and with other relatives and friends throughout their lifetime, turning to English in public as the German language gradually disappeared.

Some thirty-five miles directly to the north of the farm was St. Louis, on the opposite side of the mighty Mississippi. I was born in St. Louis, while my father was a barber awaiting the chance to find a farm he could rent, which happened some two years later. So I have no early reminiscences of St. Louis. Nor do I know when or how I was first taken there. Perhaps it was by train, for Fults then had a passenger station as well as a freight depot. Perhaps it was with our first car, a 1926 Ford, which I learned to drive sitting on my father's lap. No driver's licenses in those days. That was followed by a 1928 Chevrolet, which I recall being used to go to St. Louis. What boy would not remember such an event, with the mingling of anticipation and disgust that one had to plan two days in advance, making sure that the car was washed, had enough air in the tires, that water and oil were adequate. In those days one did not just enter a car and drive off, partly, of course, because current car reliability was not taken for granted. In this respect, the third car of my boyhood, a 1935 Chevrolet, was the harbinger of dependability.

Those early trips to St. Louis were not for cultural reasons, but to see my favorite uncle, my mother's brother. I remember that he had a sense of humor and was a good storyteller; but perhaps I liked him most because he did not live in the immediate environs. My father, who had six brothers and four sisters, had a brother who lived in Detroit, exotic both because he lived far away and was the subject of dubious adventure stories.

"How do I get out of here?" was obviously related to the mystery of these uncles. And yet, the source of that longing is unclear. The monotony of life on the farm, with its dirt, long hours, and uncertain results, obviously played its part. One could not go anywhere without returning sooner or later on the same day to milk the cows and feed the other animals. Harrowing the field or plowing was a matter of walking behind the implements pulled by horses and mules from sunrise to sunset, which in the summer could be fifteen to sixteen hours a day. The advent of the tractor, which I talked my father into letting me drive at the age of ten, turned wrestling with the recalcitrance of horses and mules into turning a wheel and being able to sit rather than walk. I do not think that it was the long hours I disliked, for long hours of work have never bothered me.

Somewhat depressing was the monotony and the lack of challenge, the lack of something different and new in one's life.

Why I felt that way when most of my companions and relatives had no such problems, and indeed thought I was a bit odd wanting to get away, still eludes me. Being in school initially was not a challenge, and I had no expectations that school would transform what I thought or did. But during the last years of grade school and during high school, I did have some excellent teachers, though I did not recognize it at the time. I would do what was expected and assume that was all I needed to know. Hence, I always had answers but no questions. Somehow, these teachers, recognizing that for me life had no questions, would ask them of me and placed journal articles in my hands that shattered my certainties, that disclosed that there were more options than one. Through that process, my attitude, how do I get out of here? was transformed. The variety I sought over against the monotony I knew began to take on the characteristics of genuine curiosity, of discoveries that reading and conversation brought. Such excursions initially were in the areas of geography and history rather than in cultural subjects. I heard my first symphony at the age of seventeen, when a high school teacher organized a trip for a class to the St. Louis symphony. While my eyes were cultivated in seeing nature and its effects on farm life, and my ears knew the sounds of nature and machinery, neither my eyes nor ears had been exposed to cultural manifestations. Indeed, my exposure to such areas occurred so late in life that it has demanded an extraordinary discipline to overtake such early deprivation.

While I recognize the pervasive urge to break out into a different world, there are, of course, individual memories, perhaps without pattern, or with unrecognized connections which simply stand alone. I was aware that there were many relatives whom we visited and that this brought some experiences that I as an only child did not have on a regular basis. There are particular early memories. When I was four or five I heard the story of the death of a young man I had liked. Having been pierced with a hayfork that fell from the barn too quickly for him to avoid it, he had apparently punctured or severed an artery. Literally scared to death, he ran and ran, with nobody being able to stop him; of course he bled to death. "Don't panic" took on a special meaning for me very early.

One of the earliest newspaper headlines I recall was the Lindbergh kidnapping, about which everybody had opinions, ranging from the equally unambiguous statements that Bruno Hauptmann was the guilty one, and should immediately be strung up and hung, to the view that he was obviously framed. The event was on everyone's mind, a drama that surrounded a folk hero whose subsequent political sympathies with the Nazis were hardly suspected. Some sixty years later, the kidnapping verdict still seems to be out.

Another early memory was the Scopes trial, first brought to my attention while visiting my mother's brother George. He was among the first in the community to have a radio with an incredible range of reception. Listening to the radio with him, while others talked of other matters, I was captivated by his humorous commentary on the trial and its major figures, the secular Clarence Darrow and the conservative William Jennings Bryan. Some thirty years later I found myself writing a chapter on the trial.

Still as vivid as a photographic memory, on one of those trips to St. Louis, is seeing the rows of shanties on the Illinois side of the Mississippi River, known as Hooverville. The shiftless moving of people, the craggy, often unshaven faces, the smoky fires used both for warmth and for cooking whatever could be turned into food, had an impact on an impressionable ten-year-old. Every time I have heard that welfare makes people shiftless, lazy, and unwilling to work, the memory of those faces rises before me. Those who have not been there seem not to understand that the sapping of ambition for change is part of the hopelessness engendered in situations of poverty in which anything different does not appear as a possibility.

As a boy, I also heard all the jokes about people leaning on shovels rather than using them in the days of the WPA. Some of the work was meaningless, like moving stones from one side of the road to the other and then back again. Some of it was doing menial things that machines could do much better. But in many cases, imaginative uses were made of such labor, and for the most part the programs saved countless people and gave them some hope. The WPA program, for instance, opened artistic paths and created books that are still standard works today.

While I was a young teenager during the Great Depression, I experienced the era differently than many. Since our food had always been what the farm produced, from vegetables to meat to home baked bread, there was hardly a change in our diet, except that there was no money to buy salt and ingredients the farm did not produce. But I remember my father and mother providing food to relatives in the city, and doing it with an indirectness that made it skirt the issue of charity, which no one wanted to receive. The clothes one wore were more tattered and the patches increased; but these were not hardships that affected one's existence. Nor do I remember how we got out of the Depression, except that it was gradual.

Related to the strange gyrations of that time, or what seemed to me to be strange happenings, was my arriving at grade school one morning only to discover that five children were absent from class – noticeable indeed in a schoolroom of about twenty – because their parents had been arrested and temporarily imprisoned for having sold alcohol, or moonshine as it was called in the local tavern. I had frequently been sent into the saloon by my parents to buy something or other, such taverns providing diverse supplies for a farming community. Of course, I saw people standing or sitting at the bar, having a drink, and frequently engaged in conversation with them, for children were usually not excluded from what was being said. I could never understand why the parents of my classmates were sent to jail for several months. At the time I had never heard of Prohibition.

I remember too a shooting on my uncle's farm, when a member of the Shelton Gang, wounded in the struggles for controlling the moonshine stills that had grown up in the wild terrain between the levee and the river, wandered to my uncle's house and demanded help, which gave my uncle temporary prominence in the paper and in the community. But even this event I understood as warfare among competing criminals as to who controlled the making of moonshine, as indeed it was. It never occurred to me that making moonshine itself was illegal. In our home, my father always made his own wine and many of the people we knew made bathtub gin. Of course, there were the town drunks, but the overuse of alcohol was not conspicuous. One prominent misuse was evident in the minister of the Protestant church in Maeystown. A loveable man, a good preacher and pastor, he took to drink to an extent that could not be overlooked: stumbling and falling in town and even being partially drunk at church events. The congregation divided between those who wanted to give him a chance and those who wanted to rail him out of town. My father and mother belonged to the first group. He reformed enough to serve for a while longer.

The Hoover-Roosevelt election of 1932, the year I entered high school, is a vivid memory for it divided families from each other. I particularly recall my father, who later became a Democrat, defending Hoover against a cousin equally in favor of Roosevelt, and carrying out his conviction by refusing for a period to buy his groceries from his cousin's store. But the saddest memory was the closing of the bank in Maeystown upon Roosevelt's election, and its consolidation with a bank in Waterloo ten miles to the north. The banker, a relative who, as bankers had been in that period, was a pillar of the community, suddenly found himself the villain, who allegedly had threatened everyone's savings and taken away a bank from the community, one of the institutions that then made a village into a real town. It was as if the town's place in the world had been taken away. It was as if its dignity was gone. The subsequent lawsuit, the outcome of which I cannot recall except that the banker left town and joined a bank in another city, was my introduction to a court trial. Being then in the early years of high school, I used to skip school in the afternoon in order to attend the trial. The twisting of statements to mean what was not intended, being forbidden to provide contexts, and having to answer yes or no when the situation was more complex than that, never seemed to be balanced by the process of cross-examination. There may be no better system, but my mind to this day focuses on miscarriages of justice, and I follow cases in which injustice seems apparent and lives have been ruined beyond all compensation.

A year or so later, another experience gripped many in the community: the escapades of John Dillinger. Although a gangster, he was nevertheless a folk hero, robbing from those who have, creating a kind of sympathy in the body politic, and he never got caught until he was gunned down in 1934. In a strange kind of way, his death added to the saga. His name was on every tongue. The result was that when my name was mentioned in writing or in discourse, it was often unwittingly translated into Dillinger. When the mistake was recognized by the person it usually led to embarrassment or teasing. The number of times when I have been introduced to speak and referred to as Dillinger is high indeed. Obviously, this seldom happens now. Still, a week before writing these sentences, a young clerk in a store referred to me as Dillinger as she asked if I needed help taking groceries to the car. The name still persists even among those who do not know who Dillinger was.

While being called Dillinger was not a source of annoyance, from early on I was not happy with my name, John Pershing Dillenberger, written as J. Pershing Dillenberger. I was called Pershing. General Pershing was a hero at the time of my birth and an appropriate name for two Germans to use. Yet, Pershing Dillenberger was just too long, and one day my parents noted that I was signing myself as Pershberger. When I reached college, I decided officially to be John. My mother eventually called me John, but not without the observation that had they had additional children she hoped she would have let them select their own names. Classmates from grade school times still call me Pershing.

In the 1930s we were also aware of the Dust Bowl, though it did not affect farming in our region, given that we received, rather than lost, soil. But for days on end, the sky was darker than usual, the sun largely obscured, and dust whirled about. There was no protection from the dust, for it seemed to penetrate everything. At the height of the storms, one shielded one's face with white cloth. Cleaning each day was a chore, for it was not unusual to have layers of dust on the kitchen table and all other spaces. It may also be noted that the country roads were dusty, and that the stirred up dust was carried along by the prairie wind. When a car was in sight, we closed doors and windows to avoid the dust billowing through the house.

The German Background

Overall, the experiences of the time had a German context. While French, English, and German peoples had settled in the area in that order, by my time the French had mainly disappeared, and the English were over-shadowed by German settlers, many from the Rhineland. The Germans were a volatile lot, feisty in dealing with issues in the community, but, like Rhineland Germans generally, with a sense of incongruity and humor. The laughter of my uncles, particularly from my mother's side, is a vivid memory, as they recounted the foibles they daily witnessed in the community. I can still visualize my mother sitting on a chair near a window, musing on such incongruousness.

But few of the Germans knew precisely the places from which they had come. For them coming to this country meant breaking the bonds of Europe, adapting to a new land, and for the children, learning English as soon as possible. While the first and second generations knew little English, the next ones were bilingual, followed by the loss of German as the language of the community and then in the home itself. The places from which these settlers came, mainly in the period from 1840 to 1860, are now known mostly on the basis of genealogical interests born in recent times. I never learned much about my mother's ancestry, except that the family came from the Darmstadt environment, between Frankfurt am Main and Heidelberg. Finding myself going to Germany in 1953 for the first time, I tried to find out from where my father's ancestors had emigrated, only to discover that no one seemed to know. In response to badgering my father with the statement that I simply did not believe no one knew where the family had come from, he canvassed all of his brothers and sisters, only to discover that a brother had a letter, still unopened, from Germany. Believing that past relatives from across the water should be ignored, he simply kept the letter, which had reached him because he had the same name as my great, great grandfather, and he never opened it. Nor could he have read it, for he could not read German script. The letter, written in 1946, was written in a situation of desperate hunger, pleading for care packages. It led to my finding distant relatives in the homestead in a small village, Nochern, on the hills overlooking the Rhine, some two miles north of the Lorelei. My visit, exactly one hundred years after my progenitors had left for the new world, made me aware of the power of language across time. Several times someone present from North Germany would smile and I would ask why, only to be told that, after one hundred years of no contact between the families, I returned to Germany using idiomatic expressions used only within a thirty-mile radius of the old homestead.

Working in the University of Heidelberg library in 1957, I stumbled on a book in the catalogue entitled, *Stammfolge Dillenberg.* In it I found a genealogical account of the Dillenberger family, written in the Nazi period, it seems, to prove sufficient Aryan ancestry, which, judging from the names, would not have been easy. Working with church records, I soon found my way in the genealogical history in the nineteenth century with a genealogy that goes back to 1493 in the town of Dillenberg. Originally, a Dillenberger was one who came from the hill on the river Dill.

Once Paul Tillich asked from where my ancestors had come and I replied I did not know, which was true at the time. His response was that it could only be the Rhineland, where Germans have a natural happy disposition. He turned out to be right about my family history, for already in the sixteenth century they had moved from Dillenberg to several adjacent towns in the Rhineland.

The distant relatives in Germany had one letter that my great grandfather had written to his brother in Germany in the 1870s. In it he wrote that he had wanted to write every week for twenty years, but that life had been so busy in the new world that something had always interfered. Even that letter was cut short by the hired man cutting his foot with an axe and having to be taken to the doctor. The letter illustrates that the ties across the waters hardly mattered.

Letters subsequently discovered indicate that when first entering the United States, the family was en route up the Mississippi, from New Orleans to St. Louis, when the river froze some thirty miles south of St. Louis – and south is the right word, because of the bend in the river. They left the boat or barge and settled not too far from the river, though the details of that venture are not known. Apparently, they knew someone in St. Louis, and at one time there was a Dillenberger street, which has long since disappeared.

In spite of the settling in the new world, some of the patterns of the old repeated themselves. With families of ten to a dozen, the land could not be inherited by all nor broken up into parcels large enough to support everyone. The result was that many looked for jobs in St. Louis in industries of various sorts. So most families had relatives in the city, and a pattern of weekend visiting started between St. Louis and the community to the south which continues to this day.

As indicated previously, although my father wanted to be on a farm, none was available after his marriage and he went to barber college, as it was called. But he took the first opportunity to move to a farm, keeping up his barber skills with all the neighbors who flocked to have their hair cut week after week. In fact, he wanted to own a farm, and the big disappointment of his life was that I was not interested. The financial possibility of owning a farm, paying for it from the proceeds of farming, could only happen if it was a family enterprise in which free labor was guaranteed for two or three decades. The alternative was renting, which my father did on three different farms, though my growing up was confined mainly to the first one. Renting generally meant that the person who owned the farm received one third of the proceeds of wheat, corn, alfalfa, pigs, cows, et cetera. In exchange the landlord provided the house and barnyard buildings, though the ordinary upkeep was the responsibility of the tenant. Moreover, the landlord obviously had jurisdiction over who the tenant would be and it was not unusual for there to be annual musical chairs among farmers and farms, either because of dissatisfaction on the part of the landlord or the possibility of a tenant moving to a farm with better land. My father's moves, made when I was away at college, were all to better land, where less work and smaller acreage were more profitable than larger acreage with poorer land.

Life on a Farm

The usual farm had a farmhouse, a barn for hay, corn, and cattle, a chicken house, an implement shed, and of course either driven pumps for water or cisterns or both. Farmhouses were usually modest; the one in which I grew up had a large kitchen, a large bedroom, and an unusable living room, called a front room, built with logs put together with mortar, and a veritable haven for rats. Above that log room, which originally was the house to which additions had been made, were two small rooms in an attic, accessible only from the outside and for the use of farmhands who then lived with us and took their meals with us as well. The most pleasant part was a lean-to porch, in the midst of some shade trees, a comfort in the hot humid summers in which the nights were only more tolerable than the days because of the absence of the beating sun. It is all too obvious that such houses had "outhouses," terribly uncomfortable in winter, both because of the cold and the distance from the house. Illumination was by kerosene lamps, occasionally supplemented by gas lamps, with their little white bags and hissing sound, fed every half hour by one's pumping more air into the gas container to keep a bright light, much brighter than kerosene lamps. Cooking and heating were by wood, coal, and gas stoves, welcome during the winter for the heat they brought, and hot for summer cooking when it was already too hot. I can remember sitting between the wall and the stove in winter, getting hot and falling asleep, with my mother and father encouraging me to go to bed, to which I usually agreed when I was sure the sheets beneath the feather bed had been heated with a hot iron that served both for ironing and heating purposes. There was, of course, no standard time for children to be in bed; they simply fell asleep and were put to bed.

The realities of farm life were quite different from the romantic notions of those who lived in the city. The hayride contrasted sharply with the making of hay, with its itchy dust, and the fresh meats and produce that city people bought from farmers on a Sunday drive to the country were far removed from the uncertain toil that produced them. Undoubtedly that contrast is not as marked today as it was then. I grew up on the farm during the period in which the transition was gradually made from hand labor to mechanization, and from diversified farming to specialization. Until my tenth year, the fields were tilled with horses and mules, with implements behind which one walked and, in some instances, upon which one sat on a contoured metal seat. The advent of the tractor brought larger implements and eliminated the need for hired hands, except for special seasons. When farmers began to buy bread, milk, and meat from grocers rather than remaining self-sufficient, and concentrated on growing grain with the elimination of animals, a greater freedom and ease, albeit with more uncertainty, entered the picture. Today, grain farmers spend half the year working and for the rest of the year can travel and virtually disappear.

During my early boyhood, we had a dozen horses or mules, and an equal number of cows that needed milking twice a day, at least fifty pigs, and over two hundred chickens. These needed attention seven days a week. I have vivid memories of returning from visiting relatives on a Sunday, only to have to take care of all the animals, sometimes after dark. Milking the cows I dreaded the most and soon made deals with my parents to take on any other chores instead of milking. It was the odor of the milk rather than the labor that I disliked. Later I learned that it may have a biological basis, for, according to my mother, I rejected milk and dairy products already in my infancy. To this day, the smell of a cheese store sends me across the street. When I was about ten, my father had an ulcer and was on a milk diet. One day he said he could not stand drinking another glass of milk even if he died tomorrow, an event that scared a ten-year-old. Within six weeks, his ulcer disappeared and it never returned. In addition, my mother, who made cheese and butter, never ate any herself. She said she did not like the taste. My hunch is that I inherited the early inability to digest dairy products from both of my parents. Friends who know my current penchant for ice cream find this hard to believe.

Working in the fields was seasonal, often calling for fifteen-or sixteen-hour days, measured by the length of daylight. In the spring it involved planting corn and in the fall wheat. For both the ground had to be plowed, a long affair with one or two furrow plows pulled by two to four horses, with usually three such teams at work at the same time. The ensuing tractor pulled the plow and accomplished more in one day than three or four plows pulled by horses. It could pull three furrowed plows at faster speed and without the rest periods required by horses or mules. In addition to plowing more soil, the tractor had the strength to plow six inches deep, then considered ideal. But the person driving the tractor kept equally long hours, for hired hands were no longer required. My father used to say that the tractor cost him nothing when not in use, while a hired hand needed to be supported throughout the year. The acres devoted to oats, rye, soybeans, and alfalfa, by comparison were small indeed, providing crops the farmer needed for feed rather than grown for market. The surplus of corn and wheat over what was required for feed was, of course, the main source of financial support.

For most farmers in the community, and for my father particularly, everything had to be in straight rows. Hence, the plow furrows had to be straight as an arrow, a feat accomplished by placing several pegs in a straight line down the field, spaced at about six to seven hundred feet apart, and heading the horses or tractor down the row of pegs. Likewise, the planting of corn had to be in straight rows, so that one could see the corn in such rows from any angle. Partly this was because farmers cultivated the corn either down the path in which it was planted and crosswise or at a ninety-degree angle. Such planting was achieved by a long wire, with knobs on it at about three-foot intervals which tripped the corn into the planter that was being pulled down the field by horses or tractor. At each end of the field, the farmer had to pull the wire tight and place it some six feet to the left or right. Obviously, the straightness of the corn in the direction in which it was planted depended on the skill of the driver, while the lines crosswise depended on the skill in pulling the wires tight and evenly at each end of the field. The straightness of line, with respect to corn, served a function. But it was also, for my father, a sign of whether or not one was a good farmer.

Corn, unlike wheat, needed cultivation as it grew, partly to keep out the weeds and partly to aerate the soil. This too went from horse-drawn corn cultivators behind which one walked, moving the prongs sideways to kill the weeds without getting too close to the growing corn, to corn cultivators on which one sat and moved the prongs with one's feet. Then came the time for one last cultivation to take place, with three or four cultivations having already been completed. This was done with a special machine that threw up soil against the rows of corn. When the corn was harvested and the stalks had been removed, the rows of dirt meant that the field was uneven. Then a machine was used to throw the mounds of dirt apart as one drove down the field, row by row. The latter was my introduction to working in the field at about the age of eight. I remember being tired as well as tired of the monotony. I left the implement and horses in the field and returned to the house. Needless to say, the spanking I got sent me back to the field.

When the corn was ripe in the fall or early winter, two options were at hand and both were used by most farmers. One was to cut the corn by hand with special knives as one walked down a row and then to deposit the cut stalks with corn on them against four uncut stalks tied together. Later the corn was taken from the stalks and shucked, as it was called, and the corn stalks were cut up by a special cutter for feed for cattle. The second alternative was simply to have a wagon with two horses go down a row of corn and stop as one picked the corn with a hand corn picker and pitched the ears onto the wagon. The picker consisted of a leather strap which held a metal pick with which one tore open the husk and broke out the ear of corn. The horses were taught to stop and go as one called to them. A farmer could do one load in the morning and one in the afternoon, unloading both with a shovel into a crib or room in the barn, sometimes pitching the corn some seven or eight feet high.

With respect to wheat, the process involved two steps. First the wheat was cut by a machine called the binder, at first pulled by horses and later by tractor. It cut and bound the wheat in sheaths, which were then assembled into small stacks to dry. The stacks were created by setting up four sheaths stacked against each other, and piling some ten or so around them, with two bundles bent, spread apart, and fashioned as a cap over the stack. It was amazing how well the cap kept water from getting inside, particu-

larly when it was done correctly. The second step was threshing the bundles, which extracted the grains of wheat. Just as the corn picker made
corn shocking obsolete, so the combine combined cutting and harvesting
into one process. Both developments occurred after I left the farm.

The big events, of course, were the winter butchering and the summer threshing seasons, both community functions. For the butchering, six
or more neighbors would arrive with appropriate knives and saws for cutting up a carcass, kettles for boiling innards, and equipment for cleaning
casings for sausage meats. The pigs or steers, of course, had to be killed,
which was usually done by a .22 caliber rifle just as morning light was
approaching. My father had let me, just a young boy, use a BB gun, a rifle,
and a two-barreled shotgun. The first one was for shooting birds (one day
the mail carrier saw me displaying a robin I had just shot and he chastised
me so much that I confined myself to black birds and sparrows) and the
shotgun was used for duck and goose hunting. But the rifle was for precision shooting and involved a good deal of practice, which I did by throwing cans into the air and shooting at them. In any case, I volunteered to
shoot pigs and steers for the butchering community. Aiming through a the-
oretical grid of the animal's head, adjusting for positions of the head being
more up or down, one should be able to fell the animal with one shot.
Only once did I have to do a second shot. In spite of doing this for several
years, starting when I was no more than ten years old, by the time I was in
high school I had lost interest in guns and eventually gave away the ones I
had.

For the threshing season some ten or twelve farmers usually combined
their resources to own a thresher and steam engine; otherwise they paid a
person who owned the machinery a fee per bushel. My introduction to the
threshing milieu was as a water boy, which meant filling jugs with water,
keeping them cool with wet burlap, and delivering them by horse and
buggy to those who pitched the bundles onto wagons, to the wagon drivers
who loaded them, and to the crew who ran the threshing machines. Being
a water boy was a matter of some abuse, for there were always those who
got thirsty before one arrived again on one's rounds or who felt the water
was not cool enough. Perspiration was the order of the day.

By the age of twelve, I was considered old enough to drive a wagon,
load the bundles of wheat as they were pitched up, and then drive the
wagon to the threshing machine, where, with a fork, one pitched the bundles into the ravenous machine, its knives whirling away as driven by the
steam engine with its long belt that turned the wheels and cogs of the
machinery. When the load was still full, it was easy enough to throw the

bundles down into the conveyer with its knives, but it was scary, for one was always afraid one might slip and fall in. There were enough stories of such happenings to make one alert. When the load was getting empty, one had to pitch the bundles up into the conveyer, and as the day went on, each bundle seemed to get heavier and heavier. It was not unusual for one or two persons each day to become sick from heat and exertion and have to quit, only to be ready to start all over again the next day.

My aversion to horses and to loading and unloading the bundles led me to ask, with my father's permission, to be allowed to be the sacker for the threshing machine. Being a sacker means what it says, putting sacks under a spout which poured the wheat into the sacks. One had to make sure that the sacks were full, which meant continually pulling them up tight. The wheat was taken in sacks on a wagon either to a grain elevator, where it was sold, or to a farmer's bin to keep either for seed for next year, for use with cattle, or in reserves in the hope of a higher price later. The wagon drivers alternated with the sacker, bag by bag, in filling the bags and piling them on the wagon. The trick was to be able to pile the sacks in time to return with an empty one and to make the transfer from full to empty bag without spilling any wheat.

My interest in the sacker's job had another basis as well. When the threshing machine was being moved to another location, either on a particular farm or between farms, I had nothing to do. Having made friends with the person who ran the steam engine that both ran the thresher with belts and pulled the thresher from place to place, I found myself being allowed to run the engine. Pulling the large thresher with an equally large steam engine, fired with coal and wood and with appropriate steam whistle, was a thrill, and I became adept at it. When the thresher was pulled into position, and the engine uncoupled, one learned to pull the engine ahead in a curve, back it up, and without further maneuvering, have it so lined up that the belt which drove the thresher, at least eighty feet long, was in such a position that it ran and centered on the pulleys without veering to one side or the other.

Two events from the threshing crew time are vivid. I had dated a girl who was claimed by one of the crew members. The result was that he wanted to fight, and while I didn't, I was drawn into it. So, on my sixteenth birthday, I had, as the language of the place put it, the hell beaten out of me.

The second event was my first participation in a strike growing out of the conflict between the old threshing crews and the new combines. One of the group of a dozen farmers who had been in the threshing circle

decided to quit and buy a combine. But when it came time for the threshing season, he wanted a straw stack for his cattle, and a neighboring farmer
who was part of the circle was willing to sell him the straw. But the outlook
was not a positive one, for the threshing crews remembered the negative
comments of the farmer with the combine that he would never need any
of us again. In addition, unfavorable winds emerged, so that chaff would
engulf us all. The result was that the entire crew refused to take the loaded
wagons from the field of the cooperative farmer to the one wanting the
straw stack. While the farmer got no straw stack that day, I had the opportunity of driving the steam engine an extra time as we moved to the next
farm.

In addition to the harvesting of corn and wheat, the growing of clover
and alfalfa for hay was a regular routine. Knowing when to cut the hay for
drying meant calculating what the weather would be for at least three or
four days in advance. Every farmer I knew in the Midwest could do better
than present day meteorological forecasts, for one learned to see clues in
the sky. One had to be careful not to put hay that was too wet into a barn,
for it would become hot and eventually break out in a fire. I remember
two incidents in which barns went up in fire. In one instance, since it happened at night and was discovered too late, the cattle inside were also
killed.

I remember well the loading and unloading of hay, especially clover,
since the dust from it was particularly itchy. The hay was pitched with a
fork onto a wagon, while the person on the wagon piled it with the center
high and the sides sloping downward but not so much that the hay would
fall off. If that was not done, the large hayfork used in barns for unloading
did not work well, pulling up just a small amount from the wagon. A good
loader in the field and a good placer of the large fork at the barn resulted
in a full load of hay being pulled into the barn by placing the fork about
six times, while less skill could result in at least twenty tries. The unloading
fork, about three by four feet, was pulled down from the top of a barn,
where a large door had been placed, by rope. One then stood on the fork,
holding oneself with the rope, and jumped up and down on the fork, forc-
ing it into the load of hay. When it was down as far as it would go, one
pulled some levers that brought arms out at the bottom designed to hold
the hay. This done, a driver with a team of horses pulled the hay into the
barn, as the rope rose to the top of the barn and ran along under the ceiling. Upon a shout from above as to the appropriate location to drop the
hay, one pulled a small rope that released the levers and the hay dropped
into place.

The next development was the advent of the hay baler, in which the hay was fed into the machine much as in a threshing machine. Only now, hay was compressed and held together by wires. Just as I pushed to be a sacker with reference to threshing, I also became a wire sticker, since each bale had to have wires inserted, which then had to be tied together. Since the bales came out on a regular rhythm, one could not get behind, or hay, not bales of hay, emerged from the machine. Fortunately, one did not need to be too precise in joining the wires together, for when the bale emerged from the compressor, the hay expanded to the limits of the tied wire. Finally, the bales had to be stacked in the field or carried to the barn. Subsequently, all these operations became totally mechanized, but that was after I had left the farm.

Most of the operations I have described not only involved considerable physical labor, they also resulted in one being dirty at the end of the day from the top of one's head to the bottom of one's feet. The last thing each evening was taking a bath in a tub of water out in the yard. Of course, that could only happen outside during the summer months. In winter the baths were less frequent and the tub was used inside, with water heated on the stove. It is obvious that rural electrification, when it finally arrived, made a tremendous difference. Just before I started college in 1936, electricity and bathrooms had become a reality for this farming community, narrowing the differences in the ways in which farming and city people lived; indeed, altering the perceptions they had of each other. Those with electricity and bathrooms looked down on those who did not have such amenities.

A farmer was necessarily a jack-of-all-trades. If you owned a farm, your own labor was free; and if you rented, the landlord was usually reluctant to spend money. I remember my father making bargains with the landlord when a new shed was needed to house implements or chicken houses needed to be built, to the effect that he would do the labor if the owner supplied the materials. This was not an uncommon practice. The result was that I learned how to do simple construction work. Years later I used these abilities that I honed as a young boy. For our summer cabin in Canada, I undertook wiring it for electricity and installing a complete plumbing system. When the inspectors arrived to approve the work they wryly remarked that it was a good job because I had not known enough to take shortcuts.

Farmers also had gardens, usually prepared by plowing an area, for spading would have taken too long, considering the size of the gardens. The women maintained the gardens. Moreover, women played a large role in working in the fields, sometimes stacking wheat bundles, turning hay with a fork to let it dry more easily, and most of all running tractors. Women provided five meals a day in the summer: breakfast, a mid-morning lunch, lunch, a mid-afternoon lunch, and dinner. All of these were big meals. At threshing time, to feed entire crews, wives joined together to provide the meals cooked at the particular farm-house at which the threshing was being done. Grant Wood's painting of the threshing scene, in which the men are eating, is regionalist art, realistic to the core.

Certainly no one doubted the worth of women in the area in which I grew up. But it was equally clear that men called the shots, except in unusual circumstances in which it was said, in a derogatory vein, that women wore the pants in the family. That women had a needed role in the economy of a society did not thereby guarantee equality. My mother's work was essential for survival; but it was a hard lot, perhaps harder than that of my father. While I remember my mother and father talking over what ought to be done, I also recall that my father made the final decisions.

As is evident, I was an only child, although I recall that my mother had a miscarriage when I was about twelve years old. Moreover, I remember when a wall with a door was built in the large bedroom, my father having made the case that I was too old to sleep in the same room with them. Given the paper-thin walls that emerged, it hardly made a difference, though it gave me more privacy, a place of my own. It was in that room, which faced south, that I learned to sleep without a light. Until that time, I would often wake up the moment a light was extinguished, be scared to death, sometimes screaming at the top of my voice. Hence, it was embarrassing to visit my favorite relatives and insist on sleeping with a light on. Knowing that I needed to solve that problem, if I was ever to leave the area, I started a regimen on the night of a full moon, placing the bed in such a way that I looked out of the window. That two-week exercise solved the problem, though I admit being uneasy to this day in total darkness, in which there is no speck of light on which one can center.

Being an only child living far from other people was a lonely existence. Sometimes four or five days passed in which I saw no one other than my parents. Even my play was by myself. I had been given a play automobile, large enough for me to sit in. I built a ramp much as garages used to have before hydraulic lifts, and proceeded to take the car apart and then put it together again in a repetitive pattern. The time spent playing garage gave me some adeptness with wrenches, and, of course, led to many grease spots on my clothes.

As I grew older, I would throw a ball hard against the side of a barn, preferably a section that had a concrete wall, and let the ball return to me. That practice, also a solitary one, made me fairly adept at throwing with the result that I sometimes pitched for small baseball teams in the area. Somehow I had learned without a teacher to throw two kinds of pitches that were fairly effective. One was a ball that had a spin that made it drop out and down as it neared the plate. The object was to confuse the batter with a ball that looked high, and then dropped over the plate for a called strike, or to pitch it looking as if it were over the plate, only to have the batter miss the ball as it sank down and out. The other pitch was thrown almost underhand, going straight as an arrow, only to rise slightly as it went over the plate. The result was that if the ball was hit, it went up as a fly ball that could easily be caught. Every ballplayer knows, of course, that such intentions do not always work. In any case, I was apparently good enough at it to have a baseball scout contact me. But I did not express an interest, remembering that a neighbor who was much better than I had been hired for a baseball farm team but soon found himself back home. Moreover, I felt that I had neither the height nor build to survive pitching balls hard for entire games.

I loved and still love baseball, no other game having the same attraction. Recently, I found myself talking with Ed Beutner about baseball and we both confessed that it was still our delight and no other sport got close. We talked about pitchers, and he recited a poem to me by Robert Francis, called *The Pitcher.*

> His art is eccentricity, his aim
> How not to hit the mark he seems to aim at,
> His passion how to vary the avoidance.
> The others throw to be comprehended. He
> Throws to be a moment misunderstood.
> Yet not too much. Not errant, arrant, wild,
> But every seeming aberration willed.
> Not to, yet still, still to communicate
> Making the batter understand too late.

That is why the pitcher is the key to baseball. It is also why Barry Bonds is such a great hitter, for he knows how to meet the deception of the pitcher. So it is not the matter of finding the ball to be hit but of seeing the deception that accompanies the thrown ball. It is why baseball is so close to life, why it is like a parable, to use Beutner's point. So, we can say, as deceivers, yet true.

My first two-wheeled bicycle was a godsend, for at times when I was free I could cycle to town and see friends. Before I was allowed to have the car for pleasure, the bicycle was a means of freedom, though at times, it was hard to peddle against the stiff prairie winds. The result was that I saved money to buy a small motor, which, when it worked, drove the bicycle with a small pulley that rubbed directly against the wheel. Compared to most people I know, I had little opportunity for childhood play. The play at home in the evenings was with adults, dominoes or pinochle, demanding and encouraging thoughtful plans. I had no siblings and lived in a world of adults, except for grade school. But even there, there was not much play but instead a kind of seriousness. I have been told, and I know that it is true, that I am not much of a general talker. I guess I am used to silences and that many of my ruminations are private, at least until I find it appropriate to speak.

On the other hand I had two close friends. One was a first cousin from my mother's side, Bob Hoffmann. The two of us spent a good deal of time together on weekends, exploring life generally and playing pranks on each other and others outside our ken. One Sunday I remember well, for Bob's sister was sent to find us and she surmised that we were in the creek that flowed through the town. She found us naked, having discarded our clothes, except that I still had on a tie that I could not untie. The second friend was Carlyle Hoffmann, son of the banker who eventually left town. Frequently, the three of us would spend hours together, exploring the countryside on top of the bluffs, with its animals and caves. Most acquaintances were German Protestants, with an occasional Catholic thrown in. In my grade school and high school days, there were no persons from ethnic groups other than European immigrants. It was not until seminary days that I encountered the Black world and the Asian world, too. The consciousness of Hispanic culture was even later on the horizon.

Upper Grade and High School Experiences

Previously I mentioned that unlike most country grade schools in the area, we had two rooms rather than one. The building was divided between the first (kindergarten was not yet on the horizon) and fourth grades and fifth through eighth. This required two teachers, one for the early grades and a second for the upper grades. Within these classrooms one heard the teacher taking turns teaching each grade. When one's own grade was not being taught, one worked on assignments. There was no homework, but a student could well spend eight hours in school each day. Some students, of which I was one, listened to the classes being taught above one's grade level. This provided a head start over others when one arrived at the next grade.

The subjects were traditional, and I hardly remember them, though obviously a base was laid for the future. My mother had taught me to read before going to school, which was not unusual at the time, but a rather normal preschool activity. I was bright enough or picked up information easily and so was promoted by skipping a grade, doing eight years in seven. One factor may have been that given my birthday is in early July, I was almost a year older entering school than those born before July 1, the latter being the decisive marker for entrance. Most of my friends had started a year before.

Totally missing in the curriculum were the arts and social studies. And the sciences were meant for high school. Learning by listening and repetition was the major method and experience.

My upper classroom teacher was a distant relative, pretty, perky, and a good teacher, who startled me once by saying that my dark brown eyes would get me into trouble, and I wondered if that was a positive or negative comment. But I noticed her eyes were dark brown too. That was my first conscious inchoate sexual stirring.

The school building sat on about an acre of land, much of which served as a play yard, including a somewhat uneven baseball diamond. Baseball was the major sport, dominated, of course, by upper classmen. Football was absent, but the baseball diamonds were places where scouts searched for future players. To this date, baseball, not football is in my being. At the time I was also playing softball and, like my male counterparts, I delighted in watching women's softball being played in regular leagues. Some of the women players were better than the men, and their uniforms attractively displayed their forms in action. Summertime brought swimming events in the deep spots of one or other of the numerous creeks, and in the evening mixed nude swimming was not unusual, particularly among high school students. Since there were many ponds in the area, winter skating was a special occasion in those three or four times each year when the ice was strong enough to be safe.

On occasion there were evening socials at the school, populated mostly by parents. The toilet facilities were on the margins of the property, one for women and one for men, without water, heat, or light; they were literally outhouses. On one of those evenings, an upperclassman got a few of us to join him in placing wet mud on the toilet seats of the building for women. The results, of course, were disastrous, particularly since it was the mothers of our classmates who first experienced our muddy décor.

The upperclassman discovered to be the main perpetrator was duly punished, but he never squealed on the rest of us. It was both a lesson on consequences and that justice, at best, was ambiguous, given that most of us were not suspected. But the event did not keep us from overturning some outhouses in the nearby town on Halloween evening.

While being in the teens has a particular cache in recent decades, that category was not in our consciousness, but age twelve was. It marked the transition from boyhood to manhood, particularly with respect to work, most of it requiring more brawn than judgment. The same was true with respect to the transition from girlhood to womanhood. There was an acknowledgment of adulthood, with the mixed feelings that one could not return to a previous time and one was not quite sure of the future. It was not that the adult world was strange, for the generations were not kept separate. It was that the new status was acknowledged, a rite of passage marked this change, and one took one's place within the community in a new way. Religiously, in the Protestant church in which I grew up, confirmation was that acknowledgment. It was the time when one knowingly and publicly affirmed one's infant baptism, now as a young adult.

The local church belonged to the Evangelical Synod of North America, a German transplant to the United States of the church created by a merger of Lutheran and Reformed churches, a government-sponsored merger that resulted in three bodies: the continuation of the Lutheran and Reformed bodies, and the union of the two. The latter merger became the Evangelical Synod of North America. Apart from a high percentage of German Roman Catholics and a scattering of fairly conservative Lutherans in Southern Illinois, the Evangelical church dominated the region. It was not evangelical in the revivalist sense and had a distinct German ethos, in which tobacco and alcohol were not considered to be vices. This church body, dominant in the Midwest, merged in the thirties with the German Reformed Church, centered in Pennsylvania and adjacent states, creating the Evangelical and Reformed Church. Thus, it was a church that was the heir of both Luther and Calvin, including their affinities and differences. Subsequently, that church in turn merged, in 1957, with the Congregational Christians to form the United Church of Christ.

Preparation for confirmation involved learning catechisms, biblical materials, and the history of the church. It consisted of six months of all day Saturday sessions, culminating in Confirmation Sunday when we were grilled with questions. Occasionally, someone did fail and had to retake the process of learning laid out by the pastor, a lanky, middle-aged man who looked old, particularly to us young persons, and seemed inflexible.

He was the kind of person who tempted one to be naughty. Confirmation Sunday concluded with participation in the rite of communion, the taking of bread and wine, with the expectation that one would be a regular participant in congregational life.

My confirmation class consisted of about sixteen individuals, equally divided in gender. Seeing each other regularly over an extended period of time, it was natural that dating patterns and various degrees of intimacies began to emerge. It is perhaps somewhat ironic that the confirmation class produced associations the church would have discouraged. The relation between boys and girls was not a part of the curriculum.

Here the habits and patterns of farming communities in the early decades of the twentieth century need to be outlined. Given the farm world, no one would have been ignorant of sex. When I was about ten, I was given the task of letting neighbors bring their cows who were in heat to meet the bull in our pasture and to end the sessions when three encounters had been completed.

In this community, dates were occasions for intimacies, which included everything except intercourse. Still there were protocols to be followed. If a young woman did not want certain intimacies, the young man was expected neither to push nor insist. Conversation about sex was not a taboo and teasing was fairly constant, with women full partners. It was not unusual for a woman to say, "No thanks, you are not enough of a man for me."

Put as directly as it was experienced, dating included sexual experimentation as a natural, if not central, ingredient. It was not that one went to the movies, or for dinner, and sexual intimacies might or might not follow. There were neither many movies nor places to go for dinner; nor could they have been afforded. The only places one could go regularly were the weekend dance halls where local bands played. Most intimacies occurred in parked cars, with two couples not embarrassed to be, as it was put, making out, respectively in front and back seats. In other words, I learned only later that the first thing about dating was not sex.

Given that setting it was inevitable that a number of pregnancies occurred. Four of my classmates married because of pregnancies. At the same time it was not unusual to hear that so-and-so had had a pregnancy terminated. I clearly remember at a community dance (meaning parents were present), when my mother asked another mother why her daughter was not dancing, only to hear that she had just had an abortion and needed to rest. Then followed the details, including naming the responsible man. The two methods of birth control were the rhythm method, which worked well if a menstrual cycle was regular and periods of abstinence were practiced, or the use of condoms. The latter were easily available in men's bathrooms, but also easily broken without the utmost of care.

My first interest in a young woman was not from the confirmation group but at a family party, where she took the initiative and introduced me to kissing and other intimacies. Margaret was my first love, and although we did not become lovers, I remember her dark eyes, dark hair and lively disposition. I dated about six women, with half of whom sexual activity was a natural part. During the last two years of high school and first year of college, I dated one person. A month after we started dating, her father told me, "All I ask of you is that you be careful." But after three years, it became apparent that sex was not enough glue to hold us together.

Once my father accepted that I would not remain on the farm, he felt obligated to do the best he could with respect to high school preparation for college. While the easiest path would have been to attend the two-year high school in Maeystown, he knew that it was not accredited and therefore proposed that I go to Waterloo High School, though that meant paying tuition, considerable travel on my part, and enduring the negative view of being too snobbish to attend the local school. With respect to travel, for three years I drove to Maeystown, and then went with my uncle in his car to Waterloo just short of the place where he was a schoolteacher. In the late afternoon he picked me up at a local ice cream parlor, which presented a daily temptation usually solved by his punctuality. Given that the first part of the trip was seven miles of unpaved roads and the last ten miles of gravel, considerable time was spent driving in cars. During the last year, my parents paid to have me stay during the week with relatives just two blocks from the high school. This had two advantages. One, for the first time I could join in high school activities in the later afternoon and evening. Two, I could spend more time with my girlfriend who, through a similar arrangement, also lived nearby.

Going from Fults and Maeystown to the county seat of Waterloo one passed from rural to city living, from the absence of electricity to bright lights, from country to city ways. This led to an ethos in which city dwellers, particularly teenagers, looked down on those from the country. I never dated Waterloo High School women. But my country background was mitigated as I distinguished myself in some aspects of school life, such as making top grades, editing the school paper, and writing for it. I remember using the paper to campaign for a new high school building, given the dilapidated three-story, elevator-less, cramped quarters. It was obvious to everyone that a new building was in order and it was built some six years later.

I remember joining a radio club, not because I wanted to know how to build them, but because, at the end of the year, one would have built a radio one could keep. Moreover, the club met during regular school hours, while most activities, particularly sports, were in the late afternoon, when, except for the last year, I was involved in traveling back and forth. Thus normal social teenage activities had been excluded until the last year, which for me was a great time, for I could also bond with male classmates. One such symbolic act was when five of us drove after school to the red light district in East St. Louis. We cruised up boldly, windows open, only to hurriedly roll them up and lock the door as hands and arms were extended toward us, as pimps and prostitutes tried to surround our car. Our driver backed up and then sped up around the human blockade. We drove back in collective silence.

But what I remember most of the last two years of high school was how two teachers — the superintendent Walter Zahnow who taught American history and Vinita Buscher, the Latin teacher – gave me special attention. As for Latin, I should have mastered it better than I did, but I was part of the strategy of getting the teacher to talk about Latin civilizations rather than spending full time on grammar. Later, I had to do a lot of remedial work. Both teachers engaged me in conversation about world issues and put various journal articles and books in my hands. Only later did I understand the full import of what they were doing. I never had the opportunity to thank Zahnow, but years later I had the opportunity to speak to my Latin teacher, for I discovered she lived with her husband in Berkeley.

In many ways, going to college, while one of the ways to "get out of here," was not the route taken by others who left the area. I was only the second person who went away to college as opposed to other alternatives. I suppose that our pastor proposed Elmhurst College. What I remember is that someone from the president's office came to visit to try to convince me to attend. He caught me on a tractor in the field and we had little to talk about. My parents took him in tow, and I assume what happened was that they promised four hundred dollars if the college could supply the rest of my needs. After that first year, I was on my own.

Moving into the future has never been a problem for me. Negatively, I grew up in a situation of cultural deprivation, though at the time I was not conscious of that lack. There was no literature in the home, only the Sears Roebuck catalogue, with its many uses from door jam to toilet paper to stuffing in floor or wall cracks when the winter winds blew, and of course, the Bible, which was indiscriminately read. Usually, my mother said short prayers at mealtime. The wider cultural world lay ahead and it dramatically changed my life as I began to claim sensibilities beyond the merely verbal.

The inevitable question arises, what were my parents like and what did I learn from them. Overwhelmingly, in my mind what I learned boils down to doing a job well, whatever it is. My mother was proud of how she ran the household and my father had a religious ideology about how one farmed better than others. He had near contempt for many farmers, because weeds were not cut, buildings not kept in good repair, and fields not cultivated.

I know nothing of how my father and mother knew or got to know each other; nor did it ever occur to me to ask. Once, on a visit, my mother saw me spank my eldest son with more passion than she thought appropriate and she said, "You too". At the time it did not occur to me to ask what she meant, partly because she did not like to talk about her own life. It was the last time I spanked either of my two sons. I have one memory of an incipient fight when I was twelve and being pushed around by my father about something he didn't like. I recall picking up a chair and saying that he would never lay hands on me again, which he didn't.

Many years later a cousin who lived in St. Louis flew his plane several hundred miles out of his way to pay me a visit at the lake in Canada where my wife Hilde, our two sons, and I spent our summers. His message was unambiguous, that my father was physically abusing my mother, that it was widely known among their relatives, and that I needed to do something about it. In the ensuing separate conversations with my mother and father, as well as with the two of them together, both admitted the reality, with my father confessing that he was angry with my mother because she had not been a virgin when he married her. My mother was several years his senior and had had a wider exposure to life in the city.

My father was a demanding person, with little flexibility, and I was much closer to my mother than to him. Still, in my boyhood, I was aware of affection between the two of them, by sound and sight. Given the standards of the time, my mother had more educational background and my father left grade school to work after the fifth grade. But in spite of that, he continued to teach himself, could hear a tune and repeat it on the accordion, and in many ways was rather savvy. Surely his belief in education made him open to my seeing a future other than farming. I recall when I left for college, my parents saying to me that I was now moving into a world about which they knew nothing, and I would need to make my own decisions apart from them. Indeed, they encouraged me to do so. On occasion

I had wondered about my father's psychic state, for he seemed so especially possessed as the years passed by. My father's head and face, particularly when he had not shaved for several days, resembled Van Gogh's self-portraits, with an intensity that seemed to border on the loss of sanity. That perception has made Van Gogh's self-portraits difficult for me to see.

Hilda and John on the Rhine

2

DISCOVERING THE MIND'S EYE
The Influence of Lehmann, Niebuhr, and Tillich

*"The farm boy in me had been given back
his eyes in theological explication."*

Elmhurst College

In September 1936 I entered Elmhurst College and on the second day, a classmate, Egbert "Tex" Schietinger, asked me if I had read Paul Tillich's *The Religious Situation* and Reinhold Niebuhr's new book, *An Interpretation of Christian Ethics*. As a potential accounting student, only slightly interested in pre-seminary work, I had never heard these names. Later, it became obvious to me that Tex was probably the only one in an entering class of over a hundred who had read the volumes, much less ever heard the names. But being in college to get an education, I borrowed the books from him (he came with something of a library) and started reading, noting immediately that part of the translation from German for *The Religious Situation* had been done by Herman J. Sander, my soon-to- be professor of philosophy. For me these books were about as ambiguous and unclear as if I were reading the Bible from cover to cover without aid or direction. In fact, these were the first books I read from cover to cover. But in the required course in religion, professor Paul Lehmann made these men, as well as a host of other men and women, come alive and I found myself, under the sheer impact of his person and teaching, switching from a business to a religion major.

Paul Lehmann studied abroad but received his Th.D. from Union Theological Seminary in New York City. While deeply interested in Reinhold Niebuhr because of his impact in the field of ethics and political analysis and friendly to Tillich in spite of his affinity to the grand liberal tradition in theology, Lehmann himself was most influenced by the German theologian Karl Barth, a pillar of church opposition to the Nazi regime. Theologically, the stress on the total transcendence of God, that is, God being wholly other than anything we know and known only in revelation, was a powerful fulcrum for doing theological work in a transitional time when the terrible force of Nazism called for unequivocal rejection and opposition. As a disciple of Karl Barth, Lehmann's theological and personal disposition involved a passionate laying out of religious commitment. The result was that one's relation to him depended in great part on agreement with his reading of the world from the standpoint of his own position. This made him a stimulating teacher, one in whom theology was a realm in and of itself, but it also had implications for how one lived. Early on I became aware that his sophisticated theology was to be seen, not as a way in which the world could be ignored, but precisely as one in which it could be engaged. For Lehmann as for Karl Barth, the Christian needed the Bible and the newspaper, which in Lehmann's case, meant the *New York Times* and the *New Yorker.*.

Given my later exposure to Niebuhr and Tillich, and their influence upon me, I was among those about whom Lehmann had doubts about my theological agenda. But that never affected our friendship, for while questioning my direction, he could never let go. Hence, we had regular contact into the 1960s, including those years while he was at Princeton Theological Seminary and I was at Princeton University, and when we were colleagues at Harvard. When he did not approve of actions, he let one know but not in a derogatory way. He believed, for instance, that I was too rapidly promoted to full professor at Harvard. He loved intrigue and gossip, but he was not mean-spirited.

In addition to his lectures, delivered with his arms over his head scratching tufts of hair on his balding top, he provided, along with his wife Marion, social events at their house, full of gustatory delicacies and conversations of import. Marion had strong opinions on most subjects, willingly and freely entering into discussion, particularly animated when she felt he was wrong. For those who got to know him, he also played a pastoral counseling role. I think he counseled most of us in our romantic relations.

It was an interesting faculty, headed as president by Paul's father, Timothy Lehmann. Timothy was a learned person and he and his wife frequently invited students with a theological bent to dinner at their home on campus. I was not then aware that there was a special relation, negative or positive, between father and son.

But the dinners at their homes, while full of meaningful conversations, were also for me, a learning about etiquette. I saw how others picked up napkins and cutlery, how to place and use them. Before that time, my only culinary experience was within the chaotic, nondescript farming culture. Much of my learning about etiquette was watching in order to know what to do, particularly in college and seminary. At Union, President Henry Sloane Coffin invited the entering class, two by two, for lunch. As was so often the case, he knew relatives of the students and while that provided relative silence for me during the early part of the meal, it gave me the occasion to watch.

The refectories at college and seminary, except upon special events, were hardly places to learn decorum. Two things I vividly recall. Most of the male students drank four or five glasses of milk. Not wanting to appear conspicuous, I started drinking milk too, only to discover that after some six weeks I was becoming ill. Having been advised to cut out the milk, since that seemed to be the only difference in my eating habits, I returned to my previous habits and within two weeks I was all right. Conversely, the dining room frequently served breaded eggplant. Given how little it was liked, there was always much going to waste. Since I happened to like it, I frequently wrapped breaded eggplant pieces in napkins and took them to my dormitory room, where I placed them, when I was hungry, on the hot radiators. To this day, I am an eggplant fan.

During my first semester, I shared a two-room suite with a fellow freshman. He turned out to be fairly demanding on how the furniture and amenities were laid out, and he simply did not like college. He lasted for one semester and for the rest of the academic year, I had the space to myself. On each of three floors there was a proctor, whose end room was replete with windows and accompanied by a bedroom. All three reported to a faculty person whose family lived on the first floor. I applied for one of the positions and was appointed to the third floor for the next three years, a financial boon since it was rent-free. Responsibility as a proctor included seeing to it that decorum and overall behavior were acceptable. My initiation into the position occurred when a group of students on the third floor dropped balloons full of water down the steps, flooding the apartment of the faculty resident on the first floor. The student punishment included cleaning the apartment as well as the entire building and probation for three months.

During my second year as a proctor, the head proctor crawled into bed with me, started to hug me and verbally expressed how much he liked me. My instinctive reaction was to tell him that I didn't want him in my bed and that I wanted to sleep. But the event made me observe his actions overall and I detected a physical piety that had sexual overtones. We never talked about it and no further advances occurred, but his relation to others now revealed a dimension I had not seen before. When I was in high school, I was a representative of the school to a conference at the state capital, and on the way by bus I sat next to a dentist who talked extensively and suggested we meet on my return, noting that he had much to teach me. When I told my father about his wanting to meet me, he told me that there were relations between those of the same sex that were similar to those between male and female and that he did not want me to pursue the matter. I really didn't know what he meant and dropped it. In retrospect, I think he handled it well.

It was a big step for me from high school, during which parental connections were still constant even as new ventures into the unknown were sought, to college, where one was virtually on one's own, though still dependent in unrecognized ways. High school involved the rural and the town, but college was in a suburban city within the metropolitan area of Chicago. Elmhurst College was two long blocks from downtown Elmhurst, some sixteen miles west of the center of Chicago. It was a denominational school, serving the Evangelical Synod of North America, but as were all such church-sponsored schools, it was beginning to broaden its religious horizons in favor of students from the immediate surrounding area. Nevertheless, it was still essentially a residential school with dormitories, dining facilities and a lively sports program, mainly centering in football. In this sense it was like hundreds of colleges throughout the Midwest. But for me it was a new world, culturally, politically, and academically. One could leave the dormitory and be in the center of Chicago an hour later. Museums were already part of the landscape, though at the time they were less of an interest to me than the social political scene. I recall visiting Socialist party headquarters and going to meetings where Norman Thomas spoke in his compelling oratorical style. It was not much of a stretch to visit Communist Party meetings, to sign petitions of various sorts, and to join in parades and picket lines. I recall picketing the importation of Japanese silk with Professor Paul Lehmann at my side.

Such involvements, very common at that time for students and faculty, were not reflective of wide-ranging political commitments but instead the result of believing that together we could make a difference in society. In short, we were mainly non ideological, though the intelligence agencies of the time did not see it that way. Things as simple as having signed attendance forms at meetings on various issues were materials assembled and reported in the McCarthy hearings of the fifties. As late as the late sixties and seventies, one could encounter the consequences of having left one's name somewhere. When I was president of the Graduate Theological Union in the sixties, the then board chair, Daphne Greene Wilkins, told me that a board member was critical of me for political associations in the past, going all the way back to college. The three of us met at Richard Miller's San Francisco office, and he pulled a document out of his desk drawer and started to read sections from it. One detailed protest activities in violation of the McCarran Act (named after Senator Patrick McCarran) and two additional subversive meetings I had attended. I said, "Is there more?" and he said "No," whereon I, much to the chagrin of Daphne, said "I could tell you more." It turned out that Miller, as a member of the Police Commission of San Francisco, had access to intelligence sources of the McCarthy era. A few weeks later, he resigned from the board.

While Lehmann had suspicions about the role of philosophy, he was convinced that one had to know what philosophers thought. Herman J. Sander taught philosophy and I took all his courses. While not a scintillating lecturer, he was thorough and did not duck issues put to him. His lectures came from extensive sheets of paper, bound in a black binder, virtually the text as he gave it. Exams and papers were based on the text of the philosophers, rather than works about the philosophers. My Bachelor of Arts thesis was on Plato and political theory. My argument was that the later published work, *The Laws*, represented a change in outlook from the idealism of *The Symposium*, with its idea of government being in the hands of a philosopher king. The failed experiment at Syracuse in Sicily made Plato, I argued, propose more complex elements as essential to government than the idea of a philosopher king. Several years later this viewpoint was thoroughly explored by Plato scholars. Both Sander and my classmate, Egbert Schietinger, eventually left academia and taught humanities, if not humanity, to military groups.

Werner Richter, formerly Minister of Education in Germany, arrived as a refugee at Elmhurst College in the late 1930s. Having been responsible for appointing professors in Germany, he had collected enough refugee enemies to preclude his being placed at a distinguished university but rather came to this small liberal arts college. We read texts, heard his lectures, and engaged in lively discussions on the issues raised by Pascal, Dostoyevsky, Nietzsche, and Kierkegaard. To this day, I can recite passages from these figures dating from that time. For me, the Richter family added a new ingredient to my life. Arriving at their house, one would hear music, mostly symphonic, and the family game was the children identifying the composer and composition. This was something I had missed and was determined to learn. Beethoven became my favorite composer, with music that dealt with the range of human life. For Barth, Mozart may have composed the music of heaven, but for me, Beethoven was of the earth, and the earth was more interesting than heaven.

The most eloquent, albeit irritating, lecturer was Thomas Clare, who used sociological and psychological approaches to life and history, making every concept conditioned by social or psychological forces. It seemed like a game being played and he was the major player and, therefore, manipulator. That there was another sociologist more sober in turn did not help. I'm afraid that for a long time I have seen psychology and sociology not as the vanguard of the future, but as the last of the scholastic disciplines, emphasizing analysis, classification and prediction. I also recall the professor of German literature, smacking his lips as he went through Faust.

While I had taken physics in high school, college presented biology and chemistry. I remember little of these classes. What I do recall is the chemistry grading system. Each Monday morning there was a test on a section of the chemistry volume. So on Sunday evening, I studied the material and could recall enough the next morning to get an A grade. A passing grade consisted of the total of the Monday morning grades, lab functions, and final exam. But if you got all As on Monday morning you had enough points not to have to take the final. Hence, a few of us got an A grade for a chemistry course that taught us nothing but temporary memory. There were no courses in astronomy, though there I had a natural curiosity.

Also among the circle of faculty members I prized was Waldemar Hille, professor of music and art. While he was known mainly for directing and producing top-level concerts, I also remember him for the other arts. For a course in art history, he let me do a paper on art and the political order, written from a somewhat Marxian angle. Given my subsequent interest in the visual arts, I am still startled that I apparently hastily wrote a paper so inadequate that I received a C-minus.

I found languages difficult. I did three years of Greek, though I never gained a sure-footed confidence. I acquired a reading knowledge of French by working through a French grammar and then placing English and French texts next to each other. German is my first language and, while my German is a dialect from the Rhineland, lacking the refinement of High German, I continue to think in both German and English. But my professor in college could not figure out why I got As in translating from German into English and C-minus working from English into German. In short my competence in languages leaves much to be desired and I have been envious of those who have such talents.

One of the requirements for graduation was passing a course in physical education. The head of that division was also the football coach, and I knew nothing of football. But he was a remarkable person and teacher. He taught me what I needed to do to pass and told me I did not need to worry about my physical fitness because I had worked all my youth in physical labor and could maintain an adequate level of fitness just by walking.

Toward the end of college, the question was, What next? While I entered college under a pre-ministerial category, this was as much for financial backing as for conviction. As indicated before, the teaching of Paul Lehmann had sent me into theology and so the natural progression was seminary. The obvious place to go was Eden Theological Seminary in Webster Groves, Missouri, on the western end of St. Louis, a seminary devoted first to the Evangelical Synod of North America, and later to the reformed tradition as well. The faculty of the seminary had names one would have recognized at the time, though not with the prominence of most Eastern schools.

Again finances played their part, though not in the anticipated way. Going to Eden could be done with hardly any independent support; moreover, it guaranteed virtual entrance into a ministerial position. As a graduate of Union, Lehmann preferred that I try Union and by then the notion of study with Reinhold Niebuhr and Paul Tillich was attractive. But how could I support the move financially and secondly, the synod under whose care I would need to proceed, would undoubtedly give future preference to Eden graduates. Given that I was willing to take a chance on a future appointment, the real obstacle was financial. If I worked each summer for three months, I could clear about five hundred dollars during that period, and I was willing to do part-time work during the academic year. Lehmann pointed out that Union had exams for one scholarship that gave free tuition for the first year. Investigation indicated that I could do two exams in philosophy of religion and one in the German language. How many competed for that prize I do not know. But I was glad I won, which helped make the financial difference, and psychically gave reason for going to Union.

There were additional advantages I had not anticipated but for which I was glad. The person who received the grant was freed for the first year from doing fieldwork in a parish and did not need to take courses in Christian education. What reasoning lay behind those provisions, or loopholes, as I called them, I do not know. But it made it possible for me to spend full time on courses that still further opened new horizons.

Going to New York City had one negative. In my third year at

Elmhurst I met a first year student, Hilde Lohans, who interested me, and we began a long courtship. Her studies were in literature and religion and we shared other interests as well. But our respective academic schedules meant that we were apart for two years, except at vacation times and in the summer months when we both took jobs at a camp near Dunkirk, New York, some forty miles south of Buffalo. Hilde and I were married after her graduation from college. We went to Union for me to complete my last year in the divinity program. She audited courses and developed an avid interest in Hebrew. I can still visualize her with alphabet cards in her hand as she tried to master the vocabulary.

Overall, college had been an exhilarating experience. I read endlessly in the areas in which I concentrated, philosophy and religion. There were wider horizons as well, as indicated with respect to the faculty members I have mentioned, many of whom opened their homes to students. Then, there were student friends, many of whom emerged from the student Christian association, for whom the advisors were Lehmann and Sander. Even at this age, there are several I recall with delight and with whom I have contact on occasion.

I learned a good deal about classes and writing, inasmuch as courses in humanities required papers instead of quizzes or so-called objective exams. When it came to papers, I consistently got As (except for the art paper that I had written without discipline and thought) and Bs on multiple-choice or true and false alternatives (except for the chemistry class). There were simply too many possible choices that made sense, and I could not bring myself to choose the most adequate or true answer. That problem plagued me during all my student life, and when I became a faculty member, I never gave a true-or-false or multiple- choice exam. Nuances were too important to sidetrack them by objective choices.

College was the beginning of the opening of many doors, although diversity, as we began to call it, was hardly on the horizon. The college had a few foreign students, but their cultures were conspicuously absent. Yet an openness was affirmed to those who were different. When I was home on a visit from college, I heard my uncle on my father's side bragging how he got a few blacks out of town by threatening them that he would have lynched them if they did not leave. It was good to hear my father and mother oppose such proposals.

Union Theological Seminary

For someone interested in living in the midst of a major city, Union Theological Seminary was ideally located. The main entrance to the neo-Gothic complex was on the northwest side of Broadway and 120th.

Directly across 120th to the south was Barnard College, on the southeast side, Columbia University, and on the east side Teachers College. On Union's north end, that is, 122nd Street and Broadway, the Jewish Theological Seminary was on the northeast corner, the Julliard School of Music directly to the north, and Riverside Church and Grant's tomb directly to the west, facing the Hudson River. The subway, as well as one of the main entrances to the Columbia campus, was on Broadway at 116th Street, where a ten-minute ride would take one to Times Square, then a symbol of the center of the city, or a bus – for a more leisurely trip – down Fifth Avenue to the Metropolitan Museum of Art or the Museum of Modern Art. On the southeast end of Columbia stood the Cathedral of St. John the Divine and to the east of Columbia, down the hill, was Harlem, then a vibrant cultural center amidst deteriorating surroundings. At the time, one could walk around in Harlem, visit jazz events, and enjoy the ambience. Harlem churches were thriving and many of the seminary students did their field work in them.

Times Square, of course, was a magnet, ranging from the Broadway theatre to peep shows, the latter being something one needed to see only once. It seemed a must for many visiting the city, who were only disappointed, to whom my usual response was, "What did you expect?" For those of us who were students, the off-Broadway theatre was particularly enticing with small intimate spaces and experimental theatre usually followed by discussion and refreshment and not to be underestimated, at prices we could afford. That is how I first saw *Waiting for Godot*. Then there were the movies, old and new, spread down Broadway.

The used book-shops on Fourth Avenue just below 14th Street were fascinating. One could spend an entire Saturday browsing for books. Half of the library I was then acquiring came from those shops. On Mondays we bragged about the volumes we had found at a nominal price, part of the game being to acquire books that were priced below what one would ordinarily expect.

What a delight it was to come from the Midwest into this wide world, indeed worldly beyond all expectations. For whatever reasons, the Chicago of my college years offered little by comparison. Perhaps the sixteen miles from downtown made a difference; perhaps there was less encouragement from faculty to experience Chicago. Union faculty encouraged knowing New York City with regard to the theatre and the arts, social and political life, and events. Their classroom lectures made reference to current productions, and they even organized theatre parties. There was a continual buzz of new things to experience. In this sense, Union provided not only a theological program; it provided a total culture which I absorbed with abandon and delight. Setting foot in New York City still gives an extra bounce to my life.

Most of the faculty members lived in apartments on the northern perimeter of Union or in McGiffert Hall, directly adjacent to Riverside Church. While married students were still discouraged, the tide could not be stopped, either in terms of marriages or single women students. Single men students lived in dormitory rooms on the east perimeter of the quadrangle. I lived in that dormitory for two years, and when I returned, married, for my last year, we had a small apartment in McGiffert Hall.

Given that my scholarship permitted me to bypass introductory courses, I could immediately enter more advanced courses and pick professors I wanted. Because of my previous exposure to the writings of Niebuhr and Tillich, I was of course interested in taking their courses as soon as possible. At the time, Union was still small enough for students and faculty to know each other. Moreover, in my case, Lehmann had seen to it that I was not anonymous. Indeed, a series of students had begun to come from Elmhurst to Union in the preceding two years and we were all known as Lehmann's Barthians. In my case, I had also come from the same church synod as the Niebuhr brothers, the Evangelical Synod of North America.

Already in 1919 Reinhold Niebuhr had proposed a union of the Evangelical Synod with the Reformed Church, but that was not well received. But by the thirties, the climate had changed, and in 1934 the two bodies united to form the Evangelical Reformed Church. That combination was unique from a theological standpoint. The Evangelical Synod was influenced by a liberal reading of Luther and to some extent by the Pietist tradition. Here it should be noted that the Luther heritage should have pointed to uniting with one or other of the Lutheran groups but they all turned out to have a rigid, orthodox reading of Luther. So it turned out that the Luther of the Evangelical Synod and the more liberal reading of Calvin in the Reformed tradition, as opposed to the Presbyterian tradition, suggested a distinct creative direction.

The question remained: in what ways were Luther and Calvin to be understood in a united church, given that the two agreed on many points but were divided on others? That was the teaser that Niebuhr threw out to me already during my first year in seminary. Then I discovered that in the States, Tillich had identified his church home to be the same religious body, the Evangelical Reformed Church. The three of us shared a consciousness and fascination about a body that combined both Luther and

Calvin. In an overall sense, my intellectual pilgrimage as an MDiv. student was to study these complementary and contradictory sources, Luther and Calvin.

So much was this my interest that I took two steps. First, there were no courses in Luther and Calvin as such and I noted this lack to Niebuhr, who said I should talk with Tillich. I did, telling him that I wanted him to do a seminar on both figures. Much to my surprise, he readily agreed, provided I found the students and managed the organizational aspects of the course. That modest working relation started a pattern that grew and continued for almost two decades, in which my responsibilities grew as Tillich's regard for my capacities increased. Perhaps that regard was helped by an easy working relation with Hilde Frankel, Tillich's secretary and expeditor of many problems, an extraordinary woman who died of lung cancer in the early fifties. I was asked to do the memorial service, but declined, doubting that I had the necessary composure to do so, having witnessed her declining life week after week.

Second, I made arrangements with three faculty members to write one comprehensive paper for their respective courses, making it possible to do the equivalent of something more like a thesis than individual course papers. This made it possible to read in depth on one figure or one theological problem. While I heard brilliant lectures, the base of my own future was laid in that freedom to do my own explorations. My reading and papers were for my own theological development. It was as if I was preparing for teaching and writing, though at the time I had no idea I would be doing that as my life work. I was interested in assignments for myself, not in meeting requirements for my teachers. I think my teachers sensed that and let me go down that path. Probably half of my time was spent in reading Luther and Calvin. The more I read, the more fascinated I became. So it is not by accident that I later edited writings of both and that most of my writings include both figures.

Clearly, the outstanding figures at Union were Reinhold Niebuhr and Paul Tillich. Originally a pacifist, Niebuhr moved away from that position as the clouds of World War II were on the horizon, and made the case that war was a necessary evil in the case of the development of Nazism. His religious and social analysis was so penetrating that he became a public figure, influencing governing agencies. Political figures, such as Arthur Schlesinger, Jr., saw the relevance of Niebuhr's thought for the public domain, but did not see the need for his Christian analysis. But for Niebuhr, it was his Christian understanding that was the basis of his social political analysis. At the same time, he made common cause with distinguished figures in the Jewish and Roman Catholic circles with respect to social issues. He utilized Christian thought, with a critical and appreciative approach, as the fulcrum from which he out thought his contemporaries, and galvanized them into action.

Paul Tillich was the first Christian professor to be dismissed by the German Nazi regime. As the intellectual leader of the German Socialist Christian movement, he was obviously a target and, through friends, including Niebuhr, he made his way to Union. While his social and political instincts were close to those of Niebuhr, theologically the two were different. Tillich was a philosophical theologian, one for whom the exploration and explication of theological topics took philosophical form. But philosophical form meant the entire range of culture, so that his work is essentially comprehensive. For the general public, his sermons were most powerful and helpful discourses. Both Niebuhr and Tillich were masters of the public platform.

Attendance at classroom lectures by Niebuhr and Tillich ranged from forty to fifty in number, and in seminars, from ten to twelve. Obviously, one got to know them well even in the classroom. One of my early memories is Tillich doing a course on the pre-Socratic philosophers. He handed out photographic renderings of archaic figures and lectured on what he saw. What a revelation! The farm boy in me had been given back his eyes in theological explication. Once in talking with his wife Hannah about Tillich and museums, she told me that she remembered him standing in front of major paintings like a dumb ox, having hardly anything to say, only to hear him six or seven weeks later give a scintillating lecture on what he had seen.

While Tillich lectured in a slow, deliberate cadence, Niebuhr kept a pace in which words jumped out and in which the dialectic of his thought overwhelmed one. While Tillich improvised on notes that formed a whole, Niebuhr's lectures rushed past his notes. Indeed, once Roger Shinn and I found that Niebuhr had left the file behind from which he lectured only to discover that, on this occasion, the papers inside were totally blank. He had turned them nevertheless; perhaps he had brought the wrong folder.

Access to Niebuhr and Tillich was easy. It happened in the halls, a place where students and faculty interrupted each other as a matter taken for granted and kibitzed as well. It happened in the refectory, where faculty and students mixed together at tables for lunch. Mostly the conversation centered either in classroom continuations or world events. Once in a pause, I blurted out what I had observed, that Niebuhr's plate was the first one that was empty each day, to which he replied "It's only fuel." I concluded there were some things in life he was missing. One day I heard Niebuhr say to Tillich "You are a Schleiermacherian," to which the reply was "Of course." For all their differences, there was an affectionate intellectual relationship between the two, something like friendly ships passing in the night.

Both Niebuhr and Tillich had frequent open houses, Niebuhr more frequently without an agenda but with the unannounced presence of persons in public life, cultural or political. That was how many of us first got to know W. H. Auden, and other distinguished political figures. A classmate, David Burgess, said of such meetings that one would not miss them willingly. Tillich's were more formalized, usually with a topic announced in advance and with Tillich making sure who had to be specifically invited for the evening in addition to those who just dropped in.

I also remember the regular meetings, usually at Union Seminary or Riverside Church, of what was initially known as the Fellowship of Socialist Christians. Organized by Niebuhr and Tillich, the group met twice a year to explore social and political issues from a Christian perspective. It was not unusual to meet persons such as Adolf Lowe, Albert Mollegen, Eduard Heimann, and Rollo May, though the dominant role of the two organizers was unchallenged.

Already in the early months of the fall of 1940, I was introduced to the religious political dynamics at Union. About twenty students professed their pacifist position and were opposed to war in any and all cases. Hence, they felt it incumbent to resist registering for the draft, even though the draft permitted one to be a conscientious objector and thus be free from being drafted. In their minds, governments had no religious right to force one to be involved in decisions about the matter. A draft as such, even if it permitted freedom from the draft, was wrong.

The number of those with this stance turned out to be eight persons, each of them known to the rest of us. Other pacifists registered as conscientious objectors, and in November the eight were sent to prison in Danbury, Connecticut, for two years. Most prominent and leader of the eight was David Dellinger, though best known to me was George Houser, a gentle thoughtful person. Both persons later became significant figures at the national level.

Henry Sloane Coffin, Union's well-known and socially privileged president, was faced with a difficult role. Since the draft permitted the rights of conscientious objectors, he found it difficult to accept the absoluteness of their positions. And while he let the law run its course, he defended the students from constituencies who wished to have the students expelled from Union. He pleased neither group, but he held his ground throughout with a tenacity and grace so characteristic of him as a person and figure. This may not be the place to comment on his wit, but it is not irrelevant, for he could make people laugh at overwrought positions and lead them to more measured responses, keeping the respect of those he could not please.

The pacifist movement was strong, with figures such as Kirby Page and A. J. Muste. But the eight Union students pushed beyond the ordinary pacifist position. Their logic was well represented in Houser's "Diary," published in the *Union Review* (November, 1940). In many ways, Roger Shinn, also a prominent divinity student, argued the opposite, namely that he could not take an exemption or delay, and so became an infantryman. A good number of us, while not pacifists, registered for the draft but asked for delay until we were eligible for the Navy chaplaincy.

Niebuhr, while he did not accept the pacifist position, did not break his personal relationship with the students. Nor did he side with uncritical promoters of war on the other end of the spectrum. He was gracious to Harry F. Ward, who followed the gyrations in Soviet policy. I took a class from Ward in his last year of teaching. Most of the course consisted of his bringing editorials from newspapers to class, condemning those he disliked, and rationalizing Soviet shifts from day to day. He represented the end of an era and there was a kind of sadness about it all.

While Niebuhr and Tillich were the stars of the faculty in terms of public attention, they did not escape negative reviews from some in the academy, including colleagues. Niebuhr was accused of misinterpreting historical figures and movements. Tillich suffered the disdain of those for whom philosophy was misleading with respect to theology. For the most part, I could comprehend such criticisms without drawing negative conclusions about either theologian.

Among scholars of note, if not of public recognition, was Richard Kroner, Tillich's German friend who came to Union in 1940. I recall being encouraged to take a course from Kroner on Kant to Hegel in order for him to have a few students. His lectures were thorough, providing every detail of the thought of these seminal figures. While philosophical to the core, Kroner thought of himself as a theologian. Somewhat ungraciously, he tried to make the case that he rather than Tillich was the theologian Union needed.

David Roberts was the star of the younger generation. His lectures in the philosophy of religion were scintillating and clear and he provided summaries of his lectures for those who wished to have copies. They were a veritable gold mine for covering the nineteenth and the early decades of the twentieth century. Indeed, I consulted them for years. He also had a penchant for conversation, so much so that he was willing to do a reading course on topics and figures that interested a few students. I remember a course in Kierkegaard made up of three of us who met every other week after dinner in his apartment. We discussed readings we had been assigned, with his role being that of providing context for our discussion. He wanted to make sure that we read the sources, rather than what was said about them by other authors. Where a particular writer was helpful to understanding an issue in Kierkegaard, he would point it out and suggest we read it. Grades for the course were his impressions of our performance in the seminar. Suddenly, we became aware that he was ill, increasingly did fewer and fewer courses, and was frequently at a sanatorium. He suffered from depression and severe back pain and died at a comparatively young age.

Of the same generation was Cyril Richardson in the field of Church History. While a bit more Anglican than some of us preferred, he covered the ground and wasted no time. It was worth listening and the attendance never faltered. But he seemed to be lecturing alternately to the right and left upper corners of the room, consulting notes as his eyes swung down in the swing from corner to corner. While a bit aloof, he had many friends, and was exceptionally helpful to graduate students. Less eloquent than Richardson was John T. McNeill, whose interpretations of Calvin and Calvinism still stand up in spite of the decades that have passed. His use of materials carried one along, though humor was scant indeed. Or was it the subject matter?

Two senior Protestant liberals, soon to join the retired ranks, were Eugene Lyman and William Adams Brown. At his peak, Lyman was as publicly well-known as Niebuhr became. Both Lyman and Brown were known for their roles in ecumenical circles and their worldwide contacts. They were stars in the early days of the World Council of Churches and the U.S. Federal Council of Churches.

Their younger colleague Henry Pitney Van Dusen, later Coffin's successor as president, was likewise of the liberal heritage and traveled even more extensively with the ecumenical agenda, with the result that students referred to his pronouncements and generalizations as Van Dusen's bird's-eye view of the world. His lectures in systematic theology appeared to be read from a written text, but with such precision that the bell at the end of the hour always rang as he completed the last phrase of the lecture for the day. He was adept at posing alternatives in ways that left no doubt of his own position, and even those of us who did not agree were swept into a kind of regard for the logic of his thought. One day I shall never forget is Van Dusen ending a lecture with the statement that one needed to accept the moral theory of the atonement, for the only alternative was a monstrosity. Out of my mouth slipped the comment, "I'll take the monstrosity," with the class response being a combination of laughter and quietness. Not known for an excess of laughter, he smiled as he closed his file and left the room. If he remembered it at all, there was no subsequent negative sign.

Several years later, when I was a graduate student, I was asked to be his assistant for a semester when Tillich was on sabbatical. Halfway through the semester, he announced he had to be away for two weeks, and would I lecture in his place, and that I should do what I judged best. Upon his return, he said he did not want to pry but that it might be helpful to know what I did to make sure that topics were not duplicated. Knowing that he had skipped Luther and Calvin and that there were no indications that he would return to them, I had decided to do the two. When I replied that I had lectured on Luther and Calvin, he said, very good indeed, for he had skipped them. It was as if I had done him a favor by lecturing on some figures he did not want to do himself. Physically, he was an imposing figure, a bit pompous, but always fair and open.

Because of James Moffatt's reputation both in biblical studies and church history and word that he was retiring, I decided to venture into his course in church history. The lectures were instructive, but they had no chronological sequence. One might be in the thirteenth century one day and the fourth on the next. The standard joke was that he had dropped his lecture notes and never gotten them back in sequence. But most of us were in awe, particularly at his translation of the Bible into a more modern idiom, though he hardly seemed the modern type. Coffin related that at the request of a club in New York City, he agreed to bring the famous man, only to discover that the chair of the day introduced Moffatt as the person who wrote the Bible. While he had come from Scotland, Moffatt was attuned to American sport, knowing the batting averages of most of the baseball players of the time.

Also in New Testament were Ernest Scott and Frederick Grant. A European, Scott's idiom never took on an American flavor, nor were his convictions very clear. Coffin was heard to say that he knew no other scholars so knowledgeable as Moffatt and Scott with respect to the New Testament but so little affected by it. Grant's lectures seemed unorganized, though unlike Moffatt, they were sequentially ordered. But they were dry as dust and Coffin heard endless complaints from those who took New

Testament courses. Grant was a doctoral level seminar genius, suggesting that doctoral work should be seminars and somewhere down the line a faculty person should tap you on the back and say, you now have a Ph.D. But in the course I took, there was a good deal of reference to social movements and one day a classmate said, "I have just read some passages on which I would like your comments." Then he read two passages and asked what Grant thought of them, to which Grant replied that "they were junk," to which the student replied, "You wrote them." Grant replied, "Wherever you quoted them from, I no longer believe them." Sympathetic laughter ensued.

Ernest Scott and Julius Bewer respectively wrote the then reigning introductions to the New Testament and to the Old Testament. If Scott's convictions were unclear, Bewer was a pietist and a pacifist. While I disagreed with most that he said, I decided to concentrate on the content of the Old Testament as we went along. Then came the exam and we all expected that the questions would cover his thoughts and lo and behold, they were all centered in concrete Old Testament content. The result was that for that course, I got the only A, much to Bewer's surprise. What a contrast it was when several years later, James Muilenburg electrified students with his interpretations and personification of biblical figures. One of my favorite Old Testament teachers was Emil G. Kraeling. I liked his quiet, thorough pursuit of texts. For whatever reasons, Kraeling was not in the flurry of the winds that blew at Union. A prominent graduate student in Old Testament was Samuel Terrien, already an instructor whose French ways delighted all of us.

In the arena of those who taught preaching there were four stars: President Henry Sloane Coffin, whose laughter taught us not to be too self-conscious, but to be careful what we said; Harry Emerson Fosdick, whose direct moral discourse made him a preacher to the nation and who said of my preaching in class that he continually had to switch between saying yes and no, making him wonder if my mind was too dialectical for preaching: in other words, make it simple; Paul Scherer was a special favorite for he could preach with power out of the Lutheran tradition and he seldom tried to change one's sentences; George Buttrick, whose sermons were works of art, and who was not happy until he could pull us into his mode. Years later, Buttrick was a charming colleague at Harvard.

Inasmuch as I did not need to take courses in religious education, I had little direct contact with Harrison S. Elliott and Frank W. Herriott. But I did have personal conversations with Herriott, as he quizzed me at times on what dialectical theology was about. He really wanted to know, but none of our talks seemed to provide lasting changed convictions on the part of either one of us. I did consult the two of them about the work with young people I was doing in a Union church in Bay Ridge for the last two years of my basic theological studies.

In the three years I initially spent at Union, the prevailing currents of thought moved gradually from the dominance of liberal theology to the currents unleashed by Niebuhr and Tillich. The liberal spirit was not abandoned, but its content was superseded by appropriating biblical and historical material in ways that illumined the present in more realistic ways, indeed in exciting ways. In addition to Niebuhr and Tillich, David Roberts and Richard Kroner became more prominent and new figures such as James Muilenburg, John Knox, Wilhelm Pauck, and John Bennett joined the faculty.

A role that kept me in touch with faculty and students was my association with the *Union Review*, published by the students of the seminary. Begun in December 1939, its aim was not to take a singular position, but to reflect the variety of student and faculty opinion represented in the seminary and sometimes beyond. The editorial board of ten was led by one of the managing editors, Roger Shinn. In November 1940, I was asked to join the board and a year later I was appointed managing editor, a position I held for two years until my graduation. Perusal of the *Union Review* indicates that it reflected the range of thinking as the US gradually moved toward and into World War II and to its end. In retrospect, I assume that my experiences with the *Union Review* fed my later editing and publishing ventures. In retrospect, I am surprised to see how many articles I had written during that period, all oriented to social issues of the time.

In sum, Union was noted for the variety of theological positions it represented. It was not only interdenominational; it already represented movements across religious lines and social movements. In the midst of that climate, I formed habits and approaches that combined a theological position with an openness to wider spectrums. If college taught me how to think within a theological position, Union taught me how to do that in a much wider setting. Union in New York City formed habits that characterized my future, though I was not conscious of that at the time. Consciously, my aim was to be as good and as thorough as possible in facing circumstances as they presented themselves. That was to be tested in the next phase, time spent in the U.S. Navy.

Being a Navy chaplain required ordination. Had I gone to the denominational Eden Theological Seminary that would have been fairly routine. In order not to be blocked, I had taken the step of keeping in touch with those who made up the committee on ordination, and on visits home, would see to it that I got to know them, or rather, they me. So I had no difficulty in being accepted and I asked the head of the committee to preside at my ordination in the church in which I had grown up in Mayestown, Illinois. Paul Lehmann came from the east coast to preach the sermon, for he had started me on my theological path. Soon after that event, I was on my way to chaplains' School.

3

BEING A NAVY CHAPLAIN
IN WORLD WAR II

*"I always had near me a book of services . . .
and when one laid it down, it fell open
to funerals."*

Differences of opinion on how to respond to the military draft have been considered. Now a word as to what it meant for some of us who took the exemption with the commitment to enter the service in some form once our theological degrees were obtained. For most of us, this meant entering the U.S. Navy as chaplains. Since graduation from divinity school did not bring much pastoral experience, those of us coming directly from seminary were sent to three months of chaplains' school set up at the college of William and Mary, Williamsburg, Virginia. The classes consisted of practical theology, designed to strengthen our lack of experience, such as in counseling, and geared to the particular pastoral needs of persons in the Navy. It also involved familiarity with the Navy ethos, protocols, and procedures. The text for the latter was mainly a thick volume we all knew as Navy Regs, that is, *Navy Regulations*. In addition, we were put through physical fitness training, that is, programs for all members of the Navy. Obviously, one of the requirements for the Navy was to be able to swim. Since I had never learned to swim, I presented a particular problem, and the minimal instruction was of little help. I still recall being pushed to the opposite side of the pool, with the officer saying to me, "For your own good, you'd better learn to swim." Later, I did learn to swim with the help of an excellent swimmer, a fellow chaplain, at Tumon Beach, Guam, though I never became a first-rate swimmer. Though I loved water skiing and became fairly proficient at it, I always wore a life vest.

Except when we were in fatigues for special purposes, we wore regulation uniforms and regularly marched to lunch and dinner. I had my share of the regular taunting cry of the person in charge, "Chaplain, everyone else except you is out of step." While in chaplains' school, my wife Hilde and the wife of another chaplain friend had taken apartments in Richmond, Virginia, and secured waitress positions in the main department store, and we visited them on weekends.

After chaplains' school, I was assigned to the Naval Training School at Bainbridge, Maryland, located about seven miles north from the point where the Susquehanna flows into the Chesapeake bay. The small town was wedged between the river and the row of hills rising some seventy feet from the water, with railroad tracks, a narrow road, and houses on the hillside of the highway. In that setting, housing was scarce. At Bainbridge, I befriended a Frenchman who owned a few buildings that he was slowly converting into apartments. Knowing something about construction, I offered to help on weekends and evenings to speed the work. In that we were successful, though I temporarily endured the wrath of the head chaplain when a chaplain friend, who was considered the best bowler on the base, broke a thumb in helping me move a hot water radiator. Fortunately, six weeks later he was bowling again.

The base itself was directly on the hills above the town. An old building from a former school was the officers' quarters, and beyond that, new construction spread out in every direction. The base was a training center for recruits moving from civilian to navy life. As such it was organized into regiments, each about a thousand persons in number. This training was what we used to call boot camp, a period of about six weeks prior to a short leave and then assignments to the Navy in various places in the U.S. and overseas. Serving these regiments was a central headquarters unit, so that supplies, health services, et cetera did not need to be created independently or separately for each regiment. But to use these services, recruits had to get special passes to move into and return from such separate areas.

While ten chaplains were assigned to the base, my particular assignment was to the neuropsychiatry group, a headquarters unit that served the entire complex. It meant that our patients came from their units to visit or, in cases of obvious breakdowns, lived in the hospital beds and rooms for whatever period necessary. The task of the unit was to determine whether a person was faking symptoms or generally ill. In the first case, people were sent back to their units; in the second case, they were separated from the Navy. Homosexuality was automatically considered a reason for dismissal, a judgment that came from on high and which neither the psychiatrists nor I were in a position to challenge. The outlook of the fifteen psychiatrists was that homosexuality was probably more biologically than socially conditioned. In the period I served in that unit, I never heard a negative remark from staff members about patients.

My task was to participate in the general assessments, particularly with respect to seemingly abnormal religious phenomena that could present problems. It was not unusual to see recruits who, without provocation that one could detect, fell into seizures of various forms. Such seizures could be fatal to themselves and others in battle. But some forms could also be feigned, and that was part of what needed to be determined, though feigning could itself be an abnormality one could not accept for battle situations. It was hard to believe that such seizures were unknown to draft boards. They were probably driven by the mandate of meeting their quotas.

Each Friday, the psychiatrists and I met with each other and sometimes with the particular persons under scrutiny. I had access to all files and read them in advance, and was a full participant in all instances, but rightly without vote on medical issues. When decisions had ramifications for family situations, I was frequently the person involved in communicating and working out the wider consequences of our actions.

Two incidents, extraordinary as they seem, may provide a picture of the wider involvements. One of our patients was found to have been involved in criminal activities and was assigned to prison in a Navy installation an hour away. At the same time, he admitted to being the probable father of the daughter of a young woman who brought her problem to our attention. Both parties favored getting married, and asked me to arrange the wedding, which was to be at the prison facilities. So some two weeks later, I arrived at the prison with all parties present, but then the man said he would not get married under any circumstances. So, the wedding was off, and having talked at length with both parties, I personally and professionally agreed that was the best decision.

The second incident occurred when the chief psychiatrist called me in to discuss the situation of a young recruit who was unsure of his sexual orientation. The psychiatrist reported that he felt that the recruit had gotten into sexual experiences with an Episcopalian clergyman at the latter's prodding and doubted that this reflected the recruit's actual orientation. Then he asked me if I would be willing to talk with him. The young recruit, then in boot camp, got permission from his regiment to come to see me. On the basis of our conversation, I thought it fairly clear that he had been under pressure from the cleric and did not enjoy the contact. But while he knew various girls socially, he had never experienced sexual activity with a woman. Had he been tempted? "Yes," he said. Did he know any women who might be interested in going to bed with him? "Yes," he said. So we agreed that on his boot leave, he would explore that interest, but that the partner had to be equally willing. So we left it that on his return he would come to see me again. So he returned from leave to the Outgoing Unit and asked permission to come to see me. The psychiatrist's hunch seemed to be confirmed, for the recruit was full of delight in his new discovery.

Quite apart from whether that was the best pastoral advice, there is a sequel. The chief psychiatrist called me in again, and with a grin on his face said, "Naval Intelligence wants to know why a recruit in boot camp got permission to see you, then returns and secures permission to see you from the Outgoing unit, when each of these groups has a chaplain he could have seen." The psychiatrist, of course, explained the circumstances, clearing me of suspicion.

While psychology and psychiatric arenas were not central to my training, my exposure in real life was educational in the concrete sense. After almost a year at Bainbridge, orders came to proceed to San Francisco as chapláin for U.S. Fleet Hospital 111, headed for the Pacific arena. Disappointed in not being sent to the European theatre with my German language background, I noted that perhaps my Navy career would center in the medical arena.

Arriving by train in Oakland and then by ferry to San Francisco, I reported to the designated office on Market Street to discover that no one knew where the hospital was but that I was supposed to check in at a base south of San Francisco. So I did, only to discover that they had no knowledge of the hospital. So back to San Francisco, where it took two days for the office to discover that the hospital staff was being assembled at a Navy base south of Mount Diablo, about forty miles east and slightly south of San Francisco.

U.S. Fleet Hospital 111 staff and equipment were being assembled for departure at an unspecified time, though the speculation was that it would be in about three months and that we would establish a hospital on a ground site, after being transferred by ship. Still, we were told that we needed to be able to leave in three days, should there be changes in the war strategy. Each week there was a Sunday evening party, welcoming the new officers with a deliberate strategy of getting them drunk at the dinner. Given that I, the chaplain, was the only officer who had arrived that week, someone took it upon himself to tell me. The result was that I did all the things one could think to avoid the effects of alcohol, such as eating a lot in advance and soaking the food in olive oil. It worked. I did not turn down drinks and remained sober. Months later, an officer could be heard saying, "Chaplain I'll buy you a drink, but only one. I can't afford to pay for what you can drink." The party was a one-time event, and in the ensuing decades, that is, until well into the sixties, I drank no more than two or three drinks per week. I started smoking in the Navy, but never got past one or two cigarettes a day. On Guam, I started smoking a cigar a day for several months, inasmuch as one could unwrap them and have a fresh smoke. Then I tried a pipe for several months. Without thinking about it, I later just stopped smoking, though I have been in a lot of smoke-filled rooms until recent decades when secondary smoke became a public issue.

The waiting time was an ideal period. A small Quonset apartment was available for my wife Hilde and myself and a number of officers and wives got to know each other well. A series of events were always being planned and carried out. By the time we left, there were at least fifty officers I knew well, a good prelude to the life we later shared on Guam.

The demands on us were not great during this waiting period. We would report each morning and then have the day fairly free. There was little to do for the physicians, the personnel support officers, and the engineers who also served as architects. One day I went to the Pacific School of Religion to visit James Muilenburg, the charismatic Old Testament professor, just appointed to Union, who signaled he would like to talk with me. We had a great day, and when I returned to Union we became fast friends.

As was frequently the case for chaplains, I inherited the broad assignment of welfare officer. So considerable time was spent going into San Francisco to secure various kinds of materials for games, magazines, movies, and athletic equipment. Under the leadership of the Spreckels family, a regular collecting place had been established to provide such materials for those going overseas. In those weeks I got to know the grand dame of the family, and it was she who insisted that I take a sewing machine for the nurses who would eventually join the hospital. She was right; it was in great demand on Guam.

While we saw the commanding officer and the executive officer on a regular basis, we did not experience the full weight of their roles until we left the United States. With about a five-day notice, we were directed to report to a ship in San Francisco to be transported to our destination. I still remember the swelling waters outside the Golden Gate Bridge, the roughest waters in the ensuing six weeks. After a brief stop in Honolulu, we headed west and docked in the flat waters of Eniwetok and its sand dunes for a three-week stay aboard ship. While we could leave the ship, the ship was more interesting than the sultry, sandy landscape. Needing a haircut and with no professional barber aboard, I went ashore and found a so-called barber. When I returned, I was teased with the remark that the barber had mistaken the front of my face for the back. Finding a mirror, I had to concede agreement. Finally our ship was sent on its way, with the explanation that we were delayed by the slower than anticipated pace of the war. Our scheduled arrival for Guam was D plus thirty, that is, thirty days after the initial invasion.

The Guam harbor, formed by a long peninsula, was a busy place, as ships unloaded materials for setting up establishments on the island. There were regular convoys of trucks that were hijacked by other U.S. units or by friendly citizens of Guam, taking advantage of the exposure to much sought-after building supplies. We spent the first few nights in pup tents, set up in a flat piece of land cleared of trees and vegetation. On the first night we woke up as water poured over all the possessions at hand. But the next night, our support staff had seen to it that newly dug trenches carried most of the water around us, though moisture continued throughout the seventeen months on Guam to such an extent that lights were used in closets to avoid mildew.

The first two weeks were spent in setting up better tents and transporting supplies destined for the hospital, some directly from the ship that brought us, others from supply distribution centers that had been set up. Given that the stealing of supplies from trucks as they passed through the countryside meant that personnel had to accompany each truck, I volunteered to do my part. Ordinarily, chaplains did not carry firearms, but we were permitted to use discretion in extraordinary situations. So keeping my lieutenant bars on but leaving the chaplain pins in my pocket, I sat on the back of the loaded truck, gun poised. There were two or three of us on each truck plus the driver and assistant driver. Hence each truck was staffed with four to five people, sufficiently armed in most instances to deter hijackers.

While we lived comfortably in tents that could house four to six people each, more permanent living quarters awaited getting Quonset buildings erected for a functioning hospital. As these buildings were being erected, some fellow officers suggested that a chapel should be built. I was willing for that to wait, but some officers said they had access to buildings that could be erected. If I would do the plans, they would do the rest. I later learned that this involved securing twenty-four bottles of whiskey to facilitate gaining priority status. The whiskey was easy to get, for one of the officers volunteered to collect rations from those allocated to fellow officers. No one ever directly involved me in these maneuvers, but on the internal grapevine the chapel was referred to as the chapel of the floating foundations.

The location of the hospital was near the main runway on the island. Outdoor movies were frequently interrupted as large bomber planes returned in early evening from their bombing runs, swooping in some three hundred feet overhead. Geographically, the hospital stood on ground about a hundred feet above sea level, a slight promontory on the west side of the island and just south of Tumon Bay, technically off limits but surreptitiously open, in fact, for beach events. On one occasion about ten of us were in the water cooling off from the heat when an unseen wave overwhelmed us, and threw us off balance, with a simultaneous undertow. About ten feet away one of the nurses screamed and was being pulled to the open sea. Being the nearest, I managed to reach her, and succeeded in pulling her to safety. My swimming lessons, such as they were, saved both of us.

The early weeks and months on Guam were a series of gastronomical transitions. At first K-rations were handed out and they served the need for food, though not for taste. Then when kitchens were set up, one could always count on Spam, served either cold or hot. Sometimes fresh fruit and vegetables appeared, secured by special forays into the countryside. Then there were the results of lend-lease where, in a planning with which one could not disagree, beef went from the states to Europe, while mutton went from Australia to Guam and the islands under U.S. control. For American tastes, the fresh mutton was at first a delight but one soon discovered that after the fifth time, one could hardly eat it because of its pungent smell. Occasionally, when ships were headed directly back to the States and had surplus food, we received such as largesse.

The construction process soon centered on hospital services for those wounded in battle. One unpleasant issue emerged when one of the doctors indicated that a respirator was needed to save a life long enough for required surgery. Unfortunately, this occurred in the early evening and the head of supplies refused to open the requisite building. So two officers, with my presence, broke a door lock and secured a respirator. For days we were threatened with a court martial, but given the uncooperative stance of the supply officer in a time of need, the charges were dropped.

While as a chaplain I was responsible for services of worship and counseling, and indirectly for the welfare of the entire staff, being a chaplain was only partly like having a parish. Aside from the support staff, persons came and went and immediate needs were served rather than long terms ones. "Dear John letters," the term for wives or sweethearts writing they had found new loves, sent many a Navy male to the chaplain's office. When nurses arrived, the inverse was also true. I recall working out a reconciliation between one of our nurses and a line officer in Hawaii. The man was so grateful that he signaled to me that he wanted to do something for me, like, did I need any extra staff. A former choir director at Bainbridge had said to me that he wanted to join my staff again, but we both knew that was unlikely. I merely mentioned the matter to the line officer and a month later the choir director arrived at my door in Guam. We had the best choir on the island.

My main task, as those of fellow officer physicians, was to serve the wounded. Between the setting up of the hospital and the arrival of patients, the doctors, who had little to do, feared they were losing their skills and were generally unhappy. To this day, my teeth show the skill of a dentist who talked me into major dental work that I could not have afforded so that he would have something professional to do.

When nurses and a Roman Catholic chaplain arrived, we knew that all our services would soon be needed. The arrival of a Catholic chaplain was important simply in terms of the number of hospital patients to be seen. Moreover, while early in the war, we had been taught what to do to wounded, dying patients in terms of specific prayers, Archbishop Spellman of New York (later Francis Cardinal Spellman), whose particular interest was the military, ordered that Catholics were to be left to die without ministrations of non-Catholics. So, a fellow Catholic chaplain was doubly important. Besides, he was older and more experienced than I was, and a wise counselor. Before the Catholic chaplain's arrival, I had arranged for a chaplain from elsewhere on the island to do Sunday Catholic services and for Anglicans/Episcopalians, a high Episcopal chaplain would arrive, toward whose ministrations I usually supplied a helping hand, for by the end of the day his thirst for alcohol required some walking assistance. For the Jewish community, a member would say the prayers, and I was asked to come and give sermons appropriate to the community. I had selected a practicing Jew to be my assistant with respect to correspondence, office arrangements, and general logistical help. Taken as a whole, cooperation across Protestant, Catholic, and Jewish lines was common practice. Only on one occasion did I need to take a stand when a group of evangelical conservatives wanted me to sponsor their activities as the personal religious position of the chaplain. The result was a policy worked out with the island commanding chaplain to the effect that it was made clear that the

Office of the Chaplain would facilitate all religious services and persuasions, but would not be identified with any particular religious outlook.

Generally, the work of the chaplain did not require much contact with the commanding officer and the chief executive officer. Still, the chaplain could have contact with them when duty indicated it was important to do so. The executive officer, Captain Flower, was not an easy person with whom to work and the medical staff in particular had a series of endless problems. To do my work, I felt I needed contact with the head chaplain of the island and other chaplains more experienced than I with hospital work. Needing his permission to see them, I was quizzed about each request, and on one occasion, he decided not to grant it. I told him that I would need to report that he was interfering with my doing my work. To that he responded, "Chaplain, I think you should respect my position," to which I added, "I respect your position sir." Then he added, "Do you think I am an SOB, as the officers generally do," to which I replied, "Yes, I do." For the next six weeks, all went well. Later we learned that most of the officers, including me, had received poor fitness reports from him. According to *Navy Regulations,* an officer is entitled to see and respond to such a report. Inasmuch as none of us had been given that option, we all received our reports directly from Washington and were asked to respond directly to that office, bypassing the usual chain of command. As far as I know, that was the end of the story. Apparently our responses were considered adequate.

But it was not the end of the problems posed by the executive officer. A nurse was killed in a jeep driven by him as they returned from a social event at which alcohol had been served. Since two members of the opposite sex required additional officers to be present, there were witnesses, and according to regulations, a board of inquiry was set up. While that group did extensive work, and according to rumors was about to make specific recommendations, the body was dismissed and the issues sent to a higher board of inquiry. Whatever the findings of that original body may have been, whether culpability or exoneration, the Navy solved the issue by sending the executive commander to another command. This was not an unusual procedure, a way of bypassing issues that would not go away, no matter what the verdict.

In the meantime, the main work of the hospital swung into high gear, for two-thirds of the wounded in Okinawa passed through the hospital. Months on end, hospital staff worked long shifts, dedicated to saving lives. Since exhaustion leads to mistakes, most of us were ordered to take some time off each week. The other chaplain and I coordinated our schedules so that one of us was always on duty. As a chaplain, one always needed to be able to be found.

Patients with similar wounds – shell shocked, limbs gone or mutilated, body organs torn by shrapnel – were placed in wards with others with similar ailments. This was both for the sake of bringing nurse and physician specialists together in one place and letting those patients with similar problems be in touch with each other. For a chaplain, making the rounds consisted of regular schedules. Those who were shell shocked were visited twice or three times a week, inasmuch as the pace of life or death was slower, with little that one could do, while those whose internal organs were damaged, one saw daily if at all possible because the movement to recovery or death was anticipated. Then there was being on call, when nurses or doctors, at the request of particular patients or sensing that certain patients needed to talk, called one's attention to the circumstances, most often that the patient was near death or dying. It was not unusual to be with two or even four persons a day as they died, and to preside at their burials.

The great mystery to me, and to doctors and nurses, was why some individuals, who according to their medical condition, should have died did not, and others who should have lived, died. The human will one way or another made a difference, but the difference it made did not illumine the reality. Of course, there were those for whom the fear of death was itself the fear that killed, and some who lived, for whom struggle and miracle seemed near each other.

Obviously, we did not have a long time with those who died, and had not known them before they were wounded. Regardless, one learned something of their family situations, of engagements and longed-for engagements, of bonds and estrangements, of hopes delayed and sidetracked. Death itself was seldom discussed, but its presence was not far away. Just as I had learned early on in the wilds of Guam that a liturgy sustained one, so prayers born of the ages and modified slightly with names and places seemed best and real with the dying. I recall talking with only a few about the services of burial. But I always had near me a book of services I had used throughout my life until it burned in 1991, and when one laid it down, it fell open to funerals. It continually reminded me of the fragility of life. As chaplains, we had been taught to take notes, however brief, of those with whom we had been present as they died. I do not recall how many such notes I had at the end of the war, but I do recall using three or four of them after the war as families wanted to visit with me as the person who had been present at the death of their loved one. Such families traveled hundreds of miles just for a half-hour visit to discuss situations I recalled from the notes I had taken.

Toward the winding down of the war, the intensity of the chaplain's role in the war tapered down. The head Navy chaplain for the area, with whom I had worked through difficult problems, called me to headquarters for a conversation in which he proposed that for the rest of my time in the service, I take on a less difficult assignment. He had known of all our difficulties with the executive officer, mainly because I had kept him informed. Moreover, a chaplain had a certain moral authority in difficult situations. Or if one had a national reputation, one carried some weight in facing difficulties. Pee Wee Reese, the famous Brooklyn shortstop, had been assigned to me as head of welfare staff. While I turned over all those responsibilities to him, we had many conversations and represented a common front in behalf of enlisted seamen. A Southerner, Pee Wee inherited many prejudices, but he was a charming person. After the war, I saw him two or three times, after games to which he had invited me, and talked about his overcoming prejudices in connection with Jackie Robinson. He knew what power meant, and in different ways, we had both used it in trying to resolve difficult situations.

In any case, I was assigned to an Aviation Repair Overhaul Unit (AROU) on another part of Guam. While there one day, dozens of army planes were seen going over the center of the island, back and forth, for at least a half hour. It turned out to be General Spaatz responding to Admiral Nimitz's having announced that the Navy had won the war in the Pacific.

In any case, as the name of the unit would indicate, AROU's function was to repair and refit fighter planes, an assignment different in so many ways from my hospital experiences. The latter had given me easy deportment around nurses, physicians, and hospital protocols, though it was fifty years later that I became a patient myself for the first time. Like most youngsters I had longed to be around planes, and I became as present in repair shops as I had previously been in hospital chambers.

I soon discovered two senior pilots who took repaired planes each Friday afternoon for testing, in runs that lasted from two to four hours. They found the tests rather tedious and asked me whether I was interested in keeping company with them on some of their runs. Crouched amidst radio equipment I stood behind the pilot's seat, resting my body against the outer cases of testing devices. The flights started out gently, but entered into rolling exercises. Then the pilot pulled the plane straight up until it shook fiercely, then dropped the nose down just before it would have spiraled down into a tail spin, followed by a push toward the earth at full speed, and then a pull up as one felt one was going down anyhow, indeed causing one to pass out temporarily as the blood seemed no longer to be in one's head. At twenty-six, I could still thrill at such excitement and got used to it enough to go up twice a month. Only once was the flight aborted and returned to base for some malfunction. An element of cruel humor accompanied us on a few flights to Rota, an island no more than about fifty miles to the north which had been bypassed in the invasions. In the early flights, of which I was not a part, the pilots would run down as if to strafe the airfield and take some modest fire. By the time of my being an accompanying person, the ammunition had run out and the persons simply ran away as the plane flying about fifty feet above ground headed for the strip.

While my Navy experience involved life and death issues, I was never in combat. However, as indicated previously, I participated in safeguarding our supplies. Once I was scared as a Japanese soldier, who was hiding in the bushes where we were bulldozing an area, ran into the clearing brandishing, as it turned out, an unloaded gun. He was cornered and surrendered to the military authorities. On another occasion, another chaplain and I were headed for a meeting in a different part of the island when bullets blazed through our jeep, leaving marks on its body. We both jumped from the jeep into a gully, with mere bruises to show for the encounter.

For most of the time on Guam, my social contacts were within the hospital compound. Sometimes when an officer had a date with a nurse away from the base, which required taking a jeep with a third officer, I was asked to be the take-along person. About the time our buildings were completed at the hospital, a jeep was found for the chaplain and one was also assigned to me at AROU. This meant I could come and go at will, only having to sign out and note my destination. For about a year, two hospital chaplains and I spent Friday evenings together. One of them had been a year ahead of me at Elmhurst College and I had met the other at Union Seminary and chaplains' school. On Friday morning, each of us would check what the chow was for the evening meal and then agree to meet for dinner where the fare was most appealing. The conversations usually covered our frustrations and delights, and our previous acquaintances turned into friendship.

Then arrived the day long hoped for, the return home. But it was not to be a leisurely ride. I received special orders to be chaplain for a ship from Guam to Port Hueneme, north of Los Angeles. The first part of the trip was very uncomfortable. Later I realized that the discomfort came from being tossed around by the tail end of a typhoon. Only when I saw that the microphone that I was to use for services was bolted to the deck and that I could use it for holding on, and when I saw those present gray at the gills, literally as well as figuratively, did I know what was happening. But things quieted down and we spent Christmas aboard ship. It was at the end of the trip that a special commendation was placed into my Navy file for extraordinary services for a special assignment in which I had to improvise. I figured that balanced out my previous bad fitness report.

After a two-day wait for train accommodations in California, I was back in New York City in early January, where Hilde and I had started our married life. We had been apart for seventeen months, the only contact being the letters we wrote back and forth to each other. My mail was censored, but through codes the Navy did not catch, my location was not a secret to her.

Technically on leave for several months, I was not given any duties but was expected to stay in Navy uniform. According to the papers, there was much discussion on what the civil and political rights were of officers in the Navy or Army or Marines. The Bell Telephone Company employees were on strike and the question was, could a person in uniform be on the picket line? I was contacted by the American Civil Liberties Union and asked to join the pickets in uniform, the logic being that it would be hard to do too much to a chaplain. So I appeared and was photographed. The next day the papers were full of the incident and I was ordered to appear at Navy headquarters in lower Manhattan. My unease was not alleviated when I ran into Reinhold Niebuhr on the street and told him what had happened. His response, as usual, was direct: "You may be a fool for Christ's sake, but the gospel doesn't say anything about being a damn fool. Now, how can I help you?" In the meantime, the Civil Liberties Union decided, for reasons unknown to me, not to challenge the matter in court as it had originally intended. Navy headquarters informed me that I had no such rights and they expected me to obey the rules until my last day, some three weeks away. Apart from the lecture, that was the end of the matter. To this day, I do not believe that the armed services should have the authority it does with respect to issues of free speech. I also felt that the American Civil Liberties Union had exposed me with no follow up on its initial commitment.

4

PAUL TILLICH'S GRADUATE ASSISTANT

"Tonight when these bottles are empty, Tillich . . .
will have agreed to write his systematic theology."
— Statement by Wilhelm Pauck to Dillenberger

Union and Graduate Division of Columbia University

It was January 1946, and Hilde and I had decided to spend the next few months at Union in familiar territory, reading and visiting classes, all prior to taking a parish. We had also decided to start a family, and Eric was born later that year. I remember giving him his bottle and getting him ready for bed, while Hilde prepared dinner for us. Then there were the walks while pushing the carriage along Riverside Drive. Those were happy times.

Intellectually, I was interested in taking another look at Tillich. While I was doing my basic theological work I was more interested in Reinhold Niebuhr. Indeed, I had done my thesis in ethics, focusing on Calvin. But my daily experiences of life and death on Guam seemed to resonate more with Tillich, for I had been dealing with "ultimacies" rather than "proximates," though the former were not absent in Niebuhr. My feeling was, take another look at Tillich.

When I ran into Niebuhr a few days after returning, he asked, "What are you going to do?" Without making reference to my renewed interest in Tillich, I talked about taking some courses and reading widely before taking a parish. The same ritual occurred as I separately met Tillich and Muilenburg. Soon thereafter, I was summoned by the three of them and was asked, "Have you ever considered graduate school and a career in teaching?" I recalled Coffin having discouraged all of us from doing that rather than going into the parish. Their response was that too many were interested in doing graduate work and teaching but that I was among those who should consider it. With that imprimatur, I found myself registering in the Columbia/Union doctoral program and assigned as an assistant to Tillich. The stipend that assignment provided plus the GI Bill provided the necessary financial resources.

In the same month a former classmate, Bob Appleyard, later Episcopal bishop of Pittsburgh, and I were asked to talk about our experiences as chaplains in World War II at a meeting of the Younger Theologians (which was actually the oldest of the theological groups) at the College of Preachers at the Washington Cathedral. Both of our papers were published in the *Union Seminary Quarterly Review* (1946). More memorable than that discussion was the new contact with senior faculty members across the country, many of whom later became friends and colleagues in various ventures. Still etched most clearly in my mind is Wilhelm Pauck returning after dinner with a paper bag full of bottles of wine and saying to me, as we met by chance at the doorway, "Tonight when these bottles are empty, Tillich, who has been so reticent, will have agreed to write his systematic theology." And so it was.

The Union/Columbia doctoral program had specific requirements from the Columbia side, what one might call the basics. First, there was the Friess/Schneider course in the history of religions, for which they had written a specific text. They also included specialists from the different religious traditions. Islam, for example, was represented by a joint faculty appointment between Union and Columbia. In short, the program intended to assure that one could not stick solely with one religious tradition.

The requirement in the history of western philosophy was met by a course given by John Herman Randall, Jr., whose prodigious book, *The Making of the Modern Mind*, was completed when he was twenty-seven. He was a brilliant lecturer and the requirement for the course consisted of two papers, each of which was to be written on a selected subject, usually resulting in about seventy-five pages per semester. Seldom did one complete the course in an academic year. I recall spending a summer on the paper for a semester. I then wrote my required comprehensive exam for the Ph.D., which included the philosophy of religion, and passed it without having completed the course. Hence, I successfully petitioned that I not be required to do the second paper inasmuch as I had already passed the doctoral comprehensive exam on the subject.

Randall stood in the naturalist tradition and had mixed feelings about religious conviction. But he agreed to do a seminar with Tillich on myth and symbol at the doctoral level, for which the dozen or so of us who took the course had to do a paper for discussion. Tillich encouraged me to move along certain lines, all counter to Randall's position insofar as we could figure it out. When the evening came on which my paper was featured, Randall responded with a mean-spirited and devastating attack and I wished I were a thousand miles away, indeed, wished I had never entered the doctoral program. But slowly Tillich joined in the discussion, hardly mentioning me, countering Randall point by point. It was evident that I had given Tillich the opportunity to counter Randall without himself having to make an attack. That bothered me for a few days, but the hurt went away when I discovered that after the heat of the evening, I had won a grudging respect from Randall.

Being a graduate student after the War was considerably different from that in the early forties. The number of students increased greatly, some having postponed entrance, others coming to seminary as a place to make decisions about the future. Being returnees was a positive situation, for we already had contact with most of the faculty and perhaps an edge in being assistants to faculty members. Roger Shinn, Paul Abrecht, and I had the privilege of sharing a faculty office. Most of the time we worked quietly, but we did take breaks together. Paul was the person who kept up with world news and we had the equivalent of a seminar each day. Roger was the balanced person, personally and intellectually, while I was trying to find my way, coming initially as a Barthian, then a Niebuhrian, then deeply involved with Tillich though I did not consider myself a Tillichian. Even today, more than a half century later, I recall that period with delight.

Having passed my comprehensives and language exams, I could now give special attention to a dissertation. My fascination with Luther continued, and I tried to suggest an area of his subsequent influence, since the whole field of Protestantism interested me. But my conversations with a half dozen faculty individually produced no unanimity of subject or direction. I then wrote down what each had said and concluded that the sum total did not permit a dissertation. So I proposed we meet; we did, and within an hour we had hammered out a dissertation, the concept of the hidden God and its place in Protestant theology. The strategy of getting faculty and candidate together early on became normal in my teaching.

My dissertation, in condensed and more focused form, was subsequently published in 1953 as *God Hidden and Revealed: The interpretation of Luther's deus absconditus and its significance for religious thought.* My colleagues affectionately referred to it as "God – hidden and revealed . . . by John Dillenberger." I may add that Tillich had listened to me and his colleagues and said "What John wants to do is work with the concept of absconditus." Even today, the concept fascinates me and has been present in a hidden way, no pun intended, in all that I have done.

In addition to a written exam and a dissertation, Columbia also required an oral exam, and when I arrived at that, I was asked to sit at the end of the table opposite that of the chair person, Horace L. Friess. Then there were four examiners on each side. John T. McNeill sat to my left at the side of the table, and Freiss asked him to start the exam, whereupon McNeill responded that he would rather wait and see how the exam went before posing his questions. So Friess said to the person on my right, "Well, let's start with you and go in the opposite direction." This meant that McNeill would be the last examiner, and if anyone on that group had a reputation of being tough, McNeill was the one. I don't think he had the slightest inkling of the pressure I felt. Actually, when McNeill's turn came, he put two questions to me about Luther of such detail that on the law of averages I should not have known the answers. But I did, and McNeill smiled, and said, "I have no further questions," thus turning out to be the shortest questioner of all. It happened that Tillich and I walked back from Columbia to Union after the exam, and in a posture so characteristic of him, he stopped, faced me, and said, "Never again will you have that many important people take you that seriously." I think he was right.

Throughout this second period at Union, and then during the time I was his colleague at Columbia and Harvard, there was pressure on Tillich to write and publish the systematic theology he had lectured on and elaborated upon for years. Doing this in English was an extraordinary challenge. But more and more Tillich thought and wrote in English, and this was a victory of language and meaning, a new reality for him.

Once as I walked into his office, Tillich handed me a reprint, and I saw that it was a German version of the "Two Types of the Philosophy of Religion." I must have paused for a moment, for he said: "Don't you see, this I wrote in English; now it is translated into German." For him, a person who had struggled to master this new language, this accomplishment meant more than I realized at the time. While Tillich had considerable help from editors and friends, I detected that his English writing style was becoming better and better, particularly with writings that were originally conceived as well as written in English.

A few years later, I bewildered Tillich by a quick response to a question after a lecture he gave at the Free University of Berlin, a response that troubled him, for even years later he kept coming back to it. After the lecture and adulation he received from friends of years ago, as we were going to his sister's house, he said, "You have never heard me lecture in German. What was it like?" Out of my mouth came, "Not nearly as profound as in English." It was one of those statements that one wishes one could take back, though I only meant that much of his thinking was natural and native to the German language, that its not quite fitting English at times seemed to give the latter a tone of added profundity in the way in which it stretched the English language.

His systematic theological program, originally conceived in German, now existed in outline form in English propositions. These propositions were distributed and were Tillich's lecture notes. It was assumed that a copy of Tillich's lectures, as he expanded on the propositions he distributed, could become the basis of a final text. President Van Dusen authorized some funds to take down Tillich's spoken text, and in the more primitive days of securing such texts, I took down his lectures in my own short hand version, and then dictated them immediately to Audrey Abrecht, whose typing speed was such that she kept up with my reading of the script. How much of the systematic theology we did I do not recall, nor do I know what happened to those pages. But what did become clear to Tillich, to me, and some others, was that the lectures as such could not be edited into an acceptable text, and that while they could be used by him, he would need to write his own new English draft, more in accord with a written than with a spoken style, and even more important, in the framework of thinking in English.

And he did. I still have visions of him with sheets of paper, several pencils, the propositions, and little else on his table or desk. He wrote without clutter, and with an unsurpassable concentration out of a wealth of knowledge accumulated by his classical German education, a background I always envied, and his oral picking of the minds of others in the United States.

Albert Mollegen and Wilhelm Pauck particularly influenced the direction the Systematic Theology had to take for the American scene. My task was limited to editorial responsibilities for volumes I and II. For volume I, I worked with Cornelius Loew on textual matters and with my wife, Hilde, to provide an English flow to the sentences. It was also my task to question Tillich on sentences or paragraphs that seemed unclear, in and of themselves, or to English readers in particular, and also to make sure that in our editing, his meaning had not been changed. Finally it was my task to meet with Tillich and go over the text, sentence after sentence. For volume II, I had sole responsibility for all of these aspects. Indeed, working on volume II was particularly memorable, for I would arrive at his apartment about three nights a week at eight o'clock, find him propped up in bed, a chair for me, a bottle of wine, and two glasses. Then we would read the text, making whatever changes seemed appropriate. After the first week, I caught on that the empty or nearly empty bottle represented quitting time.

I might add, incidentally, that Tillich's handwritten draft of volume I, with some of my initial proposed changes, is among my papers at Syracuse University, because the person in charge of the emerging Tillich archives was not interested in receiving it.

It was suggested by Tillich and others that I take responsibility for footnotes for the Systematic theology. I started that enterprise, but eventually went to Tillich and said, "I can't, for example, find what you said Plato said, but I can find passages you probably interpreted in your own way." It became clear that Tillich's memory related to what a particular text had meant to him, and it was hard to defend his interpretation as the precise meaning of the original text. So, after letting Tillich see a number of examples, it was decided that the footnoting project should be abandoned. Marion Pauck, Wilhelm's widow and writing colleague, recently told me that Wilhelm had hoped to include such documentation in his volume on Tillich, left uncompleted at his death. Given the shared classical background in which Tillich and Pauck participated from early boyhood on, Wilhelm would have been the one person who could have done it.

Tillich's increasing mastery of the dynamics of the English language is pivotal to comprehending his work. While the early stages of the systematic theology was formed first in German, his English lectures on the subject took on the character of new configurations. It was more than a translation from one language to another. It was a transformation in which the new language brought nuances of meaning not originally present. These nuances were at once suggestive of a style and a content formed by the particular philosophical and cultural patterns of the United States. The systematic theology, then, is an amalgam of German and English perceptions that give it a unique cast.

That reality created particular problems in translating the English text into German, for the danger was that the latter text could easily be devoid of those new characteristics. Tillich had not only mastered the internality of English; he had stretched it. The difference between Tillich and his translator into German, Renate Albrecht, was that the latter did not allow the English text to stretch the German.

In his sermons and smaller volumes, Tillich produced beautiful English creations in which thought and words were congruent. Those of us who edited these works found ourselves no longer finding new words for his thoughts, but facilitating the flow of the language before us. The texts of the *Dynamics of Faith, The Courage to Be* and *Biblical Religion and the Search for Ultimate Reality* are linguistically a delight to read. The latter was very special for me, for Tillich dedicated the volume to me. But he had spelled my name as Dillenburger rather than Dillenberger. It was natural enough, for Tillich knew the town of Dillenburg, some seventy miles northeast of Frankfurt am Main. My ancestors had left the town when it was still known as Dillenberg, that is before the castle was built, an event which later changed the name of the town from berg to burg. The dedication led Krister Stendahl to quip that it was an authentic dedication for in those days I played a role in everything Tillich published. Needless to say, the second edition was corrected, and I was particularly sorry to have the two editions, which were placed next to each other in my library, disappear in the Oakland/Berkeley fire in 1991.

TWO
Professional Life

A seminar at the Graduate Theological Union

5

TEACHER-SCHOLAR
Religious Studies at Princeton and Columbia

"My conception of academic life . . . required critical,
emphatic, sympathetic work."

Princeton University

In late December of 1947 I received an invitation to be an instructor in the Department of Religion at Princeton University. At the time I still had three chapters to write on my dissertation, though much of the research was finished. Still, I did not want to take a position until I was finished and so turned down the invitation. Then Niebuhr and Tillich heard what I had done, and again there came the summons. Why did you turn down an invitation to the best department of religion in the country when you are so close to being finished? And they might have added – I discovered later – since we recommended you. So I talked with my wife and we decided that we could postpone the break we had been anticipating. I called and sheepishly suggested that I would like to take the position if it were still open. What I discovered was that they were expanding the department and a sudden student demand indicated that they needed to move in mid-academic year rather than wait for the fall.

In January 1948 we moved to Princeton where I served as a preceptor in New Testament and Christian Ethics. Originally, preceptors were full professors, and they alone were considered competent to deal with freshmen and their wide interests. Moreover, it was felt that their status and standing would attract students to the various fields. By my time, full professors gave the weekly lectures which were followed by small groups of about ten students in each preceptorial. Hence, a full professor might have a hundred fifty students each week in a class and a preceptor then met with the small groups. So in my first semester I had six preceptorial sections in New Testament and five in Ethics. Initially I was unhappy, considering the duplication of materials. But in point of fact, each section soon took on a life of its own. It was in one of those sections that I first met Warren Deem, who later became a consultant, first to the Graduate Theological Union, then to various theological communities, Hartford Seminary in particular. It was there too that I met Robert Lynn, who was finishing his bachelor's thesis and later became head of Auburn Theological Seminary and then of the religion section of the Lilly Endowment, Inc.

During the academic year 1948-49, I was also able to do one course on my own, including lecture responsibilities, with the preceptor courses reduced in number. To this day, I remember the chair of the department, as he said he would, appearing unannounced to hear my lecture. It was somewhat unnerving, but it was soon evident that his comments and analysis would be helpful in every way. A senior professor had become a helper in a non-threatening way. The flip side of his kindly disposition was an indisposition to keep wheels running smoothly administratively. I remember the day when a special meeting of the department was called with an hour's notice, the dean of the college having threatened that if the course offerings were not in his office by the end of the day, the section on religion would be blank. Needless to say, the offerings for the following academic year had few changes.

At the time, Princeton had the reputation of being the premier religion department in the country. In addition to the chair, George Thomas, Paul Ramsey already had a distinguished lecture and publishing record. He once told me that he picked the ten top journals and deliberately wrote an article for each one, as well as deciding to write one book that could not be ignored. I got to know him well, since I shared an office with him in the new Firestone Library. Leland Jamison was a professor in New Testament and in American studies, having, in concert with other faculty, produced important writings in the field. He was a boisterous colleague, fun in every way. He was known to jump on his desk as he lectured. There was also a part-time appointment in Jewish studies, the occupant of which seemed more interested in demolishing the apostle Paul than in explicating Jewish thought.

The person I got to know best was Claude Welch, who had preceded my arrival the previous semester. Early on we found ourselves interested in similar projects, and through his initiative, we were asked to do a volume on Protestant Christianity. Many of the senior persons in the field had refused to write a history because it was too vast a subject. So the shift moved from the idea that a singular senior scholar might lose a reputation to the idea that a younger person or persons could gain one. Claude asked me to join him in this venture and a committee was set up to review what we wrote, an exam we passed with flying colors. Claude and I agreed that I would write the initial draft of the early chapters, he the second part, and that we would draft the final chapter together. Then we agreed to be ruthless in editing each other's materials, after which we went through the total manuscript sentence by sentence. The latter was accomplished on weekends, when we got together at our respective houses, with our wives and children off on pilgrimages while the two of us worked. It was an easy collaboration and I recall no substantive disagreement. That may be said to be surprising since Claude writes drafts after making detailed outlines and I write freely and then organize the materials. The book was published in 1954 as *Protestant Christianity; Interpreted Through its Development*. It was revised and enlarged some three decades later, again without collaborative problems. That was remarkable since we had to write about new and somewhat strident movements. While writing separate Protestant and Catholic histories would not be in vogue today and treatments might be more culturally and socially based, the volume has continued to be in print, surviving the transitions from publisher to publisher. This was only the first in a series of collaborative projects between us.

Besides those in the department, there were interesting colleagues in other areas. The Reformation historian I. Harris (Jinx) Harbison was at his prime, and the editor of the Woodrow Wilson papers and interpretative texts, Arthur S. Link, was in the early phases of his project. Whitney Oates, editor of the much used, two-volume edition of major writings of Augustine and of Aquinas, loved to drink, chat, and talk, as did the graduate dean, a devout Roman Catholic, who, returning from a weekend in New York, reported on the marvelous Roman Catholic church he had found for Sunday morning services, only to discover from his colleagues, to his great dismay, that he had gone to the high Episcopal church of Saint Mary's. Then there were the truly secular colleagues who could not leave religion alone, such as Walter T. Stace.

While the conversations among university faculty occurred readily, one had to seek out contact with Princeton Seminary faculty members. Educationally, the distance between the university and seminary was great though only a street divided them. For someone coming from Union, Jewish Theological, and Columbia, this seemed strange. Nevertheless, personal contacts occurred. Paul Lehmann had joined the seminary faculty and lived just across the street from the seminary. My wife, infant son, and I were invited to live with them for several weeks until university housing for younger faculty opened up. That context, as well as the marvelous theological library resources at the seminary, as compared to the university volumes in religion, provided a basis for a personal relation with seminary faculty.

Having come to Princeton without my dissertation completed, I was determined to finish it that first summer, and the university provided me with a special office to facilitate the project. Since the research was mainly done, I did succeed in writing the last three chapters in the three summer months. The dissertation, called *God Hidden and Revealed*, was published by Muhlenberg Press. This volume, now long out of print, was my way of working through the religious issues as I saw them. Liberal Protestant theology of the time seemed to be built on the person of Jesus as a moral personality who marked our future and was characteristic of the God Jesus portrayed. As developed, that seemed to make God the image of ourselves at our best, and ignored the ambiguities and evils around us. Having already read Dostoyevsky, Nietzsche, Pascal and Kierkegaard in college, I was not disposed toward the liberal theology of the time. A passage of Luther kept ringing through my ears to the effect that looking at the world which God created, one could only assume that God was a murderer, a tyrant, one who would lie with another's wife without regard, etc. In short, looking at the world is hardly the place to look for God. Hence, God, if there is one, must be wholly other than all that we see to be in God's favor. As I perceived it, God is hidden to us, revelation is indirect, and in a mysterious sense, God is veiled. God cannot be known directly or obviously, but in truth, as veiled in unveiling. Thus God's purpose cannot be known in and of itself. Such a God may be naked, strange to our eyes, still known for us as mystery in a positive sense. As will become evident, the God question, posed in this early form, is still with me, though differently focused.

When I went to Princeton, I assumed that I would settle in for the long run, since it was a tenure track position. But an invitation to return to Columbia in the fall of 1949 as a member of a department then being organized made me think of both Princeton and Columbia. Princeton thought of itself as special and indeed it was. But it also had a stifling ethos, with all the characteristics of a club. Among students, there was an informal dress code: khaki trousers, white shirt, and dark coat and tie for more formal occasions. All of this indicated, as we would put it today, a certain lack of diversity. That was true of major Ivy League schools in general, though I did not know so at the time. What I discovered later was that each school had a different ethos, but an ethos that was normative.

Columbia University

The invitation to Columbia presented different problems. With considerable fanfare it had been announced that James A. Pike, chaplain at Vassar, former attorney and author, had been appointed chaplain and head of a new department of religion. In those days it was considered essential to distinguish these two functions, even or in particular in secular institutions with previous religious roots. Columbia's situation was complex. It had professors who taught religion courses in other departments, usually philosophy, with orientations other than Christian. In addition, Barnard College, independent of Columbia and also connected with it at various levels at differing times, had a department of religion, headed by Ursula Niebuhr, who was married to Reinhold. Reinhold and Ursula had a good deal to say about the scene at Columbia, and with respect to James Pike, whom I did not know. A conversation with Pike convinced me that he would listen and that he counted on my help in navigating in academia. It was clear that while he did not want Christian belief to be excluded, he considered the field of religion to be wider than that. Loving the New York wider scene in addition, and with my hesitations about continuing at Princeton, I accepted the position beginning in the Fall of 1949.

For the first two years my appointment was a joint one with Barnard, and my subsequent turning solely to Columbia was a matter of being spread too wide to be focused. From a teaching standpoint, Barnard was a delight. The students were bright with excellent academic backgrounds. Advanced classes were small and frequently taught with colleagues. Memorable was a course Ursula Niebuhr, John E. Smith, and I did together, called "Interpreters of Life." Ursula had a broad knowledge and a direct access to contemporary figures, most of whom she knew personally. Her mind was like that of Herodotus, in which a story had stories within stories, but she also returned to the original story, never losing her way. She was bright, well trained, a charming companion, and an excellent chair of the department. She served tea and cheese at every meeting and I, still not liking cheese, washed it down with copious amounts of tea. I had known the other member of the department, John E. Smith, from seminary days and we soon became fast friends. John's philosophical lectures and writings were passionate expressions of his life convictions.

The joint departmental seminar, "Interpreters of Life," was designed for us to pick interesting historical figures, for each of which one of us would give an introduction, which was then followed by joint participation of the three of us with the students. We each had choices as to figures we wished to comment on. But it was also the case that one could not have first choice for all the figures. Stuck with Erasmus, about whom I had a certain ambivalence, I prepared my lecture focusing on what was wrong in his thinking, with little attention to his contributions and the total setting. But I was taken to task by one of the students, who literally dismantled my lecture. While I have forgotten her name, I can still visualize her presence. I found myself saying, in the presence of the assembled class, "Well, this lecture may have been a disaster but I will give a new one on Erasmus next year." Indeed, I worked hard and when the time came a year later, no one arrived at the classroom. Just as I was about to leave, the student arrived, telling me that the class location had changed, and would I come with her to the new location. Unsuspecting, I walked with her to a classroom where over a hundred students (as compared to the regular twelve to fifteen) were assembled to hear the professor who had said to a student, "Next year I will give a new lecture because of what you said." I gave my lecture and a standing ovation followed. I had given a well-rounded lecture. What more could a young professor want?

John Smith and I also did a seminar with Georges Florovsky, who was then the prominent star at St. Vladimir's Seminary. John and I soon discovered that we had better speak early in the session for somewhere down the line, Florovsky would take over and we wouldn't get a word in edgewise. So we began to guess at what time that would happen each week, the loser paying for beer after class. Later, Florovsky was a colleague at Harvard, always wearing his dandruff-clad robe, with his wife taking his arm and walking at his side.

In order to infuse a faculty member from religion into the required course in the humanities at Columbia College, I readily agreed to take on one of the numerous sections. The readings were extensive and the discussion wide ranging. I was literally only one step ahead of the students, only because I had more life experiences and time to have read.

The experiences at Princeton and Columbia determined my teaching style and preferences. While I was more than an acceptable lecturer, I preferred seminars, based on texts in which my role was to provide contexts and facilitate discussion. So much was that my preference that some students were uneasy because I insisted on reading and class participation, without requiring papers. "So on what would I base my grade?" asked some. In those cases where that anxiety persisted, I let them do papers.

Returning to the more administrative aspects of the new department, I worked closely with Jim Pike and we became friends to the end of his life, inasmuch as our lives continued to intersect when he was Episcopal bishop in San Francisco. At Columbia my office was between his and that of his secretary. So while I distinguished between his function as chaplain and being chair of the department, I naturally had associations with both aspects. Darby Betts, assistant chaplain to Jim, had architectural credentials and had built one of the first distinguished modern churches in Alexandria, Virginia. Sam Wylie, a conservative Presbyterian, also on the dean's staff, ministered to Protestant students, but later switched to the Episcopalian church and subsequently became Episcopal bishop in Michigan.

Sometimes Jim would involve me in the chaplain side of things, particularly when special issues were involved. One of those occasions was a morning meeting when Rockefeller interests wanted to explore prospects of a special relationship between Riverside Church and Columbia and contacted Dwight Eisenhower, who was then President of Columbia. Having been summoned to meet with Eisenhower about the issue, Jim asked me to join him in the conversation. When we arrived for an early morning meeting, the President was being shaved, but we soon moved to a more congenial setting. I doubt that anything special ever happened between the two bodies, particularly as Eisenhower learned that morning that Columbia itself had a chapel and did not need the relation with Riverside. The only other time I spoke with him briefly was in that very chapel when I was the morning preacher the Sunday before his Tuesday election to be the President of the United States. That meeting was brief enough, for I was not anxious to linger for photographs inasmuch as my name appeared that same day among others in an ad in the *New York Times* advocating the election of Adlai Stevenson. There was a kind of cruel humor going round the Columbia campus, such as this was the first time an educated man had run against a university president, or that Columbia's loss was the nation's loss. Nevertheless, I was invited by a friend on one occasion to lunch at the White House, where at the entrance to the oval office was posted the same army colonel who once had stood outside the President's office at Columbia. Somehow that amused me.

Essentially, Eisenhower represented the growing trend of university presidents in promoting the broad contours of education among those who could bring financial support. Given strong academic officers and a working bond between such officers, governance worked well. At Columbia during this period, John Krout filled the provost role. An American historian, short and stocky, keen of mind, he was direct and thorough in addressing issues. One particular incident comes to mind. At the time Union Theological Seminary and Columbia had five separate

joint MA programs in religion, each with separate protocols. The result
was considerable overlap, separate administrative staffs, and uneven numbers of students. At the same time, there were new interests not represented in the existing programs. John Krout set up a special committee
and asked me to chair it and we had a good number of conversations,
agreeing that some analogy to the joint doctoral program was in order.
Came the day for the report, Krout asked me to make the report to those
at Columbia and Union who had the authority to make appropriate decisions. Henry P. Van Dusen, president of Union, responded to me that, as
usual, I had done thorough and good work, but that he wanted the existing MA. programs to continue, with no objection to another one that met
new interests. His reason for wanting the older programs to continue was
that they defined Union's relation to Columbia. When Krout responded
that Columbia was prepared to issue new documents that more fully
defined the relation of the two schools, Van Dusen replied that the issue
was not an expanded better document, but that the historic documents
signaled a relation that could not easily be abrogated. In short, historic
documents and programs that had existed, even if there were no current
students, had a validity a new document did not, even if it was more adequate. Aside from the administrative lesson I learned that day, the subsequent situation now had six joint programs, though the new one attracted
more students than the combined older degrees. One of the later delights
was running into Krout and his wife in a London hotel and spending several days together seeing sights and plays.

Among those appointed in religion besides Pike and myself were
Norman Gottwald, Edward Dowey, and Robert Gordis. Gottwald was an
Old Testament professor, just on this side of fundamentalism, but with an
open spirit. His pilgrimage took him increasingly toward critical scholarship, where his contribution remains unexcelled. Later I was involved in
bringing him to Berkeley. Ed Dowey, whose first book is still one of the
definitive works on John Calvin, came to Columbia from Lehigh and finished his career at Princeton Theological Seminary. Robert Gordis combined scholarship with the demands of a Jewish congregation, making his
work especially enticing to scholars and students. Then there were adjunct
faculty members. Georges Florovsky has already been mentioned, as well
as Darby Betts, who combined architecture and theology, holding degrees
in both.

Within other departments, questions of religion were not foreign,
though they occurred as a part of the cultural studies of the time, chiefly
within philosophical and literary arenas. Horace L. Friess, Herbert
Schneider, John Hermann Randall (all in philosophy) have already been

mentioned. While I knew other faculty from a time three years previous, I now got to know them in a new way, technically as colleagues. Moreover, I had taken the earliest opportunity to move my office from the chaplain's arena to philosophy hall. There on the same floor, in addition to Friess and Schneider, were Joseph Blau, Gilbert Highet, Moses Hadas, Marjorie Nicolson, Jacques Barzun, Lionel Trilling, and Irwin Edman. Once the latter asked me how long I had been at Columbia, and when I said three and a half years, his response was, "in that time your accent has moved from Illinois to Ohio," to which another colleague responded, "Well, Edman's French accent has not moved at all." It was not unusual for these individuals to pause in conversation in the hallways. For me, that was incredibly important, for I was then working on Protestant Christianity and was continually bumping into cultural issues in which these fields intersected. That in their minds I was a product of and still associated with Niebuhr and Tillich, gave me associations I otherwise would not have had. Moreover, while they knew of my associations with Jim Pike, they were also aware that my conception of academic life neither excluded nor demanded a believing faith, that it required critical, emphatic, sympathetic work. In the wider academic arena, some church and academic types believed in the inculcation of faith as the aim of teaching and bemoaned the alleged secular outlook, while others insisted that interest in faith dimensions disqualified one for teaching in a college or university. Both attitudes led a good number of universities not to create or develop departments of religion. As a part of that debate, I wrote an article on teaching religion, which on rereading, I would not change much even today. (1954)

Jim Pike left Columbia to become dean of the Cathedral of St. John the Divine. While I had hoped that Columbia would now separate the chaplaincy and the department of religion, it instead continued to keep the two together. In point of fact, it made little difference in my work, for John Krumm, the new head, continued to rely on me with respect to developments in the department.

In addition to the undergraduate courses at Columbia College and some doctoral courses, I was asked by Horace L. Friess to assist in administering the graduate programs, particularly at the M.A. level. The School of General Studies, which offered courses for the general public, both audit and credit, late afternoon and evening, felt that religion should be included in the program for the public it served, and I did several courses for them.

Dating from my initial experiences at Columbia, where I first found myself simultaneously teaching, writing, and doing administrative chores, I discovered that I was spending too much time moving documents around. Suddenly, it dawned on me that I needed a separate space for each function. Usually, I had a large table and a desk, permitting three piles that I did not need to move. I discovered that doing this meant I could move my chair in seconds to any one of the three functions and know where I had been when I had last worked on it. To do that, I usually had to provide the table myself. It is not that faculty members need large offices; it is that they need space commensurate with the obligations they exercise. Some faculty solved this problem by using home offices for research and writing, and school offices for teaching and administration. I found it most convenient to be able to move rapidly from one function to another.

As I became more involved in administrative matters, I also made it my business to try to find out what the history of a project or institution had been. So I read extant minutes on specific projects or on an institution as a whole. It still amazes me how much I learned about the ethos of an institution in doing that. It also led me to ask that minutes for meetings in which I was involved contained the context of discussion as well as the concrete decisions.

My teaching centered in the history of Christian thought, a challenge enriched by the presence of blocks of students from various traditions. Usually there were about three Buddhist students who challenged my distinctions and much preferred the development of unity rather than difference. St. Vladimir's Seminary, an independent small Russian orthodox school directly across Broadway from Union, utilized Columbia courses wherever it found them congenial. The result was that I usually had at least six students from that tradition, most of whom came from afar, and who spoke English well but with varieties of marked accents. On several occasions, I had to plead with inquiring FBI agents to the effect that these individuals were legitimate students, not spies from other countries.

For those times, there were a large number of women students in the program, some registered for credit, others for audit status, some also registering at Union. Most of them were well educated and well placed in the world of culture and politics, and many invited me and others to special events. One student, through a foundation, designated a significant sum for my wife, children, and me to go to Europe to broaden my horizons, which I think for her meant to get more acquainted with the Anglican tradition. Another woman invited me to special late afternoon parties to meet the political and cultural figures traveling through, most important of whom, in my order of things, was Adlai Stevenson. Then there were television events to which I was invited, such as the McCarthy hearings. I learned at this time that it was possible to have a friendly relation with women without becoming otherwise involved, and that a special élan can be enjoyed. It is simply a fact that one enjoys the company of various people differently.

Most students discovered that I knew Tillich well and wanted some exposure to him. So I occasionally invited him to a class, not for lectures, but for questions. One occasion I remember well, for Tillich and I had gone to the faculty club for wine and food prior to an early afternoon class. The grand professor fell asleep and I could not keep him awake. He was so embarrassed and apologized on the way back, while the students, I discovered, were amused.

Having lived in student housing at Princeton, the return to Columbia was to Bergenfield, New Jersey, some seven miles across the George Washington Bridge. Bergenfield, while close to Englewood, West Englewood and Teaneck, was comparatively lower in social status. As we had a son about to enter school and another one born at the beginning of the Columbia period, a house on a dead-end street with other families with similar community and school interests was attractive, and the location made all that possible financially. But it did mean that, except for special events that allowed advanced planning, my wife Hilde missed many events in the city.

In the immediate New Jersey area, most of us were in the same age group and therefore concerned about the same issues. Inasmuch as I was a young professor at Columbia, I was prevailed upon to be, as they put it, an attractive candidate for the school board. But in terms of the opposition, I became a Communist and Jew overnight, and the attempt was made to convince Columbia to dismiss me for my alleged radical views. At a small gathering of four of us who had been invited to meet Adlai Stevenson, he quipped, "Did I do that to you too?" And Columbia called me in, talked with me about the situation, and ended it saying, "How can we be of help to you?" The fact is, I almost won the election and I am sure that the Jewish community almost made victory possible. In any case, I did well enough to be asked to be a Democratic candidate for the state assembly. The temptation to try to enter political life was real. But I also had to acknowledge that doing so would be the end of an academic career.

So I continued at Columbia, driving in each day to the Columbia area. Each morning I picked up three persons, and for the price of a bridge toll, dropped them off near the subway just past the George Washington Bridge, and they went downtown and returned on their own. The day I remember most is when one of the riders said, "This is my last day. I have decided to try being a cartoonist and we'll see whether I join you again later." That was the last time I saw Mort Walker but Beetle Bailey is still going on. For those who know New York City a bigger miracle may be the recognition that one could find street parking all day in the Columbia area. Only once did I have a problem, for I had forgotten where I had parked. It took an hour and a half to find the car, as I walked a grid pattern.

A final note on Union and Columbia: While the only formal relations between the two rested in the degree programs, the faculty contacts were extensive. Symbolic of the kind of relation was the debate I had with Edmund Cherbonnier on the theme, Athens versus Jerusalem. Cherbonnier, then an instructor at Union, was adamant that only biblical frameworks were permissible in theological thinking. For him, Tillich was the theological enemy. While I did not find myself totally in the camp of Athens, so to speak, I was more disposed toward that end of the spectrum. The Union students had organized the event and I arrived expecting some twenty people only to discover over two hundred attending, including a high percentage of faculty. I was glad that I had prepared for the occasion, as I had been tempted just to appear.

Jane and John working on an art exhibition

6

A CLOUD THAT NEVER GOES AWAY
Crises at Harvard and Drew

"We talked on my return to the states . . . about how creativity and destructiveness frequently came from the same source or demon, and that the alliance between the two sometimes has destructive consequences." — Conversation with Paul Tillich

Harvard

In June 1954, when I was summering in Dorset, Ontario, Canada, a hundred fifty miles north of Toronto, a store clerk delivered to me a note asking me to call the President's office at Harvard University as soon as possible. While I had no phone, my location was not a secret, for I was known in the little town inasmuch as we spent almost three months each summer in a cabin we owned on the Lake of Bays. There I spent each day writing for about four hours in the morning, enjoying time with my wife and two boys in the afternoon, and generally reading in the evening.

So I made my way to the store, used the general public phone, and called the number I had been given. The message from William Bentnick-Smith, assistant to President Nathan M. Pusey, was that there was interest in exploring the possibility of my joining the Divinity School faculty, and could I come for a conversation with the president sometime within the next two weeks.

While the request to come for a conversation was unanticipated, I knew the general situation and also that my name had been suggested for one of the additions to the faculty. The Divinity School, while it had a few distinguished faculty persons, such as the historian and acting dean George Hunston Williams, and Robert Pfeiffer, Old Testament professor, and two professors in the Yard, Arthur Darby Nock, early church and the classical period, and Harry Wolfson, Jewish studies, it was hardly a rounded out academic picture for a divinity school. Former Harvard president James Conant had toyed with closing the Divinity School, but finally was convinced (rumor had it that the convincing voice was Reinhold Niebuhr) to make a distinguished school with a whole array of new appointments.

Academic gossip at the time was that the Divinity School should not be accredited but one could not, not accredit a school at Harvard. In any case, when Pusey was appointed president of the university, new directions were assured.

Ursula and Reinhold Niebuhr had told me that they had nominated me for one of the opening positions at Harvard, and Paul Tillich said he had been asked for nominations and wanted to place my name on the list and would I write a draft for him? It was an embarrassing moment for me. Sensing my hesitation, Tillich orally told me what he wanted to say, so it turned out to be his thoughts at least, even if my words. At the time, Tillich had already agreed to go to Harvard in the fall of 1955.

This was the third position for which I had been nominated, with no apparent opposition. Nominations were almost the equivalent of an assured appointment. Positions were not advertised and one did not apply. It was the old boys' network, of which women could be members. In the same matrix, as I had earlier learned, one did not say no. I had no strong feelings about Harvard, only that it was an opportunity to be part of another lively scene.

In the conversation with Pusey, it became clear that he had checked me out beyond the confines of the nominators just noted. But the one point where he was not fully informed was that I was an associate professor with tenure and eligible within a few years for a full professorship. Pusey had proposed an assistant professorship, and while he was willing to think of associate professor, he said he did not have the authority to grant tenure and that such an action involved a special process. When I said, "Why should I take a gamble at Harvard when I already have tenure at Columbia," he replied, "I do appoint the committees for tenure and full professor and I think you can trust that you will qualify for associate professor with tenure and eventually for full professor," This turned out to be the case.

This was June and Pusey said they really needed me in the fall, though he knew that it would be difficult for me to leave Columbia on short notice. Columbia's response was that they could accommodate the situation if I could spend a day a week at Columbia for the first semester, and be available on special occasions for the second semester. That was agreeable, though more of a burden than I had thought.

My appointment was in theology, systematic and historical. In my first extended conversation with Dean George Williams, he suddenly asked me what I thought of the celestial flesh of Christ. Those who knew George were not surprised by such direct, somewhat unexpected questions, knowing that they came out of problems on which he was working. Fortunately, I knew enough about the concept not to flunk this first theological question.

We had managed to find a house in Arlington, and I soon discovered that George did not drive a car and that he lived nearby, almost directly en route to the Divinity School. So I asked if I could pick him up in the morning, when our schedules coincided, leaving the return open inasmuch as end of the day obligations varied for each of us from day to day. At the end of the first six weeks, I said I understood that at school we used the titles of dean and professor, but could we not use first names in talking with each other in the absence of others? To this he replied, "Don't you think it's a bit early." The next morning, as he entered the car, with great deliberateness he said, "Good morning, John." And so it was to be.

The first day at the Divinity School, I ran into the other new faculty member, Krister Stendahl. We went to lunch together and immediately became friends. At faculty meetings, others believed that we got together in advance, comparing notes and setting up agendas. In fact, that was not the case. But our instincts with respect to procedures and directions were so in tune that our differences did not divide us or become obvious to others.

The first months at Harvard were mainly spent in getting acquainted and working with protocols that were more like those at Princeton than at Columbia. One was expected to make calls on older colleagues and to be introduced to others with whom one had to become acquainted. Anyone with knowledge of the time will know of Arthur Darby Nock, learned and quirky, far out and traditional at the same time. Indeed, he was a legend. I was informed by Dean Williams that I was to write to Nock, suggesting that I go to speak with him at a time he designated, to arrive precisely on time and leave promptly an hour later. So, on a Sunday afternoon at four, I rang Nock's doorbell, and after what seemed to be a rather silent period, I heard a voice from somewhere in the recesses, saying what I surmised to be, "come in." So I opened the door, did not see him, but found him behind his desk at the end of the hall. He shook hands and invited me to sit down, but every chair had books, so I proceeded to take books from what seemed to be the obvious chair, placed them on the floor, and sat down. Tea and pleasantries were brief, then the conversation. He said he had been working on the philosopher Vico, and what did I think of him? What a coincidence, for I had been reading Vico too, and without that coincidence, I might have flunked the interview. The whole event was encapsulated in the apocryphal story of the woman student who came to see him, and finding him naked behind his desk, exclaimed "Jesus Christ," to which Nock replied, "Not Jesus Christ, just his faithful and obedient servant."

Robert Pfeiffer, professor of Old Testament, was representative of the older tradition at its best. Affable and charming in meetings and conversations, his scholarship was technical rather than inspiring. Scholarship meant making sure that theological biases did not enter into the equation. Let me give two illustrations. First, Pfeiffer said he believed in the virgin birth by faith, but not by scholarship. When I asked if that did not seem a bit schizoid, he said, "No, not if you build the walls tight enough." Second, let me mention an event at a doctoral exam. When I arrived at the Divinity School, I was told that every faculty member was expected at a doctoral exam, no matter what the field, and to participate in the examination. When my time came, I asked about the student's hermeneutical approach to a particular text. Being asked to repeat the question, but receiving no answer, Pfeiffer intervened, and said, "Professor Dillenberger, at Harvard we do not ask theological questions."

The existing faculty and students at the time of my arrival were largely in the liberal Unitarian tradition or conservative, if not fundamentalist. From both angles, the main theological traditions could be ignored. Fundamentalists could get a doctoral degree at Harvard without critical study or being confronted by theological questions. Moreover, the curriculum for doctoral degrees was set up to be able to avoid theological questions. Hence, one could enter Harvard, do the necessary work, and leave without having been confronted by other positions. The left-leaning liberals and the ultra-conservatives respected each other, but rejected positions in between.

When I talked with Dean Williams about this situation and its corroding effect on educational competence at both basic and doctoral levels, he asked me to write him a confidential memo on the subject. Unbeknownst to me the memo was given to McGeorge Bundy, then dean of the faculty of Arts and Sciences, for the doctoral program was under the aegis of that body. Upon reading the memo, Bundy asked for a committee to examine the doctoral program and make a report, which we did in writing. Nothing happened for four months, after which I was asked by Bundy to be chair of a new doctoral committee on the History and Philosophy of Religion and report to him every six weeks, which I did for the rest of my time at Harvard. It also involved my attending meetings of the Faculty of Arts and Sciences.

The new program brought discipline and depth to the curriculum and broadened the horizons. While conceptually better, its quality depended on an expanded faculty being assembled in addition to those already present – Amos Wilder, George Ernest Wright, Frank Cross, Richard Reinhold Niebuhr, James Luther Adams, Paul Lehmann, George Buttrick, Paul Tillich, John Wild, Georges Florovsky, Robert Lawson Slater. I want to add a special note about Amos Wilder. We had adjacent offices on the fourth floor of the library, with no elevators and the nearest rest room being in the basement. When an elevator was added years later, it was affectionately dubbed the Dillenberger/Wilder elevator. Amos was a poet whose graciousness touched all around him. He quietly invited me to meet his friends for lunches and dinners, a kind of who's who of people I should know. Only later did I know how carefully he had chosen them.

Nathan Pusey, the university president, was fundamental to bringing persons of both scholarly and wider Christian backgrounds into the center of the Divinity School. When Dean Williams asked Pusey to address the Divinity School Faculty and its constituency, Pusey agreed but asked two questions, who and when was the last president to do so and what did he say? Williams replied that it was Charles Eliot, a grand Unitarian leader, and then sent Pusey a copy of the address. As Williams later remarked, Pusey took the occasion to answer Eliot point by point out of a fully Christian Episcopal tradition.

The Unitarians were not too happy with the address. They felt that their role and historical relations were not affirmed, but rather ignored. It felt like the repudiation of the tradition Ralph Waldo Emerson had articulated over a hundred years before. Having been one of the early arrivals in the new series of faculty appointments, I was asked by the alumni association of the Divinity School to address them. I took the occasion to outline the Unitarian contributions and their continuing place in a wider ranging religious spectrum.

Pusey appointed Douglas Horton, known as Mr. Congregationalist, to the Deanship of the Divinity School. He was a well-known person, particularly in church circles, with a distinctive interdenominational bent. Married to Mildred McAfee Brown, former head of the Waves and former president of Wellesley College, there were affectionate quips to the effect that she would teach him administration. Horton did consult widely, but was prone to consult whomever he ran into as he ruminated on various issues. He was instrumental in promoting the inclusion of faculty in Eastern Orthodox thought and Catholic studies, making sure that such persons were active, believing members of their communities. He also strengthened the Center for World Religions. But he was not good at academic protocol and made a lot of decisions on impulse, a characteristic also evident in his leadership of the Congregationalists.

While appointed as university professor, Tillich was based in the Divinity School. But his office was next to the original divinity school building, en route from the Divinity School to the Yard. On the day of an unexpected snowstorm, I arrived at his office with snow all over my head. Seeing it, he told me to wear a spare beret he had in his office. I did, and on the way back from the faculty club, he said to keep it. I was a beret addict from then on.

Tillich's lectures in the Yard were widely attended, while his reception among university faculty was mixed. The latter was mainly because some did not find the subject matter of religion congenial, nor did they take to the notion that theology was related to all other disciplines, as was so obviously the case with Tillich. Still, he created a debate that enlivened discourse and revitalized the place of religion in the University, though the vitality of religion in undergraduate education continued to be limited. The philosophers generally were not sympathetic to Tillich, given that they were mainly logical positivists. Only John Wild was the exception.

One of the projects of special interest was a small faculty seminar on theology and science to which Tillich was invited, with the request that he secure another person from the field of religion. Knowing that I was working on a book on religion and science, Tillich saw me as the obvious choice. Among those sitting around the table were Gerald Holton in physics, George Wald in biology, and Harlow Shapley in astronomy. They were interesting, instructive sessions, though Tillich's penchant for including all knowledge in his theological outlook was obvious, leading Shapley, sitting next to me, to whisper to me deliberately loud enough to be heard, "Tillich thinks we all agree, but you and I know better." Even Tillich laughed. But what an incredible seminar it was.

During this period, I also did a seminar with Tillich for doctoral students, though I have forgotten the title. In one of the sessions, the students disagreed with him, but he was adamant in his replies. Since I agreed with the students, I waded into the debate, and the students became silent. In any case, we all forgot that the time was up and the class ended abruptly as the next class invaded the room. On the way out, Tillich said to me, "It's a good thing that you and I disagreed in public, but how can you be so wrong."

In the summer of 1957, I was appointed Parkman Professor of Divinity, the second oldest chair in the United States, and was headed for a sabbatical in Heidelberg, Germany, to complete the book on theology and science on which I had been working. I had become part of a group that met fairly regularly on religion and science at Penn State University, under the leadership of the dean, Harold Schilling, and the chaplain and professor of religion, Luther Harshbarger. A good number of German scholars had been working on the topic, among them Edmund Schlink, distinguished theologian, and a younger theologian, Wolfhart Pannenberg, both at Heidelberg. I had several conversations with Schlink on the subject and more wide-ranging ones with Pannenberg, which included walks and social occasions. Knowing of my connections with Tillich, the two of them invited me to make presentations and enter into conversation at several sessions of their seminar on Tillich, which pushed my German to its limit. Once listening to von Campenhausen's lecture, a German colleague, sensing my distress, whispered to me, "We don't understand his Basel German either."

In January of that academic year, I received a letter from Dean Horton, stating that there were rumors of my relationship with women serious enough to jeopardize my future at Harvard. Two days later, a second letter arrived, asking for my resignation. No details were given but the tone was such that it was clear my resignation was expected. It never occurred to me to ask for details or to challenge the resignation request. So I offered it.

But I was mystified. I told my wife that all I could think of was that I had been intimate with two women friends, but given the mutuality, I could not conceive of their having said anything to anyone. That reality Hilde and I had to work through, no matter whether or not they were or were not the source of concern. Only in returning to the States and to Harvard some six months later did I find that these women never said a word to anyone. Instead, I learned that two independent reports to the dean from separate professional counselors had signaled possible future relations with me on the part of two other women. Having subsequently been given the names of these persons, I can say that I know of no action that called for my resignation, and I was later informed that each one assumed the conversations were confidential. In one case the counselor rationalized the report as a caution that I probably should not be considered for the deanship, a possibility of which I was totally unaware. But I could see that two separate reports from counselors would have inordinate power. However, in retrospect, I feel that I was treated badly and that I should immediately have returned for conversations.

I discovered that faculty colleagues had not been informed of my situation until my resignation was in hand, much to the distress of some of them. I do not know what they were told. Strange as it seemed, in the spring of that year Dean Horton asked me to interview and report on a young scholar in Heidelberg, named Helmut Koester, who was being considered for the Harvard faculty. It was as if everything was supposedly normal.

Fortunately, my wife Hilde and I had become friends with Ruth and Gordon Harland. Gordon was a young faculty member at Drew Theological Seminary, using that year in Heidelberg to finish his dissertation on Reinhold Niebuhr, which was later published by Oxford University Press. We had immediately talked with them about our situation, and they were personally and professionally helpful in every way. Knowing that Drew had proposed my accepting a professorship earlier on, Gordon got in touch with the Dean about our situation. Upon exploring his options, Barney Anderson proposed that we come on a half-time visiting basis for the first year and if things worked out without too many issues, I might retroactively be given a chair that was opening up in the next academic year. That was a relief, for I had begun to think of other options, possibly in the publishing field.

Inconvenient as moving might be, it left the world of theology open and, having once considered going to Drew, it was like taking a road I had once seriously contemplated. Leaving Harvard was not a problem in and of itself. But I wished I could have left under circumstances that I controlled. I also knew that I would be marked forever, and that some possibilities would forever be closed to me.

Our living situation in Heidelberg was congenial, in spite of all that had happened. I was able to continue my work, writing at a table each morning looking out over the city and using the library in the afternoon. I was given a desk where I could work and leave books, and the staff was exceedingly helpful, particularly in helping me read eighteenth-century hand entries in bound catalogue books.

We had the lower floor of a fairly large house, with a yard view over the Neckar River with the castle directly across. It was a good place for walking and the Neckar barge traffic was always fascinating. The old city was a ten-minute walk over a nearby bridge, and of course, the shops were nearby. Eric, our oldest son, then eleven, was in an Army school, where English and German were both used, and Paul, then seven, was in a totally

German school. Within three months, he spoke perfect German and received top marks in his classes; in contrast, we assumed incorrectly that Eric was learning little German. In actuality, forty years later, both Eric and Paul spoke German fluently after a few days in Germany.

At least once a week, the Harlands and Hilde and I would go to dinner, eat and drink wine, and talk incessantly on things large and small, profound and trivial. And so it continued at Drew. Two things I remember well from the year are a trip together to Italy, and in Heidelberg a public debate on World War II, to which Gordon and I had been invited. From an American perspective, a few of the remarks were plain wrong. In the discussion, Gordon became articulate and passionate about what he had heard. Speaking in English inasmuch as his German skills were not as good in speech as in print, he asked me to translate. We both received an ovation.

By letter, I had heard from Tillich of his deep personal distress about my situation, confirmed by others as well. When we talked on my return to the states, it was the only time we talked directly about our personal lives, about how creativity and destructiveness frequently came from the same source or demon, and that the alliance between the two sometimes has destructive consequences. We both knew that the ambiguities of life were as real as their resolutions and that we – in this instance I – would have to live with that. He was aware that some had said, and would continue to say, that my alleged or apparent personal history was the product of his theological openness. That was incorrect, for in a real sense, I did not feel myself a disciple of his, even though I learned more from him than anyone else. I agreed with the late D. B. Robertson, a classmate during the Union years, who said that so many of us had learned more from Tillich than from any other teacher, but that we would have a hard time saying precisely what it was.

Tillich and I also talked about the fact that in the situation I faced, truth and untruth are curiously mixed, and that one cannot count on others' knowing or distinguishing between the two. So one is marked for life. There is a cloud that never goes away, and an element of more than ordinary uncertainty enters many associations and situations.

Alerting me to face that reality was one of the gifts Tillich gave me. But beyond that, his interpretation of faith and grace, his ringing words, "Simply accept that you are accepted," a gift in which all is transformed, and in which one has the courage to be, have made Tillich present to me in all the intervening years. Here I think particularly of the sermon, "You Are Accepted," in *The Shaking of the Foundations*. The theme of course is central to *The Courage to Be,* one of the titles we talked about at one of our lunches. Tillich was an agent of incredible grace; he made it possible for me to live in a terrain in which the contours are forever clouded; and surprises, good and bad, are always around the corner. Surely, that is nothing less than a gift of life.

Finally, Tillich said to me in words I shall not forget, "Knowing your history, people will come to you for help in sorting out their own situations and you will need to be careful, for in some instances they will be searching for more, indeed for involvements of their own." He was right in both instances.

Exactly what floated around about me leaving Harvard I do not know. Precisely the vagueness of it all made the designation of women problems more ominous than openness might have been. Leaving a Harvard chair on the best of terms raises questions and has consequences. The number of invitations I received for speaking engagements after leaving Harvard dropped by over thirty percent, just as later leaving the East coast for the West, made it drop another thirty percent. Of course, there may have been other reasons, such as working in new areas where there was less national interest.

Drew University

In spite of having to move again, it was good to be going to Drew. For the first weeks we were given a small apartment, then moved to a large house on campus, and eventually bought a lot a half block from campus and built a house. The boys found new friends, and we were welcomed into the community.

While started as a theological seminary for which it was known, Drew also had a small but growing liberal arts college, and a relatively new graduate school. Officially, the seminary served the Methodist church, though its students and faculty had a considerably wider scope. The graduate faculty was mainly drawn from the theological school and the college. The key figure and head of the graduate school was Stanley Romaine Hopper, authority in the area of literature and theology, read in the light of psychoanalytic theory. A commanding figure in every way was Will Herberg, whose volume *Protestant, Catholic, and Jew,* defined the American religious and social scene in the days prior to the new pluralism of the twenty-first century. Franz Hildebrandt, associated early on with Martin Niemoeller, came to Drew in theology and had published in Reformation history. In the meantime, he had become a spirited disciple of the Wesleys. The theological star was Carl Michalson, whose interest in existentialism was carried to the point that historic existence was set against nature at every point, as in his classic book, *The Hinge of History*. John Godsey, known for his work on Barth and Bonhoeffer, was a colleague in theology, and Carl, John, and I collaborated in an introductory course to theology. We shared the lectures and were openly in debate with each other. Indeed the exchanges among us were spirited, Carl being a thorough existentialist, John nearer Barth, and myself with traces of Tillich, all to the delight of the students.

The philosophical theological tradition was represented by Ray L. Hart, whose book, *Unfinished Man and the Imagination* has stood the test of time. The dean, Bernhard Anderson, was a star in Old Testament studies, emphasizing the covenant tradition. His *Introduction to the Old Testament*, and the companion *Introduction to the New Testament*, done jointly by Howard Kee, Karlfried Froehlich (both Drew faculty) and Franklin Young, provided the introduction to the Bible for several generations of theological students throughout the country. Robert W. Funk (whom I first knew at Harvard) was a Greek scholar, with a pronounced interest in literary criticism and rhetorical style, and stood in the tradition of Bultmann, with a particular interest in Ernst Fuchs and Gerhard Ebeling. Under Funk's aegis, a number of conferences and publications ensued on what was dubbed the New Hermeneutic. Gordon Harland has already been mentioned and there were others such as Jim Ross, David Graybeal, Jane Karlin, George Kelsey, and Nelle Morton. A special word should be said of Kelsey and Morton. George was a star ethicist and brought the theological community into conversation with the black theological voices of the time. Nelle was one of the early feminist voices and urged women to look down into their own beings to find the resources necessary to combat sexism, that is, to make it rooted and a new positive power in the world.

Taken together, this was a remarkable group of teachers and scholars, whose range of interests made the seminary an exciting place and made it necessary to broaden the horizons of the graduate program, the latter being an arena in which I was of some help. Assembling such an array of faculty involved a deliberate administrative series of acts, combining stars with individuals definitely on the rise in their fields. The strength and diversity of the faculty resulted in an influx of students. Among those whom I recall and whose own careers would make any school glad are David Miller, James Wiggins, Christine Downing, David C. Steinmetz, Steven Ozment, Conrad Cherry, William May, Sherry May, Charles Hartwick, Mike Ryan and Don Jones.

During the Drew years, my academic pursuits centered in completing and publishing *Protestant Thought and Natural Science*, and in editing *Martin Luther: Selections from His Writings*. The volume on science and theology was first published by Doubleday and Company in 1960, and then republished by the University of Notre Dame Press in 1988. While much has been written that is fresh and new on the subject, this volume continues to be a comprehensive overview, covering neglected areas of the subject. Running through most of this volume is an account of the role philosophy played in both science and theology. It still is my conviction, which I think I have documented, that both sides of the debate were influenced more by reigning philosophical debates than by theology and science per se. Catholics and Protestants, the latter mainly Lutheran and Reformed, vied with each other in the right understanding of Aristotle in relation to theology and science.

Given that history, I argued that while science and theology had implications for each other, neither should dictate to the other or fill in the gaps of the other. There is no doubt that science as we know it today does not exhibit absolute systems and is open to other dimensions But that does not merit using science in such a way that theological formulations are given free license. It is my conviction that one needs to step into the other disciplines with which one is in conversation, lest we fall into the situation of writing "theologies of" other disciplines. From both sides, we need to be open to the other, neither dictating to the other nor leaving avenues for the other to fill in.

Martin Luther: Selections from his Writings was published in the Doubleday Anchor series in 1962 and has had a steady sale since that time, and is used extensively by history departments in colleges and universities. Its limitation is that I mostly used the extant English translations of the time, a few rather dated. More recently my GTU colleague, the late Timothy Lull, had access to fresh translations for use in his volume of Luther writings.

The late Heiko Oberman once said to me that my selections were convincing and represented a definite view of Luther. In part, he made reference to my placing the Ninety Five Theses, about which every one who has been to school has heard, in an appendix, inasmuch as their content was totally in the medieval world. I belong to a group of Luther interpreters who date Luther's full conversion experience to be fairly late and understand his theological position to have developed over a period of time. While this outlook is laid out in the introduction to the volume, it is most fully developed in my last book, *Images and Relics*.

Also in the late fifties, and particularly during the Drew years, Claude Welch and I organized an editorial board to create a Library of Protestant Thought, given that many of the documents were simply not available, either for lack of translation or due to going out of print. Oxford University Press, with the interest and support of Wilbur Ruggles and Marion Hausner Pauck, committed itself to undertake the publication. I took the responsibility of chairing the editorial board and convinced Yorke Allen, Jr., head of the Sealantic Fund, a Rockefeller Brothers project for theological education, to underwrite expenses for the editorial meetings, with Oxford assuming other publication expenses. Our goal was to publish approximately twenty-five volumes, but we stopped at thirteen, given that Oxford felt it could no longer financially support the project. By that time, our chief supporter, Marion Pauck, had left the Press. In addition, the volumes are a set insofar as the color and format are identical, but they were not assigned numbers.

A look at the editorial board roster clearly confirms that the meetings were seminars of known persons in the field, who frequently exhibited differences of opinion that needed patience and reconciliation. On the board, besides Claude and myself, were Leonard Trinterud, Albert Outler, Jaroslav Pelikan, James Nichols, Winthrop Hudson, Sydney Ahlstrom, Brian Gerrish, Robert T. Handy, and Paul Lehmann. Anyone who knew Outler, Trinterud, and Pelikan also knows that there was an element of affectionate upstaging going on.

Drew was a time and place where I could bring together many of my academic interests in a very congenial setting. Yet my past still intruded on my life. While I felt that Harvard had been severe in its actions, I needed to take responsibility for the situation. I felt a need to straighten out my life. While my wife did not want a divorce, I found that for me the bond between us had been torn beyond repair. But I did not take any action until I found myself falling in love with Jane Daggett Karlin, who taught art history on a part-time basis at the theological school. A graduate of the University of Chicago with a master of arts from the Fogg at Harvard, she wanted to get a doctorate and teach in art and theology. Unfortunately, an imaginative doctoral program involving several schools was not approved. So being married, having two children, and living with her husband in Madison, she talked Drew into hiring her to teach a course each semester. Her classes were a stunning success and she began to publish books and write journal articles. She pioneered the teaching of art, particularly art history courses, in theological schools.

Our relation became serious and for a period of time we were not sure what we would do. But the die was cast and we had to make our situation clear to a few selected persons. Her husband threatened to go to the president of Drew, Robert Oxnam, and see to it that we were both fired.

So I went to see Oxnam myself and told him that we would be leaving at the end of the academic year. While Oxnam was disliked by many of the theological faculty, I found him an understanding and cooperative person. Later we learned that he had taken actions that protected both of us and Drew.

The problem became what should I do, since the combination of Harvard and a divorce would undoubtedly preclude a place in theological education. So I began to get feelers out with respect to a role in some publishing house. But in early January 1962, Theodore A. Gill, then president of San Francisco Theological Seminary, called me and wanted me to fly out immediately and talk with the faculty about a position at the seminary. I responded that I was interested but that I needed to talk with him about some personal matters that could complicate or indeed preclude my coming. He responded that he was coming to New York in three weeks and wanted then to talk with me and that I should remember they wanted me. I remember it well. We met in midtown at about five o'clock on a blustery winter day and walked to Luchow, which was then down on 14th Street, and stayed at dinner until the restaurant closed. I gave Ted the story of my life, at the end of which he repeated that he still wanted me to come out. Then he added that he needed to consult with specific individuals, both board and faculty, and that he would be in touch with me after that. Six weeks passed before I heard from him again, but in true Ted fashion, it was as if our conversation had only been a week ago. The message was come ahead, but you should come and meet the faculty as soon as you can. So, a week later I visited San Anselmo. The only lingering question was should Jane and I come separately and get married later. The mutual decision was that it would be less complicated if we were married. Indeed, with Jane's children, Bonnie and Christopher, we were given a house on campus and were readily and easily accepted. It was at Marin High School that Bonnie met Tom Farber, to whom she is married. Christopher, to the immense sorrow of all of us, died at college age of a brain injury suffered as a passenger in an automobile accident.

While I knew of divorces, it had not occurred to me that I would ever be involved in one and particularly that I would be leaving against Hilde's wishes when I was so much at fault. There were two wonderful children to be left behind, though ironically my younger son Paul and Jane's son Christopher had been close friends. Later they related how they consoled each other when they learned there were divorces ahead and almost instantly put the situation together.

When I left Drew, Eric was sixteen and Paul twelve years of age, respectively high school and junior high students. Since my position on the west coast took me to the east coast for meetings of various kinds, I did see them more often than might have been expected and they spent a few weeks each summer with Jane and me in the Bay Area. When Eric was college age, Hilde felt that it might be best if he came west. He enrolled in a college in San Diego and after two years he himself took the initiative to transfer to the University of California at Berkeley. Eric, who went from hippie to business entrepreneur while keeping his relaxed disposition, has lived most of his adult life in southern Oregon amidst the nature he loves.

When Paul arrived at college age, he and I visited various campuses, and he chose Carleton. I remember visiting him when he lived in a large house three of them had rented, that had a pool table in the basement. Paul decided to teach me to play pool. So I said nothing and deliberately shot poorly. When he had a good lead, I settled down and overtook him, leading him to exclaim, "You've shot pool before." He had not known that I had learned to play pool in the local saloon in Maeystown. He still has a pool table and when we meet, we play. Paul loved the Twin Cities area and spent his entire career as math advisor and teacher in the Minneapolis school system, winning national attention for his novel approaches. I am glad to say that Hilde and I have been present for most of the major events of their lives.

About a year or so after our leaving Drew, most of the theological faculty left over a dispute with Oxnam. I learned here that institutions can virtually destroy themselves. The theological faculty claimed that income from endowments meant for the seminary was being sidetracked to the college. In the turmoil that had emerged while I was still at Drew, I had calculated that if the theological school had received the endowment income they claimed, the school would still be in danger if new monies were not raised by the president. Among the faculty I represented a minority opinion. Probably a more important factor was that the Methodist constituency saw the faculty that had been assembled as undermining the desired Methodist ethos. In any case, it took a long time for the theological school to regain credibility.

7

ACADEMIC ADMINISTRATOR
Developing the Graduate Theological Union

*"If it is clear and not remedial, act decisively
and take the flack."*

My appointment at SFTS (San Francisco Theological Seminary) was as a professor in theology and history and with the assignment of representing SFTS in the emerging GTU (Graduate Theological Union) developments. Given the inchoate nature of the latter, I assumed that most attention would be given to my professorship. But Ted Gill had additional things in mind on both fronts. So, upon my arrival, he said casually, "Dean Gordon Oxtoby is on leave and probably will not return to the deanship. So, you might as well add that to your portfolio in an acting capacity until the faculty and I make it official." At the same time, the dean's secretary went on vacation the day I was due in the office, and in the next days I learned that she virtually ran the office of the dean. The faculty, I discovered, was waiting for the fall schedule. So I called the dean's secretary at her vacation address and she said the matter would have to wait until her return a month later. Upon further conversation with some faculty members, I discovered that delay was not unusual but created scheduling problems for faculty. So I called her again and asked her to tell me where the materials were that needed to be assembled and that I would do it. Her reply was no, and it was clear that she was not about to change her mind. So, I asked for the keys to her desk and file cabinets, so that I could do the scheduling which was already overdue. She still did not yield. So I added, "if you don't tell me where the keys are, I will have every lock broken and the scheduling will be done." Then she told me where the keys were. I went to the provost and told him the story. He smiled, said she had been a problem for years, and that they counted on my ending her tenure. After further conversations with some faculty members, I proceeded to work out

98

a retirement package, only to discover that a few members of the faculty who felt she needed to be replaced were upset by my doing it. That was the beginning of a series of administrative rules I formulated over the years, this one being, if the situation is clear and not remedial, act decisively and take the flack.

While I had had previous responsibilities for organizing projects and for running degree programs, and had been an inveterate watcher of administrators wherever I was, I had not until then had the overall responsibility for the academic functioning of an institution. In fact is was a major transition that I had made and a series of administrative rules and attitudes formed themselves out of ensuing experiences, of which the above is one. A second rule I came to is that all faculty members give one trouble, but some of them are worth it; a third, if things are not going well on an issue, never get yourself into a position that precludes your coming back to that issue, including a new approach, on another day or time; a fourth, have the patience to out sit every one else at a table, thereby assuring that no one is cut off by scheduling; a fifth, debate on the merit of a case but make sure that anger is not the reigning mood; a sixth, social occasions are important in getting to know people in wider contexts; a seventh, on major issues be sure that an initial meeting or meetings are exploratory rather than deciding occasions; and an eighth, know who the key players are and keep a continuing conversation going with each one individually. They will serve as a sounding board and you will be surprised by their contributions.

While curricular changes occurred at SFTS in the following two years, the accent was mainly on developing an excellent faculty. By the time I arrived Ted Gill had already strengthened the faculty and in the next several years appointed even more. Gill's attitude was that doctoral work required greater excellence than the existing resources of the schools. In short, joint appointments needed to be made among the schools interested in doing doctoral work.

I first heard of GTU from Yorke Allen, Jr, whom I mentioned in connection with the Library of Protestant Thought. In one of the visits with him during the last months at Drew he asked me did I know of GTU and I said I had never heard of it. He said it seemed like a good idea of cooperation among theological schools but that he was doubtful whether or not it could really be pulled off. At the time, it never occurred to me that the doctoral program for which I was to represent SFTS was the emergent GTU. Some eight months later, I saw Yorke again and said, "Now I do know of GTU, for I will be heading it." That started at least a decade of working with Yorke and the foundation, receiving sage advice and substantial funds. The concerns of the foundation were several, but most of all that the new venture must be organized in such a way that willful people could not tear it up if things did not go just as they wanted. Indeed, that had happened in the breakup of the Federated Theological Faculty at Chicago, a project that Sealantic had supported. In short, the penalty for withdrawal had to be large enough to keep cooperative programs serving the whole. Yorke insisted that our structural organization make it difficult to secede.

GTU Beginnings

Already in late 1958, that is, four years before my arrival on the scene, E.T. Bachmann, professor at the Lutheran school proposed a Cooperative Post Graduate Program in Theology for the Pacific School of Religion (PSR, Protestant Interdenominational), Church Divinity School of the Pacific (CDSP, Episcopal), San Francisco Theological Seminary (SFTS, Presbyterian) Berkeley Baptist Divinity School (BBDS) and Pacific Lutheran Theological Seminary (PLTS), working with the University at some levels. He made reference to two possibilities previously suggested by Sherman Johnson, then dean of CDSP: a) an Inter-seminary Graduate Program worked out by the seminaries themselves, and utilizing the resources and courses of the University or b) a Graduate Faculty in Religion, interfaith and ventured into jointly by the seminaries and University.

The interdenominational Protestant Pacific School of Religion (PSR) was the oldest of the schools in the Bay Area, founded in part to furnish the religious dimensions for the new state university which subsequently became the University of California at Berkeley (UCB). When Charles McCoy, whose field of interest was theology and its wider educational dimensions, came to PSR in 1959 he convinced the Danforth Foundation to financially sponsor a series of meetings among representatives of PSR, the University of California, and the other theological schools of the area. With that historical background and its Protestant ecumenical dimensions, as well as a doctoral program of its own, it was natural that PSR should think of itself as the lead school, indeed the school that could be the natural entity for spearheading any new developments. Apparently the president of PSR, Stuart Anderson, and its dean, Robert Fitch, agreed that the only solution was for them to be the leaders in such a venture and on their administrative terms. This Anderson put in writing and sent to the other schools, though McCoy had tried to persuade him not to do so, urging that PSR's role should emerge rather than possibly becoming the barrier.

In the meantime schools such as CDSP, PLTS, BBDS, and SFTS, had their own ideas of how to proceed and, since PSR did not seem flexible on what should happen, decided to move ahead when Anderson was out of town and would not be put in the position of having to try to block the future. I can testify to that absence of flexibility in cooperation in a meeting in which Anderson and other heads were present, about two years after my arrival, when Anderson said that PSR could not join in the new venture inasmuch as it was not in their master plan. Then Massey Shepherd of CDSP, noted church historian with an equal dose of not being too flexible, asked, "Where are you on the master plan?" to which Stuart replied, "Fifteen years in a twenty year plan." Hearing that, Massey asked, "Do you mean that nothing has happened in the last fifteen years to make you think of new possibilities," to which the answer was "No." The meeting erupted in laughter, but no movement occurred on any of the issues.

The four schools that organized the GTU had varying conceptions of what should occur. There was some difference of opinion as to whether the university connection was necessary, what administrative structures should emerge, whether a single entity should give the degrees, whether faculty would be paid for doctoral courses, and whether there should be a central or rotating dean from among the schools. To get started, plans emerged to add doctoral courses in church history, followed by the biblical field, with the idea that other areas would soon follow.

Concretely, a provisional organization was formed, with Sherman Johnson, Dean of CDSP, appointed also as Dean of GTU for a preliminary period. To fill his absence for a sabbatical year, Massey Shepherd was appointed acting dean of GTU and, then was followed by Johnson again for the academic year 1962-63, the year when I arrived at SFTS. Shepherd had contact with Dean Elberg at the graduate division of UCB and the letter from Elberg of January 1962 is in the GTU archives, though it was years later that I discovered it. It spelled out what the University felt it could do and was really the basis for the patterns that followed, though Elberg and Shepherd never made reference to that letter in my conversations with them. This history was not known to me when I arrived and when I first went to see Elberg, he acted as if the issue had never come up before.

My dwelling on this is only to say that the idea of the GTU was not mine. Nor do I believe that there was a single person to whom the credit belongs. But it is also apparent that for the most part there was little feeling among the four Protestant schools that what needed to happen extended far beyond a mechanism to share existing resources.

That was the situation when I arrived in the Bay Area. The geographical landscape was not entirely new to me, for I had been stationed there when on the way to Guam and later, my wife and children and I were in PSR housing as I did three weeks of summer session teaching in the mid-fifties while at Harvard. At the time, President Anderson and I had a fair amount of contact and before I left he told me that he wanted me to join their faculty. I probably would have accepted, but the formal request never came. Years later I was told that the then dean and a faculty person blocked the proposed appointment.

Aside from the personal reasons for coming to SFTS, to which I alluded earlier, I can only report what I later heard about Gill's special interest in me in particular. Apparently, Krister Stendahl was among those who recommended me as a person who had been involved in the Columbia program, reconceived the Harvard one and directed it, and broadened the scope of the one at Drew. It was undoubtedly the case that on paper, few had such qualifications. In addition, my experiences, while ecumenical in nature, were also wider than the traditional Protestant ecumenism. My graduate work and my experiences in the Navy already pushed those boundaries. I saw the ecumenical movement as the possible codification of existing historical affinities no longer separable on theological grounds. Previously, I noted the relation I had with the Evangelical and Reformed church. That union had no more than been completed when conversations began with the Congregational church, which itself had merged with another group. In 1957 that union was consummated under the name of the United Church of Christ, though there were theological wrangles on the role of the local congregation that led to some secessions. These were movements with which I was sympathetic and I knew the various players and leaders.

When Pike and Eugene Carson Blake proposed the Consultation on Church Union (COCU), I was asked to give the opening address and indeed another major one a few years later. I was also one of the representatives of the United Church of Christ. But two things occurred that ended my official association. First was the request that those willing to step aside should do so to make room for minority representation. Second, I had begun to lose interest, for while the theological differences could be overcome, it was clear that the bureaucracies would not step aside. Probably most annoying was the repeated statement by some conservatives that union was an administrative matter and that what they desired was a deeper unity than that proposed. COCU, while still extant, never moved beyond recognizing each other's ministries, and most recently was transformed into Churches Uniting in Christ.

Partly by bowing to pressure for younger and more diverse leadership and also being disappointed by the pace of things, I was sidetracked from the church world. In retrospect, I see that I moved from the church to the art world in terms of significant associations with individuals, though that movement at the time did not significantly affect my theological convictions.

Gill knew this changing world and he was determined that the emerging GTU should take on a life appropriate for the present and the future. In short, he wanted movement, expertise, and quality. I used to say that I would be his dean any day for I knew of no situation in which his thinking was less than supportive and sometimes a step ahead of what I proposed. Never did I have a more collegial relationship. I had met Ted first in the Union Theological Seminary Library, and later gave some lectures in the Presbyterian church at 106th Street where he served as pastor as he also finished writing his dissertation for Emil Brunner at Zurich. Further, I was a fan of what he did with the *Christian Century*, making it aesthetically pleasing in content and style. But little did I know what he had in mind. It was later reported that Ted had told others that it would become obvious within six months that I should head the new development. Actually, it took three months for the group to decide that, effective January 1, 1963, I should be assistant dean, reporting to Johnson and to the board and that I would be dean at the end of Johnson's term, that is, beginning with the 1963—64 academic year. It was obvious that the head of GTU, if it was to develop, needed more attention than what an existing head of an institution could give it. The idea of a rotating dean from the schools disappeared early on, though it still resurfaces on occasion as an item for discussion.

The incorporation document was registered in October 1962, which makes that GTU's official beginning date. I became the driving force on behalf of the new entity in the fall of 1962. It was not that I had ideas I wished to push, but rather that it seemed to me that there were so many favorable ingredients, human and material, that more could be expected than just accepting extant resources as the limiting factor.

One might note that the title for the head officer of GTU was dean instead of president. For this, there were two reasons. First, in the Episcopal tradition generally, the chief officer of a theological school carried the title of dean. Since that was Johnson's title at CDSP, it made sense for GTU. Second, inasmuch as there was some opposition to the head of GTU having the title president, settling on dean made sense. It indicated that the head of GTU served the schools. Moreover, it accented the academic nature of the appointment and what the institution was about.

Incidentally, several years later, I happened to drop the remark that when I was on funding missions, sooner or later the question appeared, "Who is the president or head of the institution? We would like to talk to that person." At a subsequent meeting, Arnold Come, then head of the SFTS raised the question posed by my casual statement. Without fanfare the response was, "We have come to trust you and we would be glad for you also to have the title of president."

Broadening and Shaping GTU

In the early years of my involvement every aspect to the new venture needed attention. In short, it was not a situation in which one could decide which issues came first in a string of possibilities. Setting priorities is more characteristic of established entities. Being ready for the whole called for vision that seized occasions and forged the appropriate structures.

Immediately after my arrival, teaching-load issues emerged. Should the doctoral courses be added to existing loads and the faculty paid for the additional courses? Some faculty members would have welcomed the extra money, but fortunately the central issue was faced. Faculty, if they were to have time for research, were already teaching too many hours or courses. The only alternative was to build the doctoral courses into existing requirements, which could be possible if coordination and sharing of courses across school lines became the norm.

When GTU was formed, doing doctoral work as well as teaching at other levels was an ideal for many faculty persons. But there was the additional problem that not enough faculty members had the qualifications to teach at the doctoral level. Here SFTS and BBDS took the lead, first by a wave of appointments of first-level scholars and teachers, and the second by sharing two new appointments with GTU with financial salary commitments of two-thirds from the school and one-third from GTU. It was assumed at the time that the latter arrangement might become the pattern, particularly if GTU could raise the money for its share. The model was abandoned when the Baptist constituency brought sufficient pressure to terminate the appointments of Bernie Loomer and Norman Gottwald, a revolt against two of the top liberal scholars in the country. The Presbyterian and Baptist traditions, both the most positive groups in the initial GTU developments, have continued to have problems with conservative factions about their relation to GTU. The initial Baptist school in Berkeley, a member of the Northern Baptist Convention, was moved to southern California to combine with the Covina school, where the experiment failed, with the more liberal Baptists returning to Berkeley, and now is named the American Baptist Seminary of the West (ABSW). At the same time, the Golden Gate Baptist School, a member of the Southern Baptist Convention, built a new campus in a picturesque spot in Marin County and wanted to cooperate in the GTU developments. Its president at the time, Harold Graves, was walking a thin line, and told me later sadly that they could not continue even with the cooperative library developments. Jim McClendon, who had taken me to see the campus, ironically pointed out that their library books that had just arrived were packed in liquor boxes.

Faculty competence was an issue that had to be addressed. At SFTS, where a Doctor of Theology (Th.D) program already existed, the new developments were meant to address such issues and the seminary was willing for a special committee, including UCB faculty representation, to evaluate its faculty in designated doctoral areas. As dean of the SFTS faculty, I had to write a letter that stated that unless faculty quality was a priority for all the schools, SFTS would not continue in GTU. In the case of PSR, which also had a ThD program, the willingness to be so evaluated was not well received. As a part of the negotiations to bring PSR into GTU, we agreed to incorporate those who had been doing doctoral teaching into GTU without further evaluation; a decision that I agreed to accept for the greater good, but which temporarily alienated some senior faculty members not at PSR.

It soon became apparent that GTU was taking more and more of my time, and that SFTS was contributing considerably more of the expenses than others. In addition, it was felt that a GTU dean probably should not be a member of one of the schools. When that issue surfaced, SFTS was acutely aware that employment by GTU was risky for me and that they would guarantee tenure for me. So, within two years, I was full time with GTU while living in San Anselmo. But it was obvious that the center of GTU would be in Berkeley, given the location of the other schools and the University of California. So by the end of the second year, I commuted daily to Berkeley and we began to look for a house there. We found one that was about a seven minute walking distance from the central GTU area known as Holy Hill, near enough to use the house for entertaining after various events. GTU agreed that we would purchase the house rather than have GTU do so and now, some forty years later, Jane still lives there. In the meantime, I had an office at CDSP and soon moved into a fraternity house GTU purchased at 2465 LeConte, which still serves as housing for many of the GTU offices. This was a time when fraternities were out of favor, and in subsequent years the theological community purchased several such buildings.

During the first two years, I used the secretary that came with the position of dean at SFTS. Now moving full time to GTU, I needed both secretarial and administrative help, which initially could be one person, hopefully someone who could also take care of the inevitable expansion. Besides competence, I had another criterion, namely, the person belong to an ethnic minority group. So I enlisted the help of others in the quest, and Neill Hamilton, New Testament professor at San Anselmo, came through with a person who, he was sure, could do the job, which was confirmed for me in an interview. Both her credentials and personal disposition, including an excellent background in the humanities and social studies stood out, though it was also clear that religion was not her thing. Jean Porée Merritt was my administrative assistant for five years, and during that time, she oversaw the administrative development, addressed situations of crisis, and directly managed and reorganized all non academic facets as need arose. The rudiments of many of them are still in place. There were some amusing moments, as when in my dictation "exegesis" came out as "exit Jesus" or when she offered to do a coffee hour for the Mormons. But her knowledge of religion grew rapidly in the process.

The period in which I served GTU administratively ran from the fall of 1962 to the beginning of January 1972. While administrative issues occupied much of my schedule, I did spend a good deal of time in teaching and planning with faculty. With respect to teaching, GTU did not change my teaching style, except that it was exhilarating. A Mormon student described the experience at its best: "For three years, I took nearly every class he taught. He assigned only primary sources – church fathers, scholastics, reformers, puritans, revivalists, transcendentalists, liberals, social gospelers, neo-orthodox, moderns, and post-moderns. Four to seven hundred pages a week. I was stunned. Week after week I was exposed to theologians who had addressed core issues in vastly different contexts, but all with a breadth of vision and command of the tradition unknown in my Mormon experience. Dillenberger began each class with historical and biographical background, then initiated discussion. He approached each reading fresh, open to new possibilities from his students. His own analyses were brilliant, never represented as the final word, but as openings to new directions."

Major faculty leadership roles were played by Edward Hobbs, Victor Gold, Keith Bridston, Kevin Wall, Dan O'Hanlon, John Hilary Martin, Surjit Singh, Ben Reist, Harland Hogue, and Durwood Foster. Hobbs in particular was an articulate and helpful voice in the early years. A graduate faculty was created, which met monthly and was chaired by myself as dean. It had jurisdiction over the graduate program. Given that coordination was necessary at all levels, the entire faculties of the schools also met, and the meetings were also chaired by myself as dean. The latter grouping disappeared after several years because it took too much time and the group had no jurisdiction. In its place I proposed that the heads of institutions meet monthly, given that coordinating issues needed to be faced. The new incorporated GTU board did not spell out a special role for the heads of institutions, probably because they were all on the board of the new entity. Currently, the heads of institutions play a major role in governance of various facets of GTU.

The GTU document of incorporation reads that "the primary purpose for which the corporation is formed is to conduct an educational institution offering instruction on the graduate theological level; to participate with theological seminaries and other institutions of higher learning in cooperative programs of study; and to grant such academic degrees and honors as are customarily granted in universities and seminaries of learning; either in its own name only, or in conjunction with another such institution." The incorporators, representing heads of institutions and lay members from the constituencies, had created a legal entity in its own right, based on the schools, a model of independence and relatedness. To this date, that is what the GTU is.

I do not know who wrote the document. But I do know that the first chair of the board was Philip Adams, an attorney and Episcopalian associated with CDSP. He took the wider spectrum seriously, frequently saying to me, "Where are the Buddhists and the Mormons?" But that outlook, shared by Ted Gill and some faculty, was not widely held. For the most part GTU represented the Protestant spectrum, perhaps best represented in the previously mentioned Consultation on Church Union initiated by Eugene Carson Blake and James Pike.

Now a second development was occurring: Vatican II. The contact between Protestant and Catholic scholars had been quietly going on for over a decade. But the new official stance brought emergent cooperative projects to the public front. One frequently hears it said that the enthusiasm and optimistic mood of Vatican II made it easy to work out cooperative patterns. It did make them possible, but not without having to work through bureaucratic difficulties – bishops, judicatories, and the curia itself.

Although Catholic schools had not been in the purview of most of the originators of GTU, the Union's charter certainly included that possibility. PSR, not initially a part of the founding group, kept saying that it was founded to do what GTU was doing. One evening at a public meeting, Stuart LeRoy Anderson again propounded that theme. Tired of this refrain but also believing they had a point, I announced that I had three questions, and if Anderson responded to them with a yes, I would propose that GTU go out of business and that something be worked out with PSR. I have forgotten one of the questions, but the other two had to do with granting equality to the Jewish tradition and to Catholic schools. Stuart said they could cooperate but not grant equality. Then I replied that I did not want to hear again that PSR was set up to do what GTU intended. Stuart could not move beyond his Protestant ecumenism, though he was not alone in having a congregational liberalism and an ethos that had its limits. PSR did join the GTU in 1964 and entered into the common library in 1980. In spite of the initial reluctance, PSR became one of the leaders in subsequent GTU developments.

The Unitarian/Universalist Starr King School for the Ministry joined in 1964, though its program was so unique and removed from traditional subjects and teaching style that cooperative patterns took time to develop. It also joined the GTU library in 1984, though it still has some unique and rare nineteenth-century materials under its own jurisdiction.

The Catholic scene was fairly congenial to exploration, which initially occurred almost by happenstance. I was invited to speak at a Roman Catholic parish in San Rafael on where we were with respect to Catholic/Protestant inter relations. Afterward, I met Peggy and John Cahill, devout Catholics who favored wider explorations. Soon Peggy joined the GTU Board. Also present that evening were Kevin and Antoninus Wall, Dominican priests at the local priory, but mostly anchored at St. Albert's in north Oakland. I discovered that they knew Ted Gill, and I proposed that the four of us meet to talk about cooperative possibilities, which we did soon thereafter.

St. Albert's was a Dominican college, educating students for entering the Dominican priesthood, a preparation that included advanced theological studies offered by the Dominican School of Philosophy and Theology (DSPT). The two functioned cooperatively but were distinct programs, while sharing the same Oakland campus. DSPT's focus was to provide advanced philosophical preparation, centering in St. Thomas Aquinas.

While the Dominicans needed the approval of the local bishop for exploring cooperation with GTU, that it would be given was not a foregone conclusion. Bishop Floyd Begin was a conservative Catholic, concerned to keep the faithful firm within the faith and worried about persons leaving the faith if exposed to other groups. Somehow I was invited to speak at the first commencement at St. Albert's and the Bishop was present. Apparently what I said evoked a positive response, but more importantly, we instinctively liked each other. Our conversations were encouraged and facilitated as well by his Monsignor, John Cummins. He became a wise counselor with respect to the Franciscans and Jesuits and eventually succeeded Begin as bishop, in which capacity he promoted cooperation across many boundaries and protected GTU and the schools from attacks from the conservative right. In the early days, I tried to assure the bishop that ecumenical contacts strengthened faith commitments, for the situation of exposure made one more aware of who one was and why. In any case, the Bishop attended meetings where cooperative patterns were being hammered out. Several times, he stated in public, with flair and humor, that if I promised to live forever, he would trust the ecumenical developments in Berkeley.

In addition to the approval of the Bishop, the Dominicans needed the approval of the head of the Dominican order, Anticito Alonso Hernandez. He was invited to Berkeley, with a series of well planned meetings, which the Dominicans did so well. Then came the possibility of the two of us meeting alone, except for a translator. He preferred to walk, and I recall our walking up and down Euclid for at least a half hour. He was glad that DSPT wanted to be geographically within the confines of Holy Hill, as the section north of the university is called. His concern seemed to be who would head the group, inasmuch as there was no one locally who would be supported without some reservation. I recall saying that Kevin Wall had been the moving spirit in all the planning to date and had substantial support, and that from the GTU end, he was the logical choice. I recall the relief I felt when the translator said, "The answer is that Wall will be asked." All the negotiations with the Dominicans took no more than six weeks, and the GTU schools accepted the Dominicans with a minimum of discussion.

The movement of the Franciscans from Santa Barbara to Berkeley involved less of my time than with the other orders. Although the school was related to the Franciscan mission at Santa Barbara, the situation was right for their movement to Berkeley. I remember visiting in Santa Barbara at least twice. With respect to the Oakland diocese, Bishop Begin had no reason to be suspicious of the Franciscans. They, too, were a small body, hardly threatening to the regular diocesan priests. With respect to facilities, they purchased a fraternity building at the northwest corner of LeConte and Euclid, which they initially painted a brilliant red. Most of the negotiations were undertaken with Robert Pfisterer and to some extent with Kenan Osborne, faithful professor of theology for decades. And, of course, their admission to the GTU was routine.

The Jesuits took time and energy. The seminary was known then as Alma College, located in the Los Gatos hills, a place that qualified as an area uncontaminated by the diversions of city life. Its premier theologian, Daniel O'Hanlon, was known to me from previous associations. Discovering the connection with Alma, I soon sought him out and discovered his interest in GTU. He invited me to visit with Alma's long-standing dean, Harry Corcoran, a conservative who seemed cautiously open but felt he needed to learn much more, which he made it his business to do. Educationally, it made so much sense to him and some of his colleagues. But there were special problems: leaving the idyllic location, the push from the University of San Francisco to relocate in San Francisco, the hesitation of Bishop Floyd Begin in Oakland, and the difficulties of securing permission from Rome to move from the one diocese to another.

Once convinced that it made educational sense, Harry was prodigious in his energy in behalf of the move. We saw each other frequently, and it would probably not be a mistake to say we became close friends and fellow conspirators. Indeed, Harry said I was his first Protestant friend. One of his problems was that the Catholic provincial who would have to sign off locally was a close friend of Harry's who opposed the proposed move. A story Harry loved to tell over and over, after permission to move to Berkeley was secured, was that he had taken me to meet the provincial and Father Hauck to talk about the theological implications of such a move. Arriving, Harry steered me to a wide stairwell, to a room upstairs where they usually met. Instead, the provincial said "Harry we are meeting downstairs today," and led the way to a room with seating for about a dozen people. No more than seated, the conversation began and I was pushed hard, while Harry, looking at the walls covered by paintings of the Inquisition, lamented that I was experiencing it. I was so involved that I had not even seen the paintings, though on a later meeting I confirmed it for myself. After about an hour and a half, the provincial said, "Harry, I have to go but you know where the drinks are upstairs." Harry declined, being somewhat miffed by what had happened, but then as we walked out of the building on Lyons Street in San Francisco he said, "Could we go to dinner?" My response was that I had promised my wife Jane that I would be home for dinner, but I would call to see if she could join us for dinner at Spinnaker's in Sausalito. On the way, Harry, needing a drink, wondered, he said later, what would happen with this Protestant. We arrived before

Jane did, and the waiter asked what we wanted to drink. I responded, "I know what Jane wants, a martini and I'll have one too." As Harry repeated on various occasions, that evening the ecumenical movement became totally all right. Jane too became a friend of Harry's for the rest of his life.

Slowly, Jesuit faculty members and students saw the advantages of moving to Berkeley. These included a relation with other Catholic bodies, a broad spectrum of Protestants, a working relation with a major university, and unparalleled library resources. While the country atmosphere of Alma slowly decreased as a major factor, Alma (which became the Jesuit School of Theology in Berkeley) wanted to make sure that the privileges it had become accustomed to not be lost. This meant athletic facilities, chapel, classrooms, dining facilities, all on a scale that obtained at Alma. Warren Deem, who had done a study for the GTU community, also did one that took the Jesuit concerns into account. Carrying out the Jesuit wishes would have meant demolishing several blocks of housing, a major community problem. Later, even demolishing just a single dilapidated building on land owned by GTU for the new library caused endless delay. The Jesuit-envisioned campus became obsolete when the new head of the Jesuits, Father Aruppe, who had spent considerable time in crowded Japan, vetoed the plan. The Jesuits subsequently purchased several fraternity houses and made creative adaptations.

From the Berkeley end, the only initial opposition came from Bishop Floyd Begin, who said that he could not have more Jesuits than other priests in his diocese. Translated, that indicated something of an anti-Jesuit bent, but John Cummins kept talking with the bishop. John would call me and say, "We have an appointment today with the bishop, but his psychic position is not disposed to explore such issues today." Or conversely, "The bishop is in an expansive mood today, can you come down?" Eventually, the bishop agreed not to oppose the move. From the archdiocese of San Francisco, little was heard directly. A certain lack of interest in theological education, including little support for the diocesan seminary, St. Patrick's in Menlo Park, helped our cause. It was all right for us to deal with the Jesuits, but not all right for the diocesan seminary to plan moving to Berkeley.

Harry and I were in personal contact week after week, and our conversations were always filled with what strategies were available to us. One day, I said to Harry, "I will be in Europe, including Rome, in about six weeks. Is there anything I can do?" He said, "Let me think." The phone rang the next day, and Harry said, "Could you write us a letter outlining why we should be in Berkeley, covering all the points we have talked about." One of the problems was that the request to move to Berkeley had to go through the local provincial who opposed the move. He could modify the request or make arguments against it, none of which Harry and his friends would know. I wrote the letter and was directed to be in contact with Jack Boyle, an Alma college faculty member on Sabbatical in Rome. Six appointments had been made for me and everywhere I went, xerox copies of my letter preceded me. I called it a Protestant/Jesuit end run, for they could introduce me to say what GTU had to say without going through channels. Jack joined me as an interpreter and I do not recall all the appointments, but I do remember Fathers Dezza and Small. The last appointment was with Cardinal Bea who balked at having anybody present but the two of us. It was a memorable hour, one in which he used his fluent German and I my regional Rhineland German. But we managed.

I have never known whether my letter and my presence made any difference in the matter. But Harry and I both felt that we had gotten information to critical players. Whatever letters or spoken words went on behind the scenes, we had had a chance. In any case, the provincial finally received a letter of approval for the move, but kept it to himself for a six-month period. What went on in that period, if anything, I do not know. Nor do I know if Harry ever found out. One thing is clear, if it had not been for Harry's persistence, and John Cummins' mediating role, the Jesuit school would never have made it to Berkeley and GTU.

Early on, the schools and particularly the biblical scholars were interested in a Judaic presence, the Christian term that described the interest in Jewish scholarship. Given that we had been dealing with schools, I made several visits to Los Angeles to see about the possibility of a school moving into the GTU orbit. I talked particularly with Nelson Glueck and Alfred Gottschalk. To make a long story short, I was told that we were just a year too late, that developments were so far along they could not be cancelled. To create a smaller new school for Berkeley was financially not viable, given obligations already made, all of which became transparently clear in succeeding years. So we turned to making a professorial appointment in Judaic Studies, namely David Winston. His position was funded within the GTU budget. In exploring funding sources in the Jewish community, the general attitude was, show us that you are serious and funding may follow. Subsequent appointments of three positions, the development of funding sources and special university relations have been the work of my successors.

Another avenue of exploration was the Eastern Orthodox tradition, which involved the Romanov family on the peninsula. While we talked a lot, with food and vodka, we never made substantial progress. My successor, Claude Welch, turned to the Greek tradition with considerable success. Why that did not occur to me I do not know. Perhaps it was because on the east coast my contacts at Columbia and Harvard had all been Russian.

When Philip Adams, first chair of the board, asked, "Where are the Mormons?" I could say that I did turn to them but the schools were not ready to accept them. My own contact with the Mormon tradition dated back to Harvard, when a graduate student in the philosophy department transferred to the religion program because it was less doctrinaire. Some two years later, he came to my office, saying he was about eight months from completing his dissertation, but his wife would not keep supporting him to the limits required to finish in the foreseeable future. He had been a very good student and I asked how much money he needed. He told me and disclosed his assets. So I said, come back in a few days and bring your wife with you, if you can. By the time they arrived, I had worked out a grant that, if she could continue for another two months, would see him through the time he needed to finish the dissertation. They never forgot what had happened and they stayed in touch. Truman Madsen joined the Provo Utah faculty, soon was head of religious studies, and continued to publish. Moreover, he started sending Mormon students to the GTU MA and doctoral programs. On occasion, he would give lectures at GTU and we began to talk of whether he could spend some time regularly teaching at GTU. Truman and the Mormon students talked openly of the problems within Mormonism, but added that we, as outsiders, should not have a single view of Mormonism. Just as there were fundamentalists in Protestantism, we would not be happy to be given one label. So was the situation in Mormonism. We needed to learn from each other, they said. Armed with that approach, I talked with the heads about the possibility but the answer was a resounding no. Meanwhile for several years Mormon students continued to come to GTU, and the prominent journal *Sunstone*, started in 1978, was founded and edited successively by two GTU students, Peggy Fletcher Stack and Scott Kenney. I was asked to contribute articles to the journal and did two articles, "Grace and Works in Martin Luther and Joseph Smith," (1978) and "The Sovereignty of God in John Calvin and Brigham Young."(1980)

Now to the University picture. It was clear to most faculty members that a first rate program would involve University faculty and library resources. It seemed logical to seek an appointment with the dean of the Graduate Faculties, Sanford Elberg. First, he made it clear that UCB was a big bureaucracy, one that would probably not make arrangements with any group if it meant institution to institution deliberations. That would open too many doors. Second, the way to make progress was to find ways of starting patterns that do not need permissions from on high. He asked, "How many UCB faculty do you know, and what are their interests?" When I replied that I knew ten, he said "Come back when you have fifty who are interested in religion and in working with you." I came back with a list closer to one hundred fifty than fifty, a list built by each interested person suggesting additional persons. In almost any area potentially related to GTU interests, there were more interested faculty than at Union, Princeton, Yale and Harvard put together. Years later, I asked the UCB historian Bill Bouwsma how one could account for that. He said he could reply only for the history department, where he said it was not a matter of religious conviction with respect to appointments, but that scholars who did not know religious history were poor scholars, inasmuch as religious currents were so much a part of history.

Elberg also said that given all the GTU schools and librarians, they could not and would not cooperate with each one separately, that it would have to be through a single entity, such as GTU. So we started with simple arrangements, sending the folders of candidates of which we approved to the graduate division for its approval as a way of maintaining standards. In addition, while GTU was awarding the Ph.D.degree, the understanding was that at least one Berkeley professor would be on each student's comprehensive and dissertation committees. In most instances, UCB faculty welcomed GTU students in seminars, inasmuch as they brought angles of vision not usually present with UCB students alone. Initially, GTU faculty members asked individual University faculty members to be on particular committees. Later, students had to find such faculty members on their own, a development that eroded the built-in need for GTU faculty to know faculty from both other schools and the university. While the chancellor Roger Heyns was sympathetic to these new developments, and had regular contact with people from GTU, he was not involved in any of the arrangements.

Strange as it may seem, the first working group with which GTU faculty and University faculty cooperated was the School of Environmental Design, largely under the influence of the architect, Patrick Quinn, and GTU faculty members Harland Hogue and Jane Dillenberger. With faculty changes at the School of Environmental Design, that initial arrangement disappeared. But new interest arose among university art historians, such as Herschel Chipp, Walter Horn, and Peter Selz. In the meantime,

GTU resources were augmented. We had encouraged the Dominicans to reflect their own historical past by adding a professor in the arts. So they asked Michael Morris to take a doctorate at the University of California Berkeley. In addition, Doug Adams had taken his doctorate at GTU with a concentration in the arts. Then he spent a year as a research fellow at the National Museum of American Art, where under the tutelage of Joshua Taylor, he received a first level training in art history and museum practice. We were glad to see him appointed at PSR and GTU. To this day GTU is the only theological school offering a Ph.D program in art and theology. From early on, programs developed in most of the areas of the curriculum, including biblical, historical studies, systematic and philosophical theology, ethics, psychological approaches, and others as faculty members promoted them.

Library resources were an issue from the beginning. In the early sixties, James Tanis and Raymond Morris, librarians respectively at Harvard and Yale, in an accreditation visit to SFTS, wrote that the Bay Area schools did not have sufficient library resources to undertake doctoral work. They reported that UCB had the best theological library at that level. Each of the schools had specific areas in which there was depth, but taken together, the resources were considered marginal. By and large there was much unneeded duplication among the schools. PSR, SFTS, the Jesuits, and the Unitarians had holdings in depth in limited areas. Something needed to be done.

As a step in the direction of creating a mechanism for change, all schools except PSR, agreed that a bibliographical center would be set up to do two things: one, to bring together the central bibliographical resources needed for basic beginning research, and two, to do the ordering and cataloguing for all schools in a setting in which it was agreed that budgets would not be cut but unneeded duplication would be eliminated in favor of the development of depth in specific areas. It was tacitly understood that down the road, the books would need to be brought together in a central, common library.

The theory was fine, but the expenses mounted. I did a crash course in library function and operation, mainly by consulting other librarians in the country and by extensive reading. "What can you do to make an already catalogued book cost you five dollars more," wrote one librarian and then replied "plenty," and proceeded to indicate the checking one can do to catch the mistakes the Library of Congress made and to elaborate on what it did not do. Our respective schools mainly used the Union, Dewey, and LC systems. While the LC system is not the best for elaborate cataloguing, it alone has room for all the religious groupings. However, Tanis and Morris recommended that we not go the route of LC. For me, it was clear that a national system was the future. I pushed for LC, to be told by Tanis and Morris a year later that it was the best decision I made.

Since the LC system was not created for theology, many theological librarians considered it inadequate and its work to be full of mistakes. When I asked what the percentage of mistakes were, I was told five percent; when I asked what their own cataloguing mistakes were, I received the same reply, five per cent. There is a judgment among most librarians that cataloguing is the critical part of library work and the clue to the patron finding the books that are needed. Here classification systems and browsing are in an unholy alliance. If one knows a field, one would not trust browsing, for the books could be in one of several places, depending on the particular cataloguer. Moreover, the more fully a book is catalogued, the more inconsistent the elaboration is with time, for approaches to literature are always in movement. Hence, generalized, limited cataloguing stands the test of time better than highly specified cataloguing. Likewise, the whole system is expensive, for under the classification system, books are always having to be moved to make room for the system, unless the library is new and still has plenty of room. So I say, if a book is already catalogued, take it as it comes; it is too expensive to make alleged improvements. If one started from scratch, one could place books in numerical sequence as they arrived, as at Hebrew University in Jerusalem. It saves space and the location of the book is easy to find. In fact, the computer challenges the traditional view of cataloguing.

The preceding remarks are considered heresy, however, in most though not all of the library world. Still, it was clear to me that we were spending too much time and money in revisions and procedures that were simply too expensive. So I asked the librarians (having inherited six of the librarians from the schools) to bring in a new plan that would address the rising costs within six weeks. When they arrived they said they could not find ways to save money, that the problem was that I did not want to raise the needed funds. I offered them additional time, but they declined. Finding myself boxed in, I said. "I will take your resignations as you leave." I assumed I was in deep trouble as I called the heads of institutions from whom I had inherited the six librarians. Their reply in each case was that they had not promised the librarians a place in perpetuity, that if it wasn't working, they would respect my decision. Fortunately, there were openings in the library field at the time; so other job openings took care of the matter.

PSR was not yet in the library program and its librarian, J. Stillson Judah, was all for cooperation and new systems. So I offered him the top GTU library position. Within six weeks, he turned the operation around and we were able to do what we had promised. Stillson obviously stayed on to head the new emerging library.

Moving from the Bibliographical Center to a common library was the boldest and most visible event in GTU history. Shepherding these developments was the most exhilarating of the GTU experiences of my tenure. Getting out of the agreements would involve penalties that greatly inhibited such action, and no one in more than three decades later has chosen that option. Instead, PSR, as a new president took the helm, also joined the common library. While the document and the agreements have been modified in details over the years, the essential agreement remains intact. Buying as one entity for some thirty-five years, ending needless duplication with a combined budget, made it possible to fill in gaps and extend research developments. Cooperative planning with the University also picked up speed. My experience is that I can find libraries such as Union, Harvard and Yale that are better in particular subjects than the University and GTU complex. But I cannot find a situation where the theological library resources are as good in an overall sense as in Berkeley.

The next phase was planning for a new building to house the existing collection and with enough space for twenty years of growth. In the interim, space was made available at CDSP, PSR, SFTS, and PLTS, with CDSP being the administrative center. My initial task with respect to the new library building involved seeing to it that a document was produced that spelled out a plan that could be used in selecting an architect. For that, we solicited the help of Dick Peters, a UCB professor in the field of architecture. From early on he directed the work of the committee, chaired by Bud Dinner, trustee for decades. The committee included board members mainly, my wife Jane because of her knowledge of contemporary art and architecture, and myself as president. The committee made a list of architects and took the time to see buildings of selected architects. Approximately ten architects were interviewed. I remembered most the team of Robert Venturi and Denise Scott Brown. Given their reputation, I had looked forward to their visit. But it became apparent that they had flown across country and never read the document we had prepared. The result was confusion and backpedaling on their part. They struck out. Yet it was also becoming clear that we were heading toward picking a San Francisco firm of acceptable but undistinguished work. In the midst of all this, some of us were at the edge of despair, and after some conversation during a break, Jane whispered to Bud Dinner, adjacent to whom she sat, "Why not Louis Kahn?" He probably would not have been proposed, had the prospects been better. But in that situation, Bud raised the question and Kahn looked acceptable to all. He had not been on the initial list because it was assumed he would not be interested. Several of us knew his work well, particularly the buildings at Yale and the Exeter library. According to those who knew him, his works contrasted sharply with his disheveled self. He was asked and readily accepted.

Before I left the presidency, I saw him on a few occasions. One time I recall particularly, for I said to him, "Why did you at the Exeter Library put the microfilm readers in the dark in the basement," to which he replied, "Isn't that were they should be!" But I said, "Mr. Kahn, you the architect of light, know that it is not light and dark, but the play of light that makes your architecture." In the ensuing days, he made reference to our conversations, as if, in that instance, he had not taken his own perceptions seriously. Kahn's death soon after doing several over all sketches for the building left us not knowing what he would have done with the film readers. The final building, which technically has traces of what Kahn might have done, was built by Esherick, Peters and Associates and won major architectural awards.

The GTU developments also need to be seen in the context of the Free Speech movement in the 1960's at the University. Essentially, GTU was sympathetic to those developments and had its own versions of what to do. Some faculty abandoned existing requirements and turned almost totally to experiential modes. I once had a sit-in of women students in my office. While I was in sympathy with their demands for more women faculty and additional financial support, I also had to make it clear that they could not be met immediately. I added that I would sit with them for as long as they wished to stay. When they heard me make a telephone call to my wife, telling her that I would not be home for the foreseeable period, they decided to leave.

At that time Black students and Black faculty had the least support. I encouraged the creation of the Center for Urban Black Studies, headed by Hazaiah Williams. However the Center had its own agenda, which was only tangentially related to theological education, and it finally folded. The result was that Black students and faculty were less well served during that period than other minorities and at some levels, that is still the case today. On the positive side, the American Baptist Seminary of the West has developed an imaginative program that attracts Black students.

All in all, the GTU had made major strides and, with the help of so many others, I enjoyed the role in its unfolding. The tribute by Coote and

Hadsell in their history of the San Francisco Theological Seminary reflects something of that time: "The name of John Dillenberger is almost synonymous with the GTU in its formative years. Without his pursuit of a broad ecumenism and his role in the creation of the consortium library the GTU as known today would not exist…It was Dillenberger who played the main role in extending GTU membership to the Catholic schools, in line with Gill's own concept. The libraries of the member schools were given outright to the GTU common library, virtually blocking the return of any school to independence. This policy, designed by Dillenberger, marked the essential difference between the GTU and consortia in other parts of the country and eventually gave the GTU its lasting preeminence." (193–94)

8

PERSONAL AND RELIGIOUS TRANSITIONS

*"It became apparent to me that in order to say what was said
in the past, one now needed to say the opposite in order to
convey the original meaning or emphasis."*

Leaving the GTU administration

My associations with the developing library program came to an end
when I was asked to leave the presidency in the late Fall of 1971. By 1969
I began to be exhausted. I had given up teaching in reformation history in
the UCB history department and kept to only one course in GTU, for the
administrative responsibilities were too heavy. A series of interim dean-
ships from faculty did not help enough and the lack of experience of such
appointments added to the difficulty. To solve the dean problem, Claude
Welch was brought in from the University of Pennsylvania. Anyone who
has read thus far will recall my longstanding working relation with Claude.
On a number of occasions Claude has credited me with GTU becoming
what it did; not so openly, he also acknowledged that he saved it at the critical juncture of my departure from the presidency. That he did and much
more. Between Claude and myself we administratively cover more than
one half century of GTU's life.

Remembering the alleged tenure at San Anselmo, I went to the then
president, Arnold Come, about leaving GTU administration and returning to teach at SFTS. To my surprise, he said that because of financial exi-
gency, the position had been abolished, and they simply did not have the
money for me to return. I also told Daphne Greene, GTU Board chair,
and a few others, that I wanted to leave the presidency by June 30, 1972.

Shortly thereafter, there was a board meeting, and since my future was
involved, it would be better, Daphne suggested, if I not attend. It was at
the end of that meeting that three trustees visited my office and told me to
clear out my office in three days and that my presidency was finished. They

offered no explanation and were not open to discussing it. As I began to pack up, I heard rumors that some board members were upset by not getting any answers as to the reasons for my leaving. A few days later, I walked into Claude's office and said, "What gives? Things don't add up." He said "Your relation to women has come up again and you're in trouble." But no details were given. A few days later, Krister Stendahl happened to be a houseguest. And early that evening, the chair of the heads of institutions, Charles Cooper, called and asked on behalf of the heads (later I learned that heads who had not been present did not know of this) that I resign immediately from the faculty of GTU, for they could not stand a scandal and it would be simpler if I said yes right away, so that they could immediately say that things had been taken care of. I demurred, on the basis that I should at least have a day to think about it. Krister, Jane, and I talked late into the night, Krister being a friend, good pastor, and one who knew the Harvard scene. The next morning, Krister asked "What are you going to do?" I said," What can I do but resign." He said, "Please do nothing today and we'll talk again."

Late in the day, the phone rang and it was Daphne saying, "Can you come down right away to talk?" I responded, "We have talked and I don't think there is reason to talk further." Then she added, "Krister and Claude are here." So I agreed to the meeting. When I arrived, I was told to forget Cooper's call, and that my teaching position was secure. Krister, I gather, said that he had heard nothing to indicate I should be dismissed from my teaching position, that I would survive, and that they would look bad if they persisted.

The sequel was not easy. I was upset in the sense that this was the second time I was in trouble professionally and personally, and I felt the need to get to the bottom of it. In the meantime, I heard rumors that one woman, a GTU employee, had said that I had pushed her for sex. As it happened, I later ran into her on the street, and said, "Why did you lie?" and she replied, "It was the only way I could save my job." I recalled that I had put her on warning for serious lapses on her job. But what else I picked up was more disturbing, for apparently I had propositioned women at social occasions, sometimes even in the same room when my wife was only a few feet away. That I had no knowledge or memory of such actions troubled me deeply. It made me wonder if the incident with the GTU employee may have been more complex than my memory.

I immediately went to my doctor and a psychiatrist he recommended. I kept in touch with both, maintaining a regular schedule with the psychiatrist. The report was that while I was very knowledgeable about myself, there must be something that blocked my awareness and one option was alcohol. That I was prone to dismiss, for I told them I could drink four martinis, stand still, talk allegedly brilliantly, and no one detected anything. But unwittingly I had given the clue, for I had to confess that occasionally I felt I was missing something, that I could not recall all the events of an evening. I was told that I probably had a form of alcoholism that would get worse with time, that I should never drink more than two drinks. Had I drunk in the morning was one of the questions, and I had to confess that I occasionally would prepare myself for the day with a vodka martini. Later I discovered that I had had an early morning appointment with one of the persons who complained and things began to fall into place. So I cut back my consumption of alcohol to no more than one drink, whatever the occasion.

As one of my friends put it, if you have a form of alcoholism that puts you to sleep, that may be bad manners, but it is safer than what you experienced. In my case, alcohol and sexual suggestions were tied together. For those who experienced unwelcome advances on my part, I can only say in retrospect that I am sorry indeed. Moreover, I regret that the pulse of GTU's normal life was interrupted for a period of time.

Those who wanted me to leave GTU were less interested in attacking me than in trying to avoid public scrutiny. There was talk in conservative settings of a scandal at GTU, but their investigations did not lead to anything worth publishing. Lester Kinsolving, an investigative reporter with national standing, did an article for the *San Francisco Chronicle* and I did not disagree with what he wrote. After a conversation with him and two heads of institutions, he took me aside and said, "With such friends, you don't need any enemies." Apparently, GTU hired an attorney to nail me in case things got out of control and I was advised to get one myself. Knowing Joseph Alioto, former mayor of San Francisco, I asked him to help me find an attorney. He referred me to two of his associates, who after talking with me, said "Don't worry, we know the attorney who has been hired by GTU and we doubt that you will ever hear from him." When I asked for the bill, they said I would not receive one.

Between the news report and the grapevine, various items circulated and as usual, with truth and some error. Several persons thanked me for my dignity through it all; some were indifferent; and a few would have preferred I disappeared.

Given that I was staying on as a professor, Daphne told me that she had gotten a chair for me to occupy. Later I learned who the donor was, because the donor's attorney had written a letter outlining how to do the chair, quoting extensively from a letter I had written previously to the donor suggesting a five-year period of payments. I was told later that several board members wanted to be sure that I never occupied the chair, which would not have been appropriate in any case, since the chair held my name. When the news about me broke, the donor was given the option of reclaiming the gift but declined to do so. Eventually, a John Dillenberger chair in historical theology emerged. Somehow, my salary as professor became part of the GTU budget, though some of the funds came from grant requests I wrote for endowments in the humanities and the arts.

Returning to the Professorial Role

Teaching full time in GTU had been confined to the early days, for when administrative pressures developed I dropped most of my courses and resumed them only after my returning to faculty status. Early on in my academic career I had made the decision to limit summer teaching and to substitute research for teaching, if administrative matters took over some of the time of a teacher/scholar. I had noted all too often that administrators often kept teaching, but gave up research, and the teaching dropped in quality. Moreover, research and writing were important to keep up my readiness for the classroom as a genuine future option. Fortunately, I have always been in situations where I could manage my own time, perhaps because the institutions in which I taught required no more than two classes per semester. At Yale faculty members used to say, a professor taught one course, dragged another one, and was dragged by a third.

My work had been in historical theology, that is, trying to understand how historical settings, including wide-ranging cultural developments that were not necessarily directly theological, provided frameworks for theological reflection. That preoccupation led me to write *Contours of Faith: Changing Forms of Christian Thought*. Here the aim was not to write a systematic theology in which everything was laid out, as had been the practice from the medieval period through twentieth century neo-orthodoxy, but instead to consider theology in dynamic forms, that is, in terms of change rather than as an articulation of the truth for all to see. Theology, I wrote, "is beckoned to a more drastic abandonment of its traditionally recognized forms.... Indeed, theology may have to become nontheology, just as much art has become nonart. This leaves open the question, as it does in art, whether it is theology at all. . . . The new emerging forms are strange to the eye and to the ear, and for many they appear as if they had no form at all. Some of the new is formless, decadent, and chaotic. But much of it represents affirmations and styles as valid as anything that has yet appeared in creation." (1969)

Over and over, it became apparent to me that in order to say what was said in the past, one now needed to say the opposite in order to convey the original meaning or emphasis. For example, predestination originally meant a meaningful determination characteristic of God, as contrasted with the dark powers of fate or the uncertainties characteristic of fortune. Such determination was liberating and meaningful. But when the view of predestination was identified with God controlling the details of an orderly world, the precise determiner of all things, predestination became a depressing thought, for the freedom of humanity was denied. But it should be noted that Luther and Calvin, as distinguished from Lutherans and Calvinists, did not understand predestination as the basis of faith, but rather that God could be trusted to see us through in the wavering of faith. Indeed, most traditional theological conceptions have such a checkered history, and I have delineated that history with respect to most theological terms.

After leaving administration, I decided to work full time on the nature and place of the visual arts in relation to theology, just as I once had done with respect to the natural sciences and theology. That decision was framed in part out of my study of the place of art in Tillich's pilgrimage and in the reality that it was an interest Jane and I shared. Some persons in theology assumed that Jane had seduced me into art, and two distinguished professors berated both of us for this undesired direction. In the meantime, Jane had begun to teach part time in the various schools that made up GTU and published in the field, starting with what became a standard work, *Style and Content in Christian Art*. Subsequently, she became interested in the visual arts in American religious life, which most scholars, even those in the field, believed to be meager indeed. But she collected materials, visited museums, and decided to see if an exhibition could be created. When she wrote to Joshua Taylor, former professor of art history at Chicago and then director of the National Collection of Fine Arts (now known as The Smithsonian American Art Museum) about a work of William Page she wanted to include, he immediately replied that he also wanted to do such an exhibition, that he would be in Berkeley in a few days, and could they talk. So was born the joint exhibition (shown at Berkeley, Dallas, Washington and Indianapolis) and catalogue, called the *Hand and the Spirit: Religious Art in America 1700-1900*. So when I was to be on Sabbatical, it was natural for us to turn to Washington, D.C., where

Joshua gave us space to work in the library of the museum. Jane was known as the only person who could work with this learned, opinionated person without difficulty, and I was more or less adopted in the process.

In the fifteen months at the museum, we lived in an apartment house near Rock Creek Park, with access to theatre and museums, particularly the Kennedy Center. Josh also invited us to events at his home and introduced us to his friends, most of them from the art world. Quite unexpected were contacts with Mormons, friends of Truman Madsen whom he had urged to be of help to us. It was common knowledge that Mormons held significant positions in the Nixon White House, and I received several invitations to lunch. In a conversation with the person who daily assembled what news articles Nixon should read, I noted that "this must involve difficult decisions." His reply was "Not at all," a remark that fit with what I had come to know about the Mormon outlook, that is, a clarity that had few nuances and uncertainties. One of the special events was being taken to a symphony and sitting in the presidential box, the president being out of town. Politically, it was a difficult year, Watergate hanging over us.

Academically, I worked on the relation of the visual arts and religion in the American scene, and fifteen months later, had a draft of what became two books, *The Visual Arts and Christianity in America*, and *Benjamin West: The Context of his Life's Work with particular attention to Paintings with Religious Subject Matter*. Originally the draft had been written as one volume, but the largest chapter was on West, leading Joshua to propose that I do some more work, do the history, and then extend the West material into a separate work.

My fascination with West probably was because he came from nowhere, but his gifts were recognized and he rose to prominence in England, but not without problems and affinities with George III. I never go to London without going to the crypt of St. Paul's, where are interred West and the artists of his time. Three personal notes: First, in going through the extensive drawings of West at Swarthmore, I happened to finish before Jane and a West scholar whom we had come to know, finished the piles on which they were working. So I went to the desk and asked if they had any letters of West, only to be told that they had four commercial letters of no significance. I had to be adamant to see them. They were right, but between the letters were two sheets of sketches for the placement of paintings for the Chapel of the History of Revealed Religion to be installed at Windsor Castle. It was signed by West and dated 1803. By then I had seen enough of his writing to know this was the real thing. I dashed to Jane, saying, "Is this what I think it is?" Our West scholar had left before the letters were retrieved and he had just published an article in which the conclusion was that unless new material was found we would never know the placement of each painting. Well, we do now know the scheme for 1803 and many references have been made to the sketches, now known to exist because I had found them. According to Allan Staley, who did the catalogue raisonne of West, other sketches of their placement may exist, but if so, I do not know of their existence. In any case, one of the high moments of my academic life was discovering the 1803 document.

Secondly, there are various nineteenth century lists of West's works and in order to make sense of them, I collated the six I knew about on the dining room table over about a two month period and published the over five hundred title entries as an appendix. Staley found an additional list which I had not seen. While I had done the lists for my own study purposes, I assumed they might be of help to others. It did not occur to me that for the final catalogue raissone, reference to each painting I dealt with would be appropriately included with the Dillenberger number. Third, while it was widely assumed that West was a Quaker, I discovered that he had joined an Anglican church and that much of his work was sponsored by Anglican bishops.

As a sequel to the *Hand and Spirit*, Jane and I collaborated on what became *Perceptions of the Spirit in Twentieth–Century American Art*, a catalogue and exhibition at the Indianapolis Museum of Art, the University Art Museum (Berkeley), the Marion Koogler McNay Art Institute (San Antonio), and the Columbus (Ohio) Gallery of Fine Arts. Jane did the selection of works and the catalogue entries, while I did the brief biographies and the Introduction to the Catalogue. With respect to both exhibitions, the openings were interesting events. As museum persons know, each installation makes the exhibition look different and one sees aspects one had not seen before. But more fundamentally, the public by and large is not aware of the negotiations necessary to secure desired paintings for travel exhibitions and of the problems attendant to not being able to secure specific works of art. But with persistence and/or luck, significant works of art not readily available do find their way into exhibitions.

The dynamics attendant to the *Perceptions* exhibition can be illustrated by one example. We knew that Georgia O'Keeffe had done paintings of crosses placed in the expanses of nature in New Mexico and then two paintings in Canada. She herself had commented on them. "In New Mexico the crosses interest me because they represent what the Spanish felt about Catholicism – dark, somber – and I painted them that way. On the Gaspe, the cross was Catholicism as the French saw it – gay, witty. I made two paintings of crosses when I was there in 1932." For an exhibition on perceptions of the spirit, these paintings were of particular interest, not because they were crosses but because the understanding of nature and Catholicism were intertwined in both instances, each providing a different spirituality. We had difficulty securing an example of the New Mexican subject from the museum world, but knew that O'Keeffe herself owned *Black Cross with Red Sky* and that the painting was among others in her warehouse in Brooklyn. She was reluctant to let us have it for the exhibit, according to those who spoke for her, but said neither no nor yes, while time was fleeting. In the meantime, we had secured the *Canadian Cross by the Sea*, owned by the Currier Gallery of Art in New Hampshire, and the *Cross with Red Heart*, owned by the Sacred Heart church in Margaretsville, New York. The latter had been given to the church by a local donor, who thought she was enhancing the rectangular painting by installing it in a rounded top arch window format considered appropriate for a church. No one at the church knew whether the top of the painting had been folded or cut into a round format, nor could one tell by looking, for it was high and flat against the altar wall. While they provided us with a ladder, it was too short to be able to reach the height of the top of the painting.

In the continuing conversation with O'Keeffe's agent, we learned that O'Keeffe wanted to know whether the painting had been cut or folded over and hence in principle open to restoration. Then Jane received a letter directly from O'Keeffe on the matter, stating, "I had hoped to reproduce this painting in color for my book but because of the way the frame cuts off the corners of the painting I was unable to. The frame which was made for this painting was made without my consent or approval and I do not find the idea of cutting a portion of the painting out with the frame very amusing, but such things happen. If you could find out while the painting is there if it could be removed and photographed without the frame and let me know, I would be interested." We did find out that it was folded, not cut, but did not receive permission to take it out of the frame, and we reported the results to her. Still needing the painting *Black Cross with Red Sky*, O'Keeffe's agent said it looked like the loan would be approved in the light of these circumstances but that O'Keeffe wanted to talk with us briefly first before granting the request. Jane's conversation with her was brief. O'Keeffe agreed to the loan, a kind of exchange of favors.

All of this had taken time and it was too late for the painting to be secured through the ordinary collection of paintings for an exhibit. To make the saga short, let me add that we were in New York City the day before the Indianapolis opening and dashed the next day to Brooklyn by taxi to pick it up and take it to our flight from LaGuardia to Indianapolis. The condition was that the painting could not be out of our sight, but the airlines would not let us take it on board. The compromise was that we were allowed to carry it out the gangway to the edge of the plane, hand it to airline staff, watch them place it on the baggage section, and receive it back upon landing in the same way. So, we arrived a half hour before the exhibition opened, and the painting was put in its reserved place as if everything had been routine.

As to the painting *Cross with Red Heart*, it is now owned by a private party in Minneapolis, according to Barbara Buhler Lynes, author of *1999 Catalogue Raisonne of O'Keeffe*. She further reports that the fragility of the folded part signals that an adequate restoration is probably not possible. However well intentioned the folding of the top of the painting may have been, it was an act of vandalism.

Memorable at each of the openings of the exhibition were the discussions of the exhibition. At Indianapolis, for example, there were exchanges of ideas with the art critic Barbara Rose and the sculptor George Segal.

9

NEW SPACE FOR A NEW MISSION
Rebuilding Hartford Seminary

"We had witnessed sheer genius, a listening and
creativity that required our participation but simultaneously
took us where we had not been before."
— On the architect Richard Meier

One of the schools for which Warren Deem was a consultant was the Hartford Seminary Foundation, now Hartford Seminary. Deem, it will be recalled, was a student in one of my preceptorials at Princeton University. Years later he did a series of studies for GTU and was once chair of its board of trustees. The last two activities brought him to the attention of the Association of Theological Schools, the accrediting and planning unit for theological education. He became a regular consultant to the association and to a number of its schools. In this capacity he frequently called me for extended conversations about issues he faced, indeed so much so that I felt that I should be reimbursed. But then, that is hard to suggest to a friend.

On one of the many occasions in which Hartford was the subject under discussion, Warren reiterated the new directions to which the seminary was committed, but added that it was hard to find suitable presidential candidates from the outside and there was no disposition to appoint any of the interested persons from the inside. Without thinking, I found myself saying, "What's wrong with me?" This startled me as much as it did him, for that thought had not been in my consciousness.

Two days later the phone rang, with the chair of the Hartford board asking if I would consider taking on the presidential task. Testing out the seriousness of the offer, I asked how many other active candidates there were. The reply was two, to which my response was that if they finally did not appoint either one, to let me know and we could see if our respective interests coincided. A few days later the Board chair, Carl Furniss, called again, stating that I now was the only candidate and would I come to

Hartford to meet with the search committee and the various constituencies and bring my wife Jane with me. After my initial visit, there was another request for a visit to meet again with the faculty on my management style. In addition, I had informed the chair of the board, as well as the chair of the search committee, David E. A. Carson, that it seemed more likely than not that there would be reports of my past history, both at Harvard and GTU, on which I had filled them in. Sure enough, Carl Furniss called, stating that two Board members had heard of the history and would I be willing to talk with the psychiatrist on the board who could then report to the two persons. It was clear that he did not have any doubts, but was looking for a way to take care of the issues. Hence, I readily agreed to see the psychiatrist and was glad that I did, for what I learned from him was that I could probably drink two glasses of hard alcohol without disastrous consequences but that with age, the amount would decrease. That so startled me that I then and there decided not to drink hard alcohol, though Carl Furniss, at a party at the house honoring our arrival, gave me a glass of Scotch, and with a smile on his face said, "That's your ration for the evening."

Here I want to add two matters. First, the attentive reader may wonder if alcohol played a part in the Harvard issues. My response is probably not, for in those days I seldom touched hard alcohol. Second, wine does not create the same effect as hard alcohol. But given the caution of less tolerance for alcohol with advancing age, I limit myself to no more than two glasses of wine wherever it is served. Those who have noticed that I drink wine slowly will now have the clue.

While I had been briefed on various issues, I initially missed clues on the dynamics of the faculty outlook and ways of working. But I soon learned that there were a few faculty members who had wanted the presidential position and that a segment of the constituency was in sympathy with their aspirations. But the board was clear that it wanted, indeed felt it needed, an outside person to implement and help shape the new mission. I committed myself to a five-and-a-half year contract, that is until my 65th birthday, a time when I had always stated I would retire.

Hartford had been created in 1831 to counter the more liberal theology at Yale, and for a long period of time it fulfilled that mission with an abundance of students. Over the years the fierce theological differences disappeared and Yale, Union, and Harvard competed for the same students. In that setting Hartford had no obvious advantages. Rather than fighting the odds, it looked for a new mission with a focus upon continuing education and research with respect to the mission of the church for our time. Grounded in the Congregational tradition, it saw its mission in wider terms, having had a center for Islamic studies for a long time. But to move well in that new direction meant drastic changes. A fairly large tenured faculty had to be given due notice of termination, with considerable termination funds. Since the new program demanded different competencies, existing faculty were not logical candidates even for the limited slots needed. Nor was an extended research library needed, with the result that the Protestant research portion of the collection was sold to Emory University. An agreement was signed with McGill University in Montreal to move the Muslim scholars and financial support there, with the understanding that McGill would, in addition to the faculty it had and the new additions from Hartford, add additional appointments, making the joint program the premier Muslim school in the western hemisphere. When I asked why the Islamic library was not sold, given the move to McGill, the answer of the board chair was that such a sale was proposed, but opposition to selling more of the library would have alienated too many people. A five-building-neo-Gothic campus represented a problem, made up in part with dormitories no longer needed for the new directions. What had become fairly clear was that keeping some of the buildings and selling others was not feasible. No group seemed to want truncated buildings and the extraordinary cost of renovations needed for neo-Gothic structures that had not been kept up in recent years. As is usually the case, the seminary had also acquired adjacent lands, on some of which apartment buildings had been built for student housing that was now no longer needed.

When I arrived at Hartford, the tenured faculty had mainly disappeared. President Jim Gettemy, whom I had known as a Union classmate in the 1940s, had gone, having decided that someone else should take over the reins for the rebuilding. Harvey Mcarthur, a well-regarded New Testament scholar near retirement, had been appointed interim president. We, too, had known each other for years and the transition was smooth. Several faculty members had been appointed on five-year contracts, with renewal possibilities, and some of these contracts were already at the halfway mark. Tenure had been abolished, but not without a new series of problems.

The building situation needed resolution: an unsold campus and no place to go. In the early months I saw more white elephants than I would have supposed Hartford had to offer. Before my arrival the board chair had interested the University of Connecticut Law School in the seminary campus and the matter was vigorously pursued. But the new governor of Connecticut, Ella Grasso, according to reliable reports, opposed that move because the buildings would be too expensive to renovate, though a move to Hartford would place the University of Connecticut Law School in proximity to all the legal agencies of the state of Connecticut. At a meeting of the state agencies involved and myself as the sole seminary representative, I was confronted with a proposal, coming from a spokesperson for the governor, that we extend their option to buy, inasmuch as it was due to expire in a few weeks. I swallowed hard, and said it would not be extended. I could sense the relief in the room from the law school proponents, who felt that they could win if the governor was not given more time. At the end of the meeting, I dashed to a phone and called the chair of the board, David E. A. Carson, to tell him what I had done, that I had spoken for the board without specific authorization. He laughed, and said, "That's what we pay you for, to make decisions when situations call for it and then tell us about it." I was relieved, of course, because I had known the ease with which I had worked for a brief period with Carl Furniss as board chair. Actually, I continued to work with Carl on funding and other programs, while David and I carved out a wonderful working relation. We met each Friday, as our schedules allowed, for lunch in Middletown, Connecticut, where he was head of an insurance company. I shared everything that I knew was going on. He usually responded, and when he did not, I discovered he wanted time to think. So at the next meeting he might say, "I've thought about what you said," and what he said was worth hearing. The results were that he protected me when I needed it, for he was not caught off guard. Sara and David invited us to family events with their three children and now over twenty years later, we remain friends in contact with each other about public issues and family developments.

The strategy worked, and the sale of the central campus was agreed upon. Given the time necessary for the school of law to make its plans, the seminary could remain in two of the buildings until it could work out its own plans. The final proposal, after considering many alternatives, was to build a new building on adjacent land that was not part of the original campus, though it contained unneeded seminary apartment buildings. That decision posed problems not unique to Hartford, that is, the abolition of existing buildings now occupied mainly by inhabitants no longer directly related to the seminary. Suddenly it occurred to me that the architect Patrick Quinn, whose role in GTU planning has already been noted, was now dean of the school of architecture at Rensselaer Polytechnic Institute in Troy, New York, about three hours away by car. I also knew that Patrick believed that most buildings could and should be saved, and that new buildings should not be excuses for destroying older ones. Still, we asked Patrick to consult with us. When he arrived to look at the buildings, instinct seemed to be to keep them, but as he got closer and examined the apartments, his face fell, and he said, "You know that you could be found criminally negligent for having people living in such disrepair." His judgment was that the buildings needed to be razed, apart from the question of whether or not we needed to supply housing. I could hardly disagree with him, given that just a few nights before I had been summoned by some residents in the middle of the night to see the rain leakage going on, severe enough that we decided to pay for the damage to their furniture. Given that the seminary no longer needed apartment housing, it was hard to make the case that the buildings needed to be replaced. Needless to say, the emptying of the building of occupants took at least a year.

In the meantime, time was spent with various segments of the community to talk about program directions and space needs, the end product of which was a document that could be used in an initial way with possible architectural candidates. The process for selecting an architect was worked out with the board chair, who was aware of the experience Jane and I had at GTU and was himself savvy about procedures. We advertised and sought nominations of potential architects, dealing with about a hundred names. A subcommittee of the search committee, again made up of various constituencies and marked board presence, reduced the number to a little over thirty. Then we sought agreement that each member of the search committee would need to see three buildings each of three of the listed thirty. That strategy worked well. A few members said they could not give that much time and were excused from the committee. Most importantly seeing nine buildings and having to report on them had the effect of their no longer knowing what they thought they liked. The exercise of seeing made it possible for them to see afresh. That reduced the number of architects to be interviewed to eight, including Richard Meier, Cesar Pelli, Robert A. M. Stern, and Richard Polsheck.

The format for the meetings was one hour spent on a presentation by the architect, followed by another hour in questions from the committee, and questions to the committee from the architect. To keep the impressions fresh, all of the architects were interviewed over a three-day period, followed a day later by two days for the search committee. Together the chair and I prepared a series of questions for the committee to explore with each architect, such as design competence, regard for budget constraints, doing the building on time, willingness to listen to the committee that would continue to work with the architect, etc. Finally the committee discussed and provided preferences on each issue for each architect on the list. Meier and Pelli were vying with each other, with an edge for Meier. While a few members of the committee wanted to talk more, apparently contending for another candidate, the chair declared Meier the winner as the result of an open debate and final voting.

While it is not directly relevant, it may be noted that Meier, alone among the contenders, came by himself, and he later reported that when his wife asked him how it went, he replied that he had a wonderful drive from New York on a beautiful fall day. Pelli expressed his disappointment, for he hoped, as he put it, to do a smaller building with complex functions, as over against the large skyscraper buildings he had been doing. Two formidable candidates were not interviewed. At the time, Michael Graves had done a few modest buildings, mostly facades, and later at a party in Washington when Meier received the Pritzker Award, my wife Jane sat next to Graves. He, too, had wanted the commission, he said, but that when I allegedly said to him after an afternoon together, "Mr. Graves, we've had a wonderful afternoon, but have you done anything bigger than a bread box?" Whatever I said, he got a negative message. However, I have become a fan of much of his work. Given the GTU experience in which Venturi came totally unprepared, it is obvious why he was not on the final list.

Meier's selection was mainly the result of the sheer beauty of his design and the wonderful play of light within and around his buildings. He was known already for a number of houses; The Westbeth Artists' Housing in Manhattan, the Bronx Development Center (for addressing the needs of physically disabled and mentally retarded children), the Atheneum or visitor's center and Potter's Studio at New Harmony, Indiana, a town of historic associations with the Rappites and then the utopian community of Robert Owen, more recently brought into a marvelous unity of old and new through the imaginative and indefatigable work of Jane Blaffer Owen. Immediately following the Hartford building, Meier designed the High Museum in Atlanta, though his most public recognition comes from the Getty Museum in Los Angeles and a series of buildings throughout Europe, including a church in Rome.

Planning and building the Hartford Seminary meant starting with an expanded version of the document initially associated with the search. This meant reviewing all programs, defining functions, and determining the space needs of each program or function. Weekly meetings were held with the architect with the agreement that Meier and I would decide when the meetings would end and the design phase could begin. One day, we looked at each other, and said "This is it." But in the meantime we had worked through the issue of chapel space. To keep space parameters as low as possible, we had proposed that the auditorium would also function for worship needs. But Meier told us that he felt we needed a separate space for a chapel, symbolically and functionally, and that if the issue was space, he could incorporate the chapel within required limits. So the design phase included a chapel, with the aim of serving a wide range of religious orientations, while not being nondescript. At the time, the Congregational tradition, fed also by a new group consciousness, preferred circular to row seating. But to round out alternatives, we had Meier design a cross, kneeling cushions, railing placement, and lectern. These could be removed, or used elsewhere in the room, without appearing makeshift. A small organ, with traditional pipes and excellent sound, fit the scale of the chapel but its exterior frame work was so repulsive that Meier, with our approval, approached the company with the offer of redesigning the exterior facade without charge. The offer was accepted.

Essentially, the building was erected in accord with the design plans and model, with few questions in the process. But how to have all the functions work in harmony but within square footage limitations was the biggest challenge. It meant assuring easy entrance to the building, with space that exists in its own right but also fans out from the three-story meeting room, to the bookstore and library on the first floor, to office and classroom facilities on the second and third floors. Here it seemed we were hung up with unresolved traffic flow issues. Sensing this, Meier said why don't two or three of you come to my office in New York City, where I have all the design materials, including models, and let's talk it through. He did most of the questioning, with few comments, and after about an hour and a half, he said, "Go have some coffee and give me twenty minutes." At the end of that time, he had reconceived the entire wing of the building. Was it a translation into space of what we had talked about? Was it a new creation? Neither: it was a transfiguration, something new but beyond all that we had talked about or thought about. We had witnessed sheer genius, a listening and creativity that required our participation but simultaneously took us where we had not been before.

The entrance area for the building is through a courtyard that demarks an area with a chapel on the right, a wall in front with wide aperture that marks the line of entrance and egress, and open space to the left, with a large tree and sitting space. The entrance door opens to a three-story space, with stairs to the back and elevator nearby, with a walkway to the left toward the library and book store, and a reception area which is also the entrance to the chapel and the larger meeting room. The second floor consists of classrooms and administrative offices, and the third floor is faculty offices, with areas for faculty assistance staff. The inside and outside is Meier's signature white, troublesome to some and a delight to others. One of the faculty members, somewhat unhappy with the bareness, walked in with a red rose only to exclaim, "I've never seen a rose so clearly." And so it was with the placement of furniture. The space cried out for the completeness of working spaces. But it is not congenial to messiness. Meier knew this when he requested and we gave him the right to select the furniture and signage. As he knew only too well, when buildings get near completion and budgets are tight, compromises get made in these areas.

The exterior of the building consists of three-foot-square steel panels and glass. When viewed from a distance one encounters both hidden and open areas. Fortunately, the building could be placed in an area of grass, with open space around the entire building. Adjacent buildings consist of the former neo-Gothic seminary buildings, and neo-Tudor and neo-Colonial structures, the latter two mainly houses. Although Hartford civic community support was sought and some members of the community were on committees having to do with the mission and needs of the seminary, enthusiasm could not be said to have emerged. Opponents said the nature of the proposed architecture did not fit into the community, though it is hard to know what kind of building would, in their eyes, have melded into the polyglot of fairly undistinguished buildings. The seminary community found it hard to give up its nostalgia for the neo-Gothic. By its very boldness the new building turned out to fit in remarkably well. Still, a rave review by Ada Louise Huxtable in the *New York Times* won few local converts, though it gave accreditation from outside.

Part of the hesitation stemmed and probably still stems from the nature of Hartford as a city. The core of the city establishment consisted of about eighty families of a distinctly New England frame of mind. To make it in the community, as a seminary president needed to do, one still had to be introduced. That introduction, in our case, came less from the religious community than from the artistic, since both of us had credentials in that arena. Given that the Wadsworth Atheneum, one of the oldest and still distinguished museum, was at the core of the cultural life, moving into that circle was not difficult. At most city-wide events, symphonies, and plays, one inevitably encountered the same people, and for special events at various institutions, there was the core of eighty.

Another real estate venture may be noted. The seminary had been given one of the fairly prominent older spacious landmark houses near

Farmington, on about five acres of property, with a few attendant later buildings, about seven miles from the seminary. This had become the president's house. The gift had the stipulation that before twenty years from the time of transfer, the property could be sold, but the endowment, which brought in about sixteen thousand a year, would need to be given to Trinity College. If one waited over the twenty-year period, the house could be sold and the endowment kept. So I asked the business person to give me a breakdown of the expenses and it became clear that maintaining this country place cost considerably more than the endowment brought in. Noting this at a meeting of the executive committee of the board, the response was that they knew that the seminary would be ahead selling the property but giving the separate endowment to Trinity. They had assumed that this was where presidents would want to live. The decision was made to see what the alternative might be. Directly across the street from the new seminary building was a house that had been turned into several small apartments, all of which were in poor repair. It should be noted that the poor repair in most of the seminary buildings was a natural development, for investing money into buildings whose future use was unsure was deliberate benign neglect. In any case we asked Patrick Quinn to see if this building could be transformed into the president's house and he did a marvelous renovation. The point of the story is that the *Hartford Courant* carried a front- page headline, "Seminary president moves from Farmington to Hartford." Symbolically, that was an important event, though that had not been in our consciousness.

Educationally, I assumed that I would not need to give much attention, if any, to the three faculty members in Islamic studies, given that McGill University and Hartford had agreed on an arrangement to the effect that the Hartford professors would be working in an expanded McGill program. It looked as if the only remaining issue was what to do with the Islamic library which remained at Hartford. But signs began to emerge on the radar screen that all was not well. The senior Islamic scholar did not want to move to Montreal and had arranged for most of his work to be in Hartford. One of the other scholars was at McGill, but not very happy, while a third was quite content to stay at McGill. More importantly, there were beginning doubts about McGill's capacity or willingness or both to raise the funds called for in the expansion of faculty needed to become the best Islamic program in the west, if not in the world. This is not to say that McGill was mediocre; quite the contrary.

But to Hartford it increasingly seemed as if it had given a present to McGill, without any indication that the agreed contractual goals would be reached. I proposed to David Carson that we disclose our problems to our board members, and then go to McGill to talk about negotiating out of the contract if they could not meet its terms. When we met with the McGill constituencies, there was little indication that we were being taken seriously. They kept referring to the contract, while we indicated that there were no concrete signs that it was being implemented. In the frustration that ensued, I finally suggested that David and I return to Hartford to consult with our attorneys about next steps and that from then on, our attorneys would take our place. I then folded my papers and rose from my chair. Surprisingly, this immediately changed the mood for the better, and having played the role of bad cop, David could temporarily be the good cop. So we talked about how we could work out an interim financial solution as part of abandoning the contract. We agreed that Hartford would provide forty thousand per year for five years. In my calculation, though that was never formally said, this would make it possible for McGill to keep the person who wanted to stay at McGill until his retirement, while bringing the others back to Hartford. While this was an annual loss to the seminary for a five-year period, it saved face for all parties. I felt sorry for McGill's Charles Adams, a great Islamic scholar with excellent program instincts, and a wonderful disposition. I assume that he was told that McGill could not keep the commitments at a juncture when overall finances at the institution took a dive. In these conversations tenure was an issue, for unlike the new contracts at Hartford with limited terms, tenure was still part of the Islamic faculty agreements.

What to do with the Duncan Black McDonald Center, as the Hartford Islamic program had been known, on its return to Hartford was the next agenda. Its past history had been distinguished, with excellent degree programs, and an agenda that wanted to make sure that Islam was known and appreciated by the Christian world. Known widely, too, was *The Muslim World*, published by the Seminary from the early years of the twentieth century. It seemed as if the thrust of the Islamic scholars would take Islamic studies directly to the churches, as was the case with other programs. But in the midst of this thinking occurred the Iran crisis, which brought new attention to Islam as a religion. To use but one example near home, Hartford's United Technologies discovered that it had ignored Islam as a religion and culture in its work abroad, with the result that instead of appreciating the religious culture, it had contributed to misunderstandings.

In the ensuing years the Islamic scholars were busy doing educational programs for various industries and for a public that was awakening to the role of religion in general and Islam in particular. That need and public interest has increased over the last decades. While I had included Islam as part of my doctoral program at Columbia, I became indebted to Willem Bijlefeld, director of the Hartford Center, as we worked through programs addressing the future. I remember with fondness asking Vim, as he was known, something about a thought or practice in Islam and he would respond, "Which country do you mean?" and then give me a mini lecture. Pluralism was not only across; it was also within.

While transitions always pose special issues, total transitions compound them visibly with respect to staffing. Imagine having residential buildings no longer needed and reducing the major buildings from six to one. In our case, just figuring maintenance persons, the number needed moved from over six to fewer than one. My critics accused me of getting rid of close to fifty people. My answer was that they were wrong, that it was closer to sixty. Most every function of which one could think had somebody in charge. Actually in an interim period old and new functions need attention. The result is that a staff is at its height just before the reductions become both possible and necessary. A bookstore that served two hundred students for regular classes now served a small group of faculty, nonresident students, and community persons. Here changes meant that one could combine the library and the bookstore and operate with fewer people than either had before. So one could go on. Yet most who were let go felt that they were indispensable and that the institution owed them a position for the rest of their working lives. We tried to transfer individuals to new positions, but in many cases that did not work. Just as at the faculty level, the new positions demanded talents and training that existing staff mainly did not have.

The assistant to the president had served the previous president for years, and was competent and gracious, but set in her ways. She was near enough to retirement for her to think of a retirement package. For her successor, I decided, as I had at GTU, to aim for a competent person from an ethnic minority. Several faculty members advised me not to go that route, for if it did not work out, I would be stuck with the person, it being allegedly impossible to fire minorities. Through consulting with the Black community and a board member who had particular contacts in that community, several promising candidates emerged. In that group, Mary Williams stood out. She held a major position at one of the larger Black churches, and had the requisite skills, personal and technical. Some two weeks after being on the job, she came to me and said that there were two Black staff members who were not competent to do their jobs, and that to keep them was to send all the wrong messages, for equality also meant equality in having the appropriate skills or being able to acquire them. She saw no possibility of the latter being the case. The same faculty members who had urged me not to hire an ethnic minority person confessed that the two Black secretaries were incompetent. So the changes were made and Mary saw to it that the vacancies were filled. Mary was a gift to anyone for whom she worked. When I left, she came to tell me two things: first, that my trust in her judgments and my support were beyond anything she had ever experienced and second, she appreciated, using her language, that I had been a gentleman throughout. I need not comment on why I appreciated both comments.

Another appointee I enjoyed was Wally Matsen, vice president for development. He was an excellent advisor on many issues and knew the political dynamics in most settings.

Faculty and church issues were complicated and I should have seen this sooner. That might have changed what I did. My first mistake was a meeting of the local Congregational association on a Sunday afternoon at which I was asked to speak. Little did I realize that the meeting was for several hours and that I was scheduled to speak around four in the afternoon. I had chosen a subject on the church and the visual arts. Not only was the audience not sympathetic nor interested in the arts but I think I was expected to talk about the school and its relevance to the church. That I bombed out was confirmed by my friend of long standing, a seminary classmate at Union, Robert L. Edwards, then a figure of standing in the church. I should have asked Bob in advance what was expected of me. In retrospect, I could not have picked a topic less tuned to their sensibilities.

The second situation gradually became apparent, namely, that some of the pastors in the area had campaigned for one or another of the existing faculty members to head the seminary. Indeed, I had made it clear in an interview with the faculty that I would be consulting on all issues but that we might not always get unanimity. Some individuals believed in process discussion to the point of consensus on all issues, and they were willing to block any directions if there was no consensus. In that setting I began to make proposals for consideration and then schedule specific follow-up meetings, so that ad hoc meetings would not be the place where official actions were taken.

Before my arrival, Hartford had adopted the practice of appointing senior officers to five-year terms with the possibility of renewals, tenure having been abolished. Several of the officers needed to be reviewed, and if denied another term, given the time to find other positions. Two of the officers were denied another term. Ordinarily, the deliberations were kept private, as was the precise vote. Given that the vote was advisory to the president, he or she made the final decision, making the reasons clear as to its basis. The two not recommended for another contract spread the word that their future was cut short solely by the president, circulating that opinion among the group who had wanted a different outcome. Given this situation, the chair of the board met with the two persons, telling them that their conversations were in violation of agreed-upon privacy of deliberations and that the disclosures were in fact not true. What was true was that as president I was against another contract, but I was not the deciding vote in the committee. I do not know if knowledge of my judgments influenced some on the committee. The two persons involved found other academic positions, where they had distinguished careers beyond what they might have had at Hartford.

Rebuilding the faculty staff turned out to be exciting. Prominent among those already on board were Jackson Carroll and David Roozen. Both were researchers on the nature of congregational church life, and its factors in decline and renewal. While Carroll eventually moved to Duke, Roozen continues his scholarly projects at Hartford. Miriam Winters had just received her doctorate at Princeton Theological Seminary, having worked with Karlfried Froehlich, whom I had known from Drew days. She brought not only a knowledge of historical theology, but also leadership skills in feminist thought and a background in music as a composer, with a gentle, lilting voice. Tom Hoyt, with a doctorate in New Testament studies, came not only to teach in that area but also to create programs in the Black community on the north end of Hartford. The public and degree programs he initiated became the pride of the community. When Tom left to become a bishop in his church, the program continued. Clifford Green from Australia, with a deep grounding in Bonhoeffer, focused on ethics and community agendas. For several years, Dikkon Eberhart, a novelist with a love of books and a knowledge of merchandising, guided the changing needs required in the bookstore and library developments.

Geographically speaking, the Hartford research projects served the country as a whole. Classroom teaching was focused in Hartford and New England. The Islamic program, while centered in Hartford, served a wider public.

Twenty years ago Hartford was, in some respects, nineteenth-century Boston, small enough to have centers of culture that lived side by side but with few patterns of cooperation. Educationally, the city was well served by Trinity College, several Catholic colleges, the Hartford Graduate Center, and the University of Hartford. Heads of these schools, including that of the seminary, met with each other but did not forge significant patterns of cooperation. The city was still the home of insurance companies and the extensive United Technologies group. Together, they sponsored a vibrant cultural life. The north end of the city comprised an extensive black community, which was mainly isolated from the rest and unequal in opportunities. Coordination and extensive reorganizations were needed. As a city, Hartford, in its own way worked on social issues with as little fanfare as possible. One of the unknown facts about the seminary was that it came to be a place where these groups met with each other and tried to change the dynamics of the city for the better. The meetings were not official ones, and the absence of publicity made it possible to talk honestly. But the reality is that Hartford is still one of the major cities where little social and economic equality exists

While in principle Hartford Seminary was interdenominational and pluralistic, the reality was less encompassing. With respect to Roman Catholicism, the ethos of a Congregational and Presbyterian setting was not the most hospitable climate. Moreover, while there was an extensive Catholic diocese, the archbishop was fairly conservative and more prone to talk than to act. Perhaps the problems in the diocese that he was working through were simply all that could be handled. Similarly, I was disappointed in not making cooperative progress in the Jewish community.

However, since those years, much has changed and the seminary has played a leading role. The various programs have grown and been strengthened by faculty additions, all with a new focus. In the last decades, Hartford has become the major vehicle in the country for analyzing and proposing directions for congregations, partly facilitated by the financial backing of the Lilly Endowment, Inc.

10

A SECOND HOME
Professional Societies and the Art World

*"I had moved from the world of church and academic
religious leaders to the world of the visual arts and art
museums. So I began to feel at home in both worlds."*

Throughout much of my professional and administrative career, I was
fortunate to be active in a number of academic and artistic circles.

While I was a member of the New Haven Theological Group during
my stay on the east coast, the Pacific Coast Theological Society while on
the west coast, and a member of the national group, the American
Theological Society, I was never in a leading role in any of them, though I
did papers when asked to do so. I simply did what was expected and participated in the conversations.

I had a more active role in serving a four-year term in the seventies
on the executive committee of the Association of Theological Schools in
the United States and Canada (ATS) and for years served on special committees and accreditation visits. When GTU sought accreditation from the
Association, it refused to accept the application because it had no criteria
for institutions that served a coordinating role, even if they had some faculty members and granted degrees in their own right. GTU took two
actions. First, it successfully offered to help write rubrics for entities such
as GTU. Second, it immediately sought accreditation from the Western
Association of Schools and Colleges (WASC) . In so doing it unwittingly
set a precedent for seeking joint accreditation from the two entities on the
part of many theological schools. By definition, accreditation agencies are
conservative, and while interested in the future, they seem to need to
accent criteria applicable to all members. Perhaps that is why my experiences at both GTU and Hartford Seminary with respect to accreditation
visits were always somewhat unpleasant.

More congenial in the eighties were the five years spent on the board
of the American Academy of Religion (AAR), during one of which I

served as president. The AAR grew out of an early group known as National Association of Bible Instructors. While I was a student at Union, I used to attend their meetings, numbering at most fifty people. In the subsequent developments Bob Funk played a dominant role in respect to NABI and SBL, and in other groups extending beyond scripture. He promoted their scholarly and theological endeavors and cooperation with each other. During my active period, the Academy had already reached several thousand members and was trying to come to terms with its growth and with it, the opportunities that brought. Up to that point, the offices were located where the executive director held a professorship. Given the expanding size, it became apparent that the time required of a director could no longer be part time and that the office staff needed to expand. Still, it seemed important for the head of AAR to have faculty status. I was a member of a committee to explore these issues and subsequently was appointed chair of a committee to make concrete proposals for the future.

While we explored about ten options, it soon became obvious that Emory University was interested in encouraging a wide range of professional societies to locate on its campus, including the Society for Biblical Literature. So I spent considerable time with Jim Waits, dean of the School of Divinity, and Jim Laney, president of Emory. Laney had credentials in theology and was a well-known public figure, later becoming Ambassador to South Korea. While Waits and Laney both wanted the AAR to be situated at Emory, there were limits to the resources it could provide. What made the negotiations difficult was that the provost, with whom I was to do the negotiations, was not as open as we had been led to believe. My problem was how to bring the problems to Jim, whom I knew, in such a way that did not focus on the perceived differences between the president and the provost. On that point Waits was most helpful. While we had one rocky meeting, we managed to come to an agreement with Emory to provide temporary space at a nominal rate, with the hope that a new building would emerge for various societies, chief of which would be AAR and SBL. That occurred later. Simultaneously the committee had come to unanimous agreement that the new executive director should be Barbara DeConcini and Emory's department of religion was open to giving her an academic appointment.

Two additional groups in which I was invited to participate were the Interfaith Forum on Religion, Art and Architecture (IFRAA) and the Society for the Arts, Religion and Contemporary Culture (ARC). Initially, IFRAA sponsored thematic conferences and featured the stars in the respective fields, crossing many boundaries. Gradually, it moved its meetings from city to city and the programs centered on seeing local architectural buildings and allied arts. For my taste, it became more and more a show-and-tell enterprise and less an avenue for critical scrutiny of wider issues. The same change of direction was evident in its stellar publication, *Faith and Form*, edited until recently by Betty Herndon Meyer. Instead of discussion of issues, it more and more featured the work of its members, increasingly architects. Given both financial reasons and the increasing domination by architects, IFRAA became an interest group in the American Institute of Architects (AIA). I was glad to have published several articles in *Faith and Form* and to have received one of IFRAA's awards in recognition of contributions made in the field of religion, art, and architecture. While I was interested in conversations with architects, I was less interested in the trade aspects of their craft.

ARC has had half a century of history, aspects of which I have detailed in *The Visual Arts and Christianity in America* and which has received more extensive treatment in the recent history written by Betty Meyer. ARC was dedicated to serious conversations on the arts and culture, and was founded by such figures as Marvin Halverson, Wilhelm Pauck, Truman Douglass, Paul Tillich, Alfred Barr, Jr., Stanley Romaine Hopper, Howard Spragg, William Conklin and Amos Wilder. It sponsored various volumes on art, religion, and culture, based on some of the conferences, and from time to time, it issued smaller publications on various subjects in the field. What has continued amidst the ups and downs of financial gyrations are the three annual meetings on the first Saturday of February, May and November, usually in New York City. While the attendance varies from about thirty to sixty, I try to attend as many as possible, for I learn more and my spirits are nourished in the delight of what conversations at their best can do. So I have continued on its board, whose main agenda is to develop programs that stretch the horizons of the arts and culture, and their religious dimensions.

Two other projects in which I had a founding role are Art Christianity Enquiry (ACE) and the Center for Art, Religion and Education (CARE). The spelling of enquiry indicates that the project has something to do with Great Britain. So let me explain. During an extended visit in England, Jane and I were interested in what was going on in England in contemporary art and religion/theology. Several individuals pointed us to Tom Devonshire-Jones, the curate of an Episcopal Church in Regent's Park, London. When we reached him by phone, he immediately declared that he had read all of our writings and could we come to dinner with him and his wife, Susan. Thereafter there occurred a series of meetings in which we decided to ask about thirty people to join us for a conference in the field of art and theology in various countries. So we met in London in the summer of 1991 with representatives from the visual arts and interested clergy and theologians from Great Britain, the U.S., Australia, Germany, Italy, the Netherlands, and Switzerland. The meeting, while originally intended to be a one-time event, was of sufficient merit that the members wanted to meet again in 1993 in Dresden. This was followed by a third in 1995 in Berkeley, California, a fourth in 1997 in Amsterdam, a fifth in Oxford in 1999, a sixth in Minneapolis in 2001, a seventh in St. Petersburgh in 2003 and an eighth is scheduled for New York City in 2005. While the membership has changed, the amazing thing is that at least 50 percent of the attendance of individuals has been constant throughout the years. This is all the more astounding when one takes into account that costs are borne by the participants, either from their own resources or grants they have secured. That the meetings have continued surely means that we are learning a good deal from each other.

In addition to the 1995 ACE meeting in Berkeley, several of us decided to add a five-day conference on a world-wide basis for the general public, crossing from ecumenical to inter religious dimensions. Four international conferences had preceded us, including the double-tiered New York City/Montreal event, Brussels, Jerusalem, and San Antonio, with a major leadership role played by Robert Rambusch. But this one was more wide ranging in terms of religious representation from artists and the theological field, reflecting developments in Islam, Buddhism, Hinduism and other religious groupings.

It is not an understatement to say that Doug Adams, my wife Jean, and I together articulated the scope of the international conference and were responsible for seeing to it that the various elements came together, including the mundane matter of seeing to it that the hard pews had foam rubber cushions.

In 1987 Doug and I had decided we needed to create an independent non-profit research and program entity in the visual arts called the Center for the Arts, Religion and Education (CARE). We formally created a corporation and appointed a Board, whose chair for a protracted period was Tim Nuveen, followed by Joan Carter. At the time we assumed that grants could easily be funneled through GTU, with the Center paying a modest management fee. But GTU was slow in fulfilling requests for reimbursement. In the case of payments for the installation of *Winged Figure* given by De Staebler to GTU, the Center's board members, with the leading gift from Joan Carter, gave $60,000 to GTU to cover all costs of casting and installation. But it took months for GTU to issue the checks to reimburse the artist for those expenses. So we set up our own system, which required little administration effort to get things done in a timely manner.

On the other hand, we did not wish to be isolated from GTU and so we asked to become an affiliated member. In the time that has elapsed, the CARE has provided courses in the various arts – dance, drama, worship and the arts, and art history. Such courses have been given at all levels, MA, Doctorate, MDiv, and continuing education. These courses are approved by either a school or GTU. At the same time, conferences are featured and supported. Most of the developments, including funding programs, have come through the energy and imagination of Doug Adams. The Center has moved far beyond its initial phase and is developing a financial base for a future beyond the lives of the current board.

The riches of Rome and the Vatican collections were well known to Jane and to me. So in the 1970s, we were pleased to be invited to a series of conferences in Rome, established primarily for patrons of art who could give art works or help finance funds for art and art care. We were asked not because we could give works of art or financial support, but because they wanted a small group of persons present who were conversant in art and theology. It was during these conferences that I got to know James Flexner, the virtual dean of early art in the U.S. He gave one of the papers for a conference in which Paul VI also spoke, a group of about thirty-five people. What I remember most was Flexner, then already well advanced in age, directing traffic on a excursion outside of Rome when our buses got jammed on a narrow street. It was not that he was a better policeman than historian; it is just one of those moments one remembers, for the historian who mapped our historical byways could also sort out contemporary road entanglements.

Among the public persons of note at the Rome conferences was Larry Fleischman. Larry was head of the Kennedy Galleries and had been the direct and indirect source of much of the contemporary art in the modern part of the Vatican collection. He had also given a room and equipment for cleaning sculpture. I had known him in New York and he and I frequently found ourselves standing near each other at one event or another at the Rome meetings. He wanted to make sure, out of his graciousness, that I knew everyone of note, particularly clergy with visibility. When Paul VI entered to give his address, Larry was first in line and this Jew knew the protocols better than the rest of us. While appreciative of his gestures on my behalf, I was amused to switch roles in one instance. Just as he had told me that Cardinal Baum was next in line and I should meet him, the Cardinal stepped out of line and said, "John, I'm so glad you are here." Larry could not have known that when the Cardinal was a monsignor we knew each other well in ecumenical circles and that the two of us had a particular affinity in that our understandings of the early church were in sync with each other's views.

While most of the meetings were educational by nature, the late afternoon gatherings and dinners were social events in which there was much talk and delight. At a dinner in Castel Sant Angelo, especially preempted for the group, I found myself placed at a table where Baron Hans Heinrich Thyssen-Bornemisza and his fifth wife, Tita Cervera, were sitting. That was before the Thyssen collection went to Madrid, virtually next door to the Prado. In addition to the exquisite beauty of Carmen (Tita), and the obvious graciousness of the two, I was impressed by their wide-ranging knowledge and their interest in those about them.

These meetings also introduced us to persons in the Vatican museum(s), including its director and his assistant, Patricia Bonicatti. The latter became a special friend, whom we saw thereafter on our visits to Rome. Knowing of our interest in the Sistine ceiling and the cleaning then underway, she volunteered that if we wrote about the cleaning of the ceiling, she could give us a press pass to take the elevator to the scaffolding to see the cleaning in process. At the time, half of Eve had been cleaned and I was allowed to touch Eve at the not yet cleaned part. We spent an hour on the scaffolding viewing and talking with the workmen, many of whom knew English. As everyone knows, there was considerable controversy over the cleaning, mainly led by James Beck of Columbia University. I might add that the only heated discussion we had on the matter was with George Segal, a critic of the cleaning. The main issue was whether or not the cleaning took off a level that was a sealer done by Michelangelo, and which left a sheen that was not the bright level we now see. But there are paintings by Michelangelo that have the same brightness. Suffice it to say that the *Bible Review* published our article, "To Clean or Not to Clean: the Sistine Ceiling Restoration" (1988). Beck said it was the only sane article from the opposition, a dubious compliment.

The cleaned ceiling in its entirety does present the whole as Michelangelo did it, and we now see it as it was during its first twenty years, that is, before the smoke from the stoves in the chapel began to cloud the scene. But it is hard to study it with the hordes that daily push into the space. Fortunately, Jane and I once had a half hour by ourselves in the room before it officially opened, with the instruction to come out when we were finished. Later, on my eightieth birthday in 1998, celebrated with some twenty friends in Rome, we had the room to ourselves before the official opening time.

Working in art and religion means seeing the art objects themselves, for which there is no substitute. Moreover, they need to be seen repeatedly. So our travel in cities was usually determined by which museums needed to be seen. In the United States alone we visited more than two hundred museums over a two-year period, all of which were useful for our exhibition planning and writing projects.

Most interesting to both Jane and to me were friendships with contemporary artists that emerged in the course of our work in theology and art. In effect I had moved from the world of church and academic religious leaders to the world of the visual artists and art museums. So I began to feel at home in both worlds.

In connection with a project which featured Barnett Newman's *Stations of the Cross* (usually referred to as the *Stations*), Jane wanted to check some aspects that only the artist would know. How to be in touch with him was the question, but it was solved when a director of a New York museum offered to call to see if we could have an appointment. We were asked to come to their west-side apartment at five on the same day, expecting to spend an hour. The apartment was full of his paintings, set in rooms of the apartment with peeling paint on the ceiling and walls. He answered Jane's questions, and we talked freely on all issues of the time, including theology. We could not get away, nor did we want to, and were prevailed upon to join Barney and his wife Annalee for dinner at one of Barney's favorite restaurants on the east side. We parted company with hugs at two in the morning.

So started a friendship that lasted throughout his life and that of Annalee. We could not come to New York City without visiting with them and subsequently we were invited to all his openings. Among one of the special evenings was dinner with Victoria and Cy Newhouse, Jr. at their apartment. I recall that Barney had arranged the event so that the four of us could see the paintings that they had bought from him, the story being that Barney would not sell the paintings until he was sure that they would be prized. Victoria is an architectural historian of distinction and Cy has seen to it that the *New Yorker*, among all the publications he nurtures, continues to be, in my estimation, the best journal of moral discourse in America.

Upon Barney's death, Annalee sent us one of his works related to the *Stations* and two more especially for Jane. As is known in art circles, Annalee had made Barney's work possible by teaching school over the years and by taking steps to protect his legacy. She became wealthy enough to live in River House, whose elevator companions were persons one recognized. Mugged one day, she had decided to move from the west end, but she never lost her touch across the social spectrum. An opera buff, she traveled the world, and on occasion asked us to join her at Lincoln Center. After Barney's death, she took us to see his studio, a kind of sanctuary few were permitted to enter.

Among the abstract expressionists, Barney was known as the intellectual. Well read and a lively conversationalist, he was idolized or bemoaned, depending on the person. For example, Jackson Pollock and Barney liked each other; but his relation with Mark Rothko was rocky. Jane and I had one afternoon with Rothko, sitting, talking (instructive but not as scintillating as Newman), and looking at two of the paintings for the Rothko Chapel in Houston. They were propped up against the walls of his ex-firehouse Manhattan studio and the play of color is a strong memory. Being there from about four-thirty in the afternoon until six-thirty, we saw the full spectrum of light playing on the paintings as they took on a life of their own. The grimy windows of the firehouse were a good filtering medium. But when the paintings were finally installed in the chapel, they did not seem to have the rich grading of color, inasmuch as the Texas sun was so bright that the contrasts did not work as well as had been envisioned. Dominique de Menil tried every conceivable way of filtering the light, and today the light is as good as one could reasonably expect. The day of dedication, which also included seeing Newman's *Broken Obelisk* on the same plot of land, was a grand event. Standing on the sidewalk and after saying goodbye to Dominique, I remember her taking the crook of her walking stick, hooking it around her husband's elbow, and pulling him to the waiting car. She was a gracious and determined person, a major patron of the arts. The chapel and the nearby art museum, which houses her collection, together symbolize her life on behalf of the arts.

George Segal was probably more known to the general public than Newman or Rothko. His sculptures of figures, such as the *Bus Riders* or the *Diner*, were seen by wide audiences, particularly since they were placed in public corridors and one did not have to go to museums to see them. While Duane Hansen spoofed figures through a naturalness that is eerie, and Edward Hopper disclosed figures who are simply lonely, Segal's figures have an interiority that link the medium and the message. Known also for the figures of Abraham and Isaac because they were rejected by Kent State and then purchased by Princeton University and located between the chapel and the library, Segal had a kind of notoriety which always puzzled him. He was a gentle person, trying to illumine life through his art and using biblical figures and events, not because he was interested in a predetermined religious interpretation but because they were paradigms of human life in its variegated forms. Probably best known is his *Holocaust Memorial* placed near San Francisco's Legion of Honor Museum, where the ocean and bay meet outside the Golden Gate Bridge. Controversial too at the time of its installation, it has come to be accepted as a place of pilgrimage. One seldom sees it without flowers that have been left by visitors.

We were privileged to see his studio space on several occasions, where one saw religious figures that had not been sold and works in process. Like Newman, Segal was an eloquent speaker. But while Newman held forth, forming his thoughts as if they were lectures, George responded to questions in a way that made you see him forming his thoughts. I asked him twice to give lectures, once at Princeton in front of his sculpture at the university and once at Union Theological Seminary in a classroom setting. For the Union experience, I assumed he would come with a prepared speech and he at first startled me by saying he wanted to respond to questions instead. So I introduced him and put one question to him, to which he responded with such ease and graciousness that the questions and discussion with him just naturally happened. At the dedication of the Holocaust sculpture, the rain came down in torrents, so the talk and festivities were inside the museum, with the group moving outside only for the brief dedication. As we moved outside, I saw that George did not have an umbrella, that no one had thought of providing him one, and that he was stepping into the drenching rain. Since my wife and I each had an umbrella, I gave him mine and said "It's yours to keep." Those without raincoats or umbrellas were literally drenched. At a second Princeton event, we tried to get the seminary to enter into conversation with Segal about securing and placing his work, *Abraham's Farewell to Ishmael* on campus, but nothing came of it. For the theological students, that sculpture was a powerful image of the family dislocations they witnessed in their own work. Of all the artworks they saw on slides, this one captured them most.

One evening at an exhibition opening in honor of the sculptor David Smith, I found myself in conversation with Cleve Gray, but knew little about him. We exchanged pleasantries and decided that since we were not more than an hour away from each other, we should get together. On our way back to Hartford I mentioned this to Jane and she said she had always wanted to meet him. He in turn mentioned my name to his wife Francine, who said, "John Dillenberger. Was he there? I was in one of his classes at Columbia." So it was natural that we got together, had regular dinners at a restaurant halfway between Hartford and Warren, frequently with John Smith and Chickie joining us. John, whom I have mentioned before, was Francine's major teacher.

Jane and Cleve talked art incessantly and from time to time we talked for hours in his studio, a barn that David Smith had converted into a studio. Just a hundred feet away was a house whose graciousness was exceeded only by its occupants. Francine du Plessix Gray is a novelist whose many works I need not mention. Most of them have historical themes and are exceptionally instructive. The art form and the thought live together with equal grace. Those who read the *New York Times* book review section or the *New Yorker* will recognize her name as a reviewer, a person who is reviewed, and an essayist. Once at the American Academy in Rome, they discovered that there was extra space available for guests. So they arranged for us to join them for over a week and we deeply enjoyed the Academy, where I previously had done some research, and Rome in particular. They also asked us to join them for a weekend retreat where silence was the order of the day. I went reluctantly, and enjoyed it more than I thought I would, with Francine, a great conversationalist, being the one person at the edge of being admonished for talking. Francine has many interests, once telling me that she was deeply interested in monasticism. When I said she was so far from being monastic herself that I found it hard to understand, she responded "But John, I know what they are giving up."

Cleve confesses that he is mostly torn between abstraction and figuration, that when he does figures, he finds himself retreating to abstraction, and that most of his figures emerge out of his abstractions. He loves to do series, all meditations on the world he is experiencing, such as his Roman Walls, Prague, and Zen paintings. His most monumental work in paint, as contrasted to his enamel walls at the Hartford train station, is *Threnody*, a series of paintings that cover the walls of a large space designed by Philip Johnson at the State University campus at Purchase, New York. Unfortunately, these paintings, which cover the wall space, are installed only occasionally. But when they are they provide a totality, with dark forms moving toward the center of three walls, where mutations of brilliant red anchor the room. The paintings, according to Cleve, create a dance of death and life around the room. They provide an ambiance of hope in the midst of despair, a positive ambiguity. I confess that I prefer the *Threnody* installation over the Rothko chapel.

Cleve also did a series of vestments, with lyrical line and colors of the church year, for the Episcopal Church in Farmington, Connecticut. They were unveiled at the Hartford Seminary with great excitement. My only hesitation was that while Cleve used sensuous colored line with great grace, the depictions of the cross were very traditional. In our discussion I raised the question of why the cross was so inhibiting that he could not form it in nontraditional ways. We both left the question dangling between us.

Our most recent time together occurred in Berkeley just a few months before I began writing these reflections. In the morning Cleve, Francine, and I walked about in the University Art Museum, seeing, ruminating, talking in ways familiar to us over the years, and then headed for the Faculty Club where my wife Jean was waiting for us. The four of us had started lunch and drank some wine, when, as the report has it, I fell silent and unresponsive, though still seated in my chair. Some ten minutes later the medics, in response to a 911 call, arrived with gurney and stretched me out. I revived, awake enough to have a conversation with the medics on the way to the hospital. Tests revealed that I had an attack of vasovagal syncope, a fainting spell with a fancy name. So my latest direct human contact with Cleve and Francine was from my hospital bed, though beyond that, Cleve sent me a watercolor sketch from the work he was doing, and Francine sent a book. For days the phone rang, the two of them wanting to be sure we were all right.

Stephen De Staebler has been a part of my life from the early sixties, that is, the time spent on the west coast. For my book, *The Visual Arts and Christianity in America*, I chose for the cover his *Crucifix* from the Newman Center ensemble in Berkeley. Although not religious in the traditional sense, De Staebler, like many modern artists, is enamored by the subject and his clay and bronze figures exhibit a respect for religious issues, in non conventional terms. For me personally, the *Winged Figure* in the rotunda of the GTU library has a special place. Stephen said in public that his relation with Jane Dillenberger, Doug Adams, and myself had been the context for thinking of GTU as a location for one of his figures. One day, he said, he knew that he had done a figure that seemed to say, "This is the one ". So Stephen gave the figure to GTU and the Center for Art, Religion and Education took financial responsibility for all the attendant matters of installation. Initially the gift was not welcomed, and it took many a meeting before the GTU board approved going ahead, meetings in which Stephen's presence, his personal aura, made all the difference, as did the support of the president of GTU, Glenn Bucher.

Stephen has done many public sculptures in the Bay Area, both in San Francisco and the East Bay. But one of his major patrons has been Jane Owen, leading figure in the restoration and rejuvenation of New Harmony, Indiana, home of the initial Rappite group and later the Owenite community in the nineteenth century. I met her first in connection with our common interest in Paul Tillich, and attested in her case in the creation of the Paul Tillich Park in New Harmony which is home to a bust of him and inscriptions from his writings. Jane Owen restored many of the old buildings, created new ones that fit into the ambience, and created a score of new modern buildings, including Richard Meier's Visitor's Center and Potter's Studio, Philip Johnson's Roofless Church, with its Lipchitz sculpture and the *Pieta* and *Annunciation* standing figures by De Staebler. In addition, De Staebler did a sculptural wall, called the *Vision of St. Benedict*, for one of the meeting rooms, an outdoor fountain, and a small chapel. Jane Owen's husband was the grandson of the original Robert Owen, though it is Jane who has had the vision and tenacity that has made this small town into a national treasure. There is a certain serendipity in De Staebler and New Harmony, for he originally comes from that area of Indiana and he and Jane Owen were great conversation partners about the work he undertook. Indeed, conversation is so characteristic of Stephen. I recall conversations with him about art, but beyond that, moving verbal explorations of a personal nature about issues that affected both of us. I was touched just a few weeks ago when Stephen called to ask how I was, noting that I seemed unduly quiet at a meeting we had attended several evenings before. Of such sensibilities deep friendships are made.

Let me mention two more artists. In connection with the art program at St. Peter's Church under City Corp in New York City, it was hoped that Frank Stella would lend some paintings for an exhibition. Annalee Newman agreed to ask him if he would do so and the reply was positive. My wife Jane and I were asked to come to his studio to make the selections. There were at least three dozen choices and he gave us time to view them all, interjecting a comment here and there. When we came to the two we wanted, he ventured, "One I call Augustine and other Aquinas. Take them both, but Augustine is the most profound." Later we were able to see some more of his nonpublic works in the intimacy of Meier's apartment in New York, Stella being the artist that Meier most appreciates. That may seem strange, but the two styles fit together.

The other artist I want to mention is Richard Lippold, whose baldacchino over the altar at St. Mary's Cathedral, San Francisco, made of wires and metal, is one of my very favorite pieces of art. It focuses psychic energy over the altar without creating a fence, and the shimmering created by actual movement of air and reflections of light give the impression that beauty is the forming of space. So that we could talk about the piece, he invited us to his studio apartment in New Jersey. We did not know that we were to stay for dinner and that he was the cook. I can still see in my mind's eye how he used his knife with the agility and grace that marked his work. Moreover, the drawings that became the basis of his particular works were themselves works of art. We kept in touch. In how far his hope to do more commissions for religious spaces was the motivation, I do not know. When he heard about our commissioning Meier for Hartford Seminary he asked if he could visit us. When he came the building was near completion and he looked at the three-story open space over the entry that cried out for a different kind of baldacchino. He even offered to help raise some funds, but Meier was not interested. His work was a work of art and did not need additions, he said in his own words. It was the one point on which Meier and I disagreed.

During the Hartford years, Meier and I spent considerable time together and frequently went from place to place in New York City by taxi. I knew him as a great taxi hailer. A few years later I experienced that it was easy for me, too, and events fell into place. At the Metropolitan Museum, shops on Madison Avenue, and restaurants, I was confused on occasion with Ed Koch, and it still happens when I am in New York, always to my advantage. Perhaps the taxis were stopping for me, the alleged Koch, and I had attributed it to Richard's particular gift or recognized prominence. In San Francisco, to a lesser degree, I was confused with the columnist, the late Herb Caen, whom I met on several occasions. I have never met Koch, though once sat near him at a restaurant table probably originally meant for him, considering that he arrived after I did.

11

CONTINUING PROJECTS
The Return to Berkeley

"To be claimed with respect to all our senses
is nothing less that having our full humanity restored."

Writing Projects

When the summer of 1983 was on the horizon, I reaffirmed to the board of trustees at Hartford Seminary that I had no intention of going beyond the five and a half years I had promised. I felt I had done what I had been asked to do and that the time had come to return to my research interests as the focus of my retirement years.

We had not sold our house in Berkeley, and after five winters of heavy snows, we were ready for a more benign climate. Besides, we still had friends in Berkeley. Some of the persons in Hartford found it hard to understand our leaving, inasmuch as we had made it in the Hartford establishment. Said one of them, "Now you would be welcome more than ever, for you would no longer need to raise money for the seminary."

So we returned to Berkeley to a life of research and writing. I was interested in how various religious traditions defined humanity and how the various secular disciplines also provided such profiles. Over a two-year period I drafted what was subsequently published as *A Theology of Artistic Sensibilities: the Visual Arts and the Church* (1986). My draft version and the draft by Wilson Yates of *The Arts in Theological Education* (1987) were distributed and discussed at a Lilly supported Consultation on the Arts and Theological Education organized by Emory's Candler School of Theology in 1985. By the late eighties a good number of art and theology programs had emerged, including those at GTU, Yale Divinity, Candler, Wesley, Andover Newton, United at the Twin Cities, Union in New York, and Christian Theological in Indianapolis. Robert Lynn at Lilly and, subsequently, John Cook at the Luce Foundation saw to it that these developments were both supported and creatively conceived. Now, almost two decades later, these and additional programs seem destined to be part of the continuing landscape. GTU continues its doctoral and exhibition programs, accents that distinguish it from most of the other programs. United may be singled out for an ethos in which the arts are part of its very life. From the paintings and sculptures throughout the buildings, to the classroom ingredients that seem to touch each discipline, to publications, including *ARTS*, to its active involvements with the museums, the visual and other arts are everywhere. We have Wilson Yates to thank for those developments.

A Theology of Artistic Sensibilities, in addition to being an overall historical sketch, dealt with the contemporary scene and laid out an agenda for the future. Essentially, the approach was similar to the much earlier book on theology and the natural sciences, laying out an approach that respects the integrity of each discipline. I resisted positions in which theologians incorporated the arts on their own theological terms, or positions in which the openness of science made it possible for theologians to develop fairly conservative positions. Moreover, I made a plea for the use of all our senses as a way of broadening the parameters that make up our humanity.

An experience at a service of worship at St. Peter's Lutheran Church on All Souls Eve at 54th and Lexington in New York City may illumine what is involved. That evening the music was exceptional, the incense pungent, the sermon excellent, the bread and wine good to the taste, and behind the altar, there was a sinuous triptych by Willem de Kooning. For the first time every sensibility was simultaneously claimed in a service of worship. But to do this every sense must be at its best and one must be trained and attuned to all of them. To be claimed with respect to all our senses is nothing less than having our full humanity restored. In many ways the verbal may be central, but it is not enough in and of itself.

This is not the place to go into detail about the de Kooning work, but it should be noted that a liturgist, then a member of the congregation, opposed having the work installed. She wrote that the better a work of art, the more it interfered with the center of worship — for her, the verbal liturgy. Such a viewpoint is totally opposite to what, I think, worship should be. Worship is not one thing, but a concentration of various modalities in a common gestalt.

While I believe that all of our senses and sensibilities need to be claimed, in the above volume I centered on the visual arts. For much of Protestant history there was a split between the alleged purity of the intellect and the moral over against the seductiveness of the sensual in art. That split needs to be overcome, not by taming the art but by a discipline in the act of seeing. I have previously written that "precisely because art has a seductive character, sensuous to the core, a discipline of seeing is essential in order for one to be illumined beyond the sensory embodiment. The discipline of seeing, learned by repeated seeing, . . . forms the seductive into a discriminating sensuousness that is more than itself. Horizons are stretched, formed and filtered, as creation's images are regained in their sensuousness. . . ." (244)

A second writing project centered on *Protestant Chrisianity,* first published in 1954, still in print but no longer up to date. Claude and I made changes where we felt they were called for and added new chapters covering the interim years. Between 1954 and 1988 new philosophical currents had appeared, including process theology, analytical philosophy, the new hermeneutic, and theologies of hope. In addition, aspects of radical religion appeared in the death of God books, and on the opposite pole, in new conservative movements. Black, liberation, and feminist theologies emerged with vigor and in new forms of scholarship. Finally, there appeared the recognition of religious pluralism, with tentative steps toward inter religious dialogue.

A year later *The Visual Arts and Christianity in America* (1989) was completed, which was the updating of a previous volume that had stopped at the end of the nineteenth century. For someone wanting a comprehensive view of the range of issues and subjects in the American scene, this is still the fullest account. In this, as in my other publications with Crossroad, I was sorely disappointed, in that there was little promotion of the books, and as the staff left for another publisher, Crossroad abandoned the books. Neglect from both sides was fatal. Indeed, I have decided that this book, in particular, needs resurrection.

During the same period, Jane and I decided to bring together Tillich's writings on the visual arts. This was published as *Paul Tillich, On Art and Architecture* (1987). Given the pronounced interest he had in the arts throughout his career, it seemed strange that this had not been done before. Jane selected the plates, and helped edit the texts that had not been published previously. I wrote the introduction, in which the case is made that the arts lay at the basis of his theological work.

Personal Transitions

After returning to Berkeley, Jane reestablished her academic life. In the period before going to Hartford, she had been doing a good deal of teaching, directing dissertations, and promoting art exhibitions at the GTU library. While Hartford Seminary faculty had indicated they wanted her to teach, they did not move in that direction, and I felt I could not be her promoter. So she did a course on occasion at other schools, but given her training and genuine interest in the museum world, she spent most of her time doing projects at the Wadsworth Atheneum. By the time when the new Hartford Seminary building emerged, we had moved to the building across the street and her study faced the new construction, which she enjoyed, as well as the times we spent with Richard Meier. While there were special friends, the Hartford ethos was not encouraging. She said there were few interesting men, by which she meant vibrant conversational partners in the still male-dominated culture. I think what she missed was the lively faculty exchange at Berkeley in the sixties and seventies, and which she succeeded in rebuilding at many levels upon our return. To understand Jane one needs to know that art and religion were and are her life; there is nothing second.

Several years after our return to Berkeley, Jane and I were divorced. I was acutely aware that this was a second divorce but finally that did not deter me from making the decision. Divorce is not easy, and many of those who say that it is have probably not been there. It colors everything one is, has been, and will be. Just as the rupture of both marriages was real, equally real is that for most of the years together life was good.

In 1992, I married Jean Poree Kresy, who for five years in the sixties had been my administrative assistant. In the first part of the intervening years we occasionally found ourselves at the same events but then that ceased. When our lives intersected again by chance some nineteen years later, she was deputy director of the Office for Civil Rights for the U.S. Department of Education for the western region, headquartered in San Francisco. Her second husband had recently died after a long illness and she had moved to Hiller Highlands in north Oakland, a planned community of townhouses of various sizes. It was there that I eventually joined her. The house was small for both of us with her furniture and my books, and we thought of moving elsewhere. But before we got that far the Berkeley/Oakland fire of 1991 swept through the area and totally burned all of our possessions. Fortunately, we had taken one of our cars and gone to the First Congregational Church in Berkeley where I was giving an address, only to walk out of the church thereafter to see the billowing smoke and raging fire on the horizon. It was some four days later that we were taken by police van into the area where nothing but ashes and melted metal greeted us, except for a small Shona sculpture from Africa that a friend had given us.

That we were away probably saved our lives inasmuch as the fire came from an angle where we would not have seen it approaching. As it was, eleven persons lost their lives on the short street on which we had lived. Starting over on every front is daunting indeed, though at times our bitter humor rejoiced in not being burdened by possessions. I am acutely aware of the many painful transitions in my life, but intensely grateful for the good that has been in them.

After a few weeks we moved into a condominium which turned out to be a mistake and we were able to negotiate our way out, mainly through the graces of a friend who is a real estate broker who pled that we were not of sound mind at the time. That stated characterization was hard to accept, but later we came to understand that we needed time to sort things out and that we had made several mistakes. Subsequently we settled into a two-bedroom high-rise apartment on the south end of Lake Merritt. Had the apartments been available for purchase, we might have done so, but they were not. Still our stay there gave us the time to decide what to do. We vetoed rebuilding on the lot because of the restrictions and covenants. Jean did the negotiating with the insurance company on our housing loss, and I started the initial looking for a house to purchase, all of which already had high costs, given that over three thousand homes had been destroyed and many were looking for places to buy. We did do all right with the insurance company and were able to sell the lot on which the house had stood. In the meantime, I looked at about thirty houses and saw one that looked feasible. So Jean and I looked at it and saw possibilities. We think it had not sold because it was so depressingly dark and the kitchen needed redoing. But on the horizon there was a marvelous Bay view. Those who saw the house initially and what we did with it say it is not the same house. Both of us have a sense of space and were I to start over, I would probably be an architect.

Location was also a factor, for given that my library was entirely con-sumed, I needed to be near the GTU and UCB libraries. Losing one's working library is a blow, but more than that was the loss of irreplaceable paintings. In addition I had completed research for a book and a begin-ning draft was underway, but all was destroyed in the fire. In the mean-time, I had discovered that while living on the south side of Berkeley made access to San Francisco shorter, access to the library was easier from the north. The house we purchased is in El Cerrito, three miles to the north of GTU. Given the time needed to reestablish a household, there was little time for academic work. So the book was stalled and I wondered if I should return to it at all. But eventually I did. I had to start over, including visits to see works of art again in Europe, given that photographs and doc-uments had been burned. I think what emerged, *Images and Relics: Theological Perceptions and Visual Images in Sixteenth-Century Europe* (1999) is a better book as a result of having had to do it twice. It is a book that combined my continued interest in the reformation with the world of art, a kind of coming home in which old and new interests coincided. Central to the volume are chapters on Grünewald, Dürer, Cranach the Elder, and Michelangelo, seen in terms of the religious currents of the time.

I might add that Jean and I had thought of moving to Washington, D.C., where she had been offered a position. We both loved that city and felt that it might be easier for all concerned if we left Berkeley. But the fire also made us aware of the friends we both had in the area, in Jean's case going back to forty years of regular contact. She has a remarkable capacity for friendship and I have inherited many of her friends, just as I lost some as a result of the last divorce.

Ours is an interracial marriage, and for most of her life, Jean has lived simultaneously in both the black and white worlds. This has enriched both of us, though on occasion, particularly in traveling, we have been made aware that our state is not the usual. We have had wonderful experiences, particularly in traveling abroad. Turkey was delightful, for Jean, who did half of the driving. She was both a woman driving (in three weeks we saw one additional woman driving a car) and from another race, the subject of approving glances and conversation. Lingering U.S. prejudices manifest themselves mainly in restaurants, in table locations and service. But in the London Tate, where the restaurant was mostly staffed by blacks, we were taken out of the waiting line and given the choice table location. Sometimes it works both ways.

In addition to my reading and research interests, I continued to be involved in the life of GTU. From 1988 to 1993 I was a member of the GTU board under a faculty emeritus category. I had some hesitations about a former president being on the board and I knew that two presidents were uneasy about it. But when I decided to resign, the two said not yet; we need you. So I waited until my term expired.

In addition, I had been asked in my retirement to serve on several search committees at GTU, including the search for a dean. I declined heading that committee but agreed to serve as executive secretary. The top candidate had superb credentials, but most of the women faculty could not accept him for he was a white Anglo-Saxon male. So there was a kind of crisis. Early on in the search, I had contacted Margaret Miles at Harvard, whom I had known for years as a friend and colleague in history, art, and theology. She had said that under no circumstances would she consider an administrative position. So I used her as an advisor, running person after person past her and talking with her two or three times a week. In the midst of the crisis, I had a phone call from Margaret, who said that she had come to the conclusion that the job was meant for her. So I said, "Margaret, is this as unequivocal a yes as was your previous no," and she answered "assuredly." So she came for interviews and was resoundingly voted to be the vice president for academic affairs and academic dean, and appointed to the John Dillenberger chair in historical theology.

When she arrived Margaret asked me to do spade work in other searches, including an appointment in Jewish studies and for the librarian.

Acting Librarian

I was startled when Glenn Bucher, the President, and Margaret asked me to be the interim librarian for a year or two, depending on when a librarian could be found. Knowing of my role in the creation of the GTU library and hearing my comments on libraries during the search (based on an address to the American Theological Library Association, published in *Theological Education* as two articles, "Traditional Library Functions and the Economic Factor" in 1969 and "Unraveling the Library Mystique" in 1989), they saw the proposal as a natural choice.

Their reading, with which I agreed, was that the library needed attention, that things had been drifting for some time, particularly from the perspective of faculty. Given that I was technically not a librarian, they added that funds would be available for me to have a library consultant who could meet with me and occasionally with them. Why would I take such a position? I have been asked. Well, I had invested a good deal of time in the creation of the library and, on reflection, felt I could do the job in a situation needing urgent attention.

Andrew Scrimgeour, then of Regis University in Denver and now librarian at Drew University, seemed to me to be the ideal person as a consultant to me and to Margaret and Glenn. I had known him for years and we were on friendly terms, but I also knew he would be professional in all that he did. Andy and I agreed that first of all he would interview library staff and review various documents and then he and I independently would make a list of problems as we saw them and compare what we had listed. We were astounded that our lists, except for one item, were identical.

At the top of the list was that acquisition purchases were too low. In fact, the accreditation agencies had already pointed out that taking inflation into account, we were standing still rather than increasing our acquisitions budget. So the first order of planning meant increasing acquisitions on a three-year step plan. Bluntly put, acquisitions is the last place to cut from an educational standpoint, but the first place some administrators, including librarians, want to cut.

Second, given that the workforce seemed overstaffed, attention would need to be given to those aspects. Organizationally, the library had three centers of power, virtually unrelated to each other: the office of the director, the area of public services which also included reference functions, and the area of technical services. When I arrived I discovered that the public services and technical services met without the director; in fact, that the director was not invited. At first I assumed that was because I was not a trained librarian, but instead it turned out to be a matter of turf or power. They were comfortable in their fiefdoms. So initially I just insisted that I be invited, inasmuch as I needed to be educated in what they were doing. It became apparent that some staff members were almost exclusively supervising. The library seemed much too small for that. But most of the supervisors resisted taking on extra responsibilities.

Third, the overall posture was that of thinking of internal working relationships, with little awareness that a library is a service-providing entity, that its internal functions exist for the sake of making resources available to students, faculty, and the public. There was too much of being nice but not helpful. One incident was illustrative of the problem. Two faculty members came to me complaining that they could not access the library from their own office computers and that the library was not helping to solve the problem. Indeed, they had been rebuffed by the librarians when they initially requested help. So I asked one of the librarians who appeared to be both competent and courteous to meet with me and the two faculty members. The librarian listened to them, asked some questions, and then told them that if they did the following, it would probably work, but if it did not, to call her and she would immediately come to their offices. Her instructions worked and word quickly spread throughout GTU that the library was becoming more helpful and courteous. In short, the library culture needed to change and many staff members began to discover the joy of serving a public.

Still, the staff transitions were not easy. Two terminations appeared necessary and working with our attorneys we made the case for their leaving and were generous in the severance packages. Several persons resigned when they discovered that working patterns would change and that the staff would be reduced over time. Fortunately, there was a group of younger librarians on the staff, competent and ready for advancement. Let me mention but two, Danny Wilson, who became the head of technology developments and Ann Hotta, who spearheaded the educational technology program for GTU and its relation to the schools.

The area that gave me the most difficulty was that of cataloguing. Given that this had been a problem already in the early phases of creating the library, it was not surprising to me. Part of the reason may well be that I am least in accord with aspects of that area, believing that when a book has been catalogued once, why would one want to change it or improve on it. Better records, considering the costs, may not be the top priority. More importantly, our five cataloguers were processing only about one-half of what their counterparts were able to do in other theological institutions. It never became clear whether the lack of productivity was due to over-cataloguing details or to lack of effort.

The second cataloguing issue was the choice of which network to use for the protocols of cataloguing. GTU had been using RLIN (Research Library Information Network), initially sponsored by Stanford and the University of California at Berkeley. Although RLIN was a fine system, it was so expensive that these universities, along with others, had abandoned it in favor of OCLC (Ohio Computer Library Center). OCLC was also the preferred system for most theological schools. We simply could not, at the time, justify the expense that would have been entailed by remaining in RLIN.

While negotiating cataloguing changes, we were able to secure two state grants and one private grant for cataloguing two groups of materials not yet known to our public constituency, namely, the marvelous collection of our oldest, and in some sense, finest scholarly books that had been placed in the basement for storage, and the magnificent collection of orthodox materials of the Patriarch Athenagoras Orthodox Institute, an affiliate of GTU. Credit for these grants goes mainly to Susan Carpenter, my administrative assistant, a superb researcher and writer.

My calculation was that our cataloguers, if the output could be increased, could do the newly acquired materials, and still do the recon over a period of five years. "Recon" refers to the cataloguing of scholarly books in the basement that had not been re-catalogued when first contributed by the schools to the library, and therefore not yet entered into GRACE, the GTU on-line catalogue. In short, at the end of five years, the GTU library collection would be fully catalogued and we would then not need more than one or two professional cataloguers.

Shepherding the preceding developments occurred mainly through the creation of a new management team of five members representing the major segments of the library. This group met every other week and hammered out conceptions and concrete plans. Thus the issues facing the library were always developed with the whole in mind.

Finally, in my term as librarian, I began to work with an architect and library consultant as to the space needs for the future. The original architects for the library had projected that the library would be full in twenty years, and so it was. In addition, while there was talk that technology would replace books, in point of fact technology has increased the space needs. In the meantime, moveable shelves, installed by my successor, Bonnie Hardwick, have taken the very immediate pressure off and given time to do more extensive planning, not only for the library but also in relation to building needs in the whole GTU area. I was glad to be part of the preliminary planning and funding endeavor.

During my two years in the library, I spent a good deal of time with Jim Spohrer, who at the time was both in charge of the Germanic collection development and in the inner circle of the University of California library administration. He is a gem, and I miss seeing him and hearing his wise comments. We were responsible for one major joint development, an agreement on mutual acquisitions development, to be reviewed annually by a joint standing committee.

President

Toward the end of the interim librarian venture, Jean, who was now retired, and I were looking forward to several months in Europe, partly travel and partly research. But then the issue of serving a year as president emerged, for Glenn Bucher, who had been president since 1992, announced that he would be leaving to head the Boyer Center, a position of great interest to him. Glenn appeared to have lost the full confidence of the heads of institutions, partly because he believed that GTU had no future if it could not hire additional faculty and add additional support resources. He felt reasonably assured that the money could be found. But one major venture was sidetracked when he signed a twenty-year project in Jewish studies, with major support from segments of the Jewish community, only to find that three trustees challenged the contract. They said that Glenn had not been authorized to sign the contract without further approval of details by the board, all of which they found unacceptable. While the original contract had been written with the approval of GTU legal advisors, the contract was rewritten under pressure from the three trustees. The new document was not acceptable to members of the Jewish community, and the initial financial grant had to be returned. Later when I talked with members of the Jewish community, they said, why should they be positive about an institution that does not honor a contract signed by the president. The three trustees, in concert with the chair of the Board, pressured Glenn to leave, buying out his contract, apparently not fully aware that he had an offer which he would have taken under the best of circumstances.

Throughout its history, GTU has been torn between two directions, one, building the doctoral program on the existing resources of the schools, which hopefully would be strengthened, and two, GTU hiring enough faculty to give an independent base to each of the areas. Put in succinct terms, should GTU be something like a tenth school with respect to the doctoral program? The direction of hiring additional faculty for graduate work in GTU was spearheaded in the presidencies of Michael Blecker and Glenn Bucher. Blecker was formidable, but his intentions were halted by his sudden illness and death. Sanford Elberg, former dean of the graduate division at UCB and the person who had been so helpful in working out the shared doctoral program, served as interim president for a year. Then Bob Barr served for four years, with great administrative skills. But he did not believe that GTU could raise the money needed and was ready to give many of the functions back to the schools. Glenn Bucher, like Blecker, wanted to build more GTU resources, but like Blecker, made only a beginning through the full endowment of a chair in theology and art history, as well as expanding the general endowment. Most promising was his creation of a president's council, which to this day is a source of insight and support.

My own judgment is that if GTU found money independently and coordinated appointments with the schools, both would profit. But the reality is that the schools pay substantial funds for GTU administrative expenses and considerable money for Jewish studies. If the schools were freed of some of these financial responsibilities, they would be more open to cooperative and independent appointments that enriched programs across the board, including the doctoral program. Instead, they are afraid they might have to help GTU meet its own expenses. Without a breakthrough at this level, the potential of the whole is limited. The GTU president and staff exist in a form of tension with the schools, pushing them beyond what their constituencies think they want when in fact they merely look inward. To ensure such a future, GTU needs to push continuously for wider horizons and to seek financial resources to undergird them.

Interest in me apparently centered in the fact that I knew GTU's history, and because of my library stint, was up to date on current issues. Since the heads of institutions and the Board saw major planning aspects as immediate priorities, there was no interest in hiring an interim person who would simply hold the operation together. Rather, they wanted to move forward. This was symbolized in that the board appointed me president, rather than acting or interim president, thus making me the first and sixth president. The heads of institutions and the GTU board chair met with me to see how I responded to several issues and how I would address them. I sensed no difference of opinion on any major issue, though the inevitable question of my past emerged. I was grateful that happened because it gave me an occasion to talk about it in an overall sense. Previously, Michael Blecker, when he became ill, suggested that I be the interim but that was vetoed by the then senior board members.

In the first week I was in office, Dean Margaret Miles came to me, pleased to announce that a foundation had given money for a part-time appointment in feminist studies, with the understanding that we would commit ourselves to endeavoring to raise money for a full-time chair by the time the grant ran out some five years later. Moreover, the funding specified a definite person. Not having heard of it before, I naturally raised some questions, and discovered that the Catholic schools also had questions about the specific appointment. Examination of documents indicated that the dean could make interim appointments, the length of which were not specified. The same document assigned all academic issues to the dean, with the president having little voice in the overall academic direction. While the GTU dean and the heads of institutions had differences of opinion about the nature of the doctoral program, the deans of the schools were frequently not on the same wavelength as their presidents. In spite of these complications, Margaret created a good climate for the doctoral faculty to be working in and instituted new models of work, particularly in interdisciplinary studies and in the creation of a faculty advisory board for the dean. Moreover, her national and international stature as a teacher and scholar modeled and captivated her colleagues and students.

Rather than spending my time on current academic problems, I turned my energies toward the future, which indeed is what the board and heads of institutions had asked me to do. A good deal of energy went into developing a strategic plan, including the work of a governance committee. All of this involved extensive discussions with the heads of institutions and officers of the board of trustees, particularly the board chair, John Weiser, vice-chair Rita Semel, and academic chair, Joan McGrath. Work in these areas was completed after my departure. But while I was still there, agreement emerged on directions for the future, centering on work on Jewish Studies, on potential Islamic resources, and on a coordinated thrust to focus the issues inherent in a plethora of programs in Asian religions and Christianity. The board, in its last meeting with me — with the presence of the new president, Jim Donahue — voted these three areas as priorities for exploration. I might add that from the moment of Jim's appointment, I made no decision of import without talking with him and providing him with the appropriate documents.

That finishes my extensive involvement with GTU. As a friend put it, "You have been so present throughout its entire history, it is simply time to be absent."

Westar Institute

For several years I have been a fellow of the Westar Institute, though given its major attention to the Jesus Seminar, I have not been active, since biblical subjects are not areas of my competence. Nevertheless, I had a decided interest in them and read a good deal of the literature. But three factors recently have made a difference in my involvement in its work.

First, while a not-for-profit institution, Westar has not spent much energy on exploring what this can mean with respect to organizational structure and funding potential. Sensing those issues on the horizon, Bob Funk, colleague and friend for over four decades, asked that I be elected a member of the board and become its chair. We have made some progress in creating structures that integrate the academic and organizational aspects in terms of mutual responsibilities and directions.

Second, while still active in studies that bear on the Jesus tradition, Westar is rapidly expanding the horizons of its work. Work on the Book of Acts and the Pauline corpus, together with new translations and fresh interpretations, will soon be published. In addition, a seminar on the history of Israel is in the process of formation. Beyond that, attention is moving toward the nature of theological reflection. In short, what is theology to be in the light of what has been gong on in other fields of knowledge and research beyond the biblical field? The latter is of particular interest to me, intimations of which have been signaled in my teaching and writing to date, particularly within the natural sciences and the visual arts.

Third, it is a joy to see the Westar scholars at work. Instead of persons upstaging each other in their presentations, they bring their insights to each other in a collegial atmosphere and learn from each other. Their work strives for provisional consensus, but also revisits positions taken decades before. Moreover, results of their work are shared with the public. This has two important facets, first creating religious literacy and, secondly, incorporating the insights of the lay public.

Essentially, it stands for a new liberalism in religious and social life, one in which openness is accompanied by vision without the development of orthodoxies. While I am happy to be identified with such directions, it has also become evident that I no longer have the energy needed to be as active as I have been in the last two years.

THREE
Continuing Reflections

John Dillenberger caught in concentration

12

BUILDING FOR CHANGE
Reflections on Theological Schools and the GTU Experiment

*"Deans and presidents are not the custodians of the
past, but the harbingers of change."*

While critical of the actual role many institutions play, I am not anti-institutional. Quite the contrary, I believe they are the agencies through which both stability and change are maintained in society. It is obvious that stability without change ossifies the achievements of a particular society, and that change without stability and continuity turns the potential of creativity into chaos. When the orthodox, whether in religion or the social political realm, becomes an orthodoxy, the leavening of the new is stifled. That is the nature of the religious right, both religiously and politically. It wants to turn to the past as the basis for a viable future.

But the new, without grounding, is romantic about the possible, as if good intentions alone could guide the future. The anti-institutionalism of the sixties pointed to major issues in society that were not being addressed. But it had no sense of the structures necessary to institute genuine change. It gloried in visions of revolution, without the discipline and know-how through which revolutions take place. Change does not take place without the promotion of new or modified institutional structures.

Translating this approach into the political world, it is obvious that the absolutes of the right and the left need to be rejected. Ideally democracy is that middle ground, but we should not act as if it is the only form that human associations must take. The experience of the United States, given how widely different world cultures are, is not ideally or structurally the path for all to follow.

With respect to the religious/theological spectrum, we will probably see many groups retreating more within, trying to recapture what makes them unique, but doing that in a culture that they know will be more diverse than we have ever experienced. California may only partly be the knell of the future, but it is surely relevant to note that by 2005, there will be no ethnic or religious majority in that state. That is a different world in which to live and work. Wrongly approached it will lead to discord, but with some imagination and discernment, it can become a glorious future.

By and large, denominational seminaries are less venturesome than those related in some ways to colleges and universities. Their chances of survival are greater, even when they are less needed than they once were. In my experience, Drew and the San Francisco Theological Seminary were denominational schools that once vigorously pushed beyond their initial boundaries but returned, for a complex number of reasons, to a more traditional posture. Denominational seminaries, as educational entities, should not only express but also stand in critical relation to their sponsors, a built-in uneasiness. Union Theological Seminary in New York City, once the premier school of ecumenical Protestantism, moved to expand its interreligious interests, but became bogged down in bending to the social demands of the sixties to the point that existing financial resources were deeply depleted and new financial support was not on the horizon. Its current president, Joseph C. Hough, has worked diligently and creatively toward a new future in association with Columbia University, building on past collaboration to forge new programs and to save its unexcelled library. In one bold stroke the new constellation will have major resources in Buddhism, Christianity, Hinduism, Islam, Judaism, and other Chinese and Indian religious traditions. Its former role in ministerial training will obviously take on new though modest forms. At the same time, its financial future looks viable again.

Yale Divinity School, too, has had a rocky road in its relation to Yale University, involving decaying buildings, programs, financial matters, and leadership issues. But it seems to be emerging from this complex of problems without major changes in mission. Harvard Divinity School and the University of Chicago Divinity School, with long histories of financial viability and strong faculties, seem relatively untouched by major crises. But the futures they see for themselves are less clear, which can become a problem if new directions for our time are too slow in coming.

Given that I have not directly experienced working in the world of divinity schools in universities generally, or been on a traditional denominational school faculty, I do not trust myself to say much about them. I do, however, want to add some comments on theological consortia, where I have more direct knowledge. It is true, I think, that GTU has gone further in that direction than other areas in the country. But that may have come about because of special circumstances that do not obtain elsewhere.

First, geography, particularly proximity, played a role. Of the nine schools, five were in Berkeley, three moved into Berkeley, and one did much of its teaching in Berkeley. Most of the theological schools are located on Holy Hill, as the area adjacent to the north side of the university has been dubbed. It is a five-minute walk from the GTU library to the UCB library, less than from Union to the Columbia library or from Harvard Divinity to Widener library. Most of the classrooms for GTU are in this central area, making it possible to schedule classes by a common registrar.

The GTU library is a paradigm of what should be possible across the spectrum, though in a different way than is usually suggested. In the GTU one hears it said that there is too much duplication, each school having one dean and one president when the total student body of the schools taken together ordinarily would only need a dean and a president. Yet, a dean and president is precisely what each school needs, both to symbolize and to actualize what the school is about. But libraries, classroom allocations, business offices, personnel policies, maintenance, etc., can be centralized. Several individuals in the world of business have said to me that GTU has centralized the educational aspects, which for the most part, has been a failure elsewhere. Nevertheless, GTU has not been able to centralize what business enterprises take for granted.

While there is truth in the above, the situation is more complex. As some of the smaller schools discovered, the common library was a real bargain in what it provided. But they had been accustomed to cutting back on acquisitions and/or staffing when budgets became critical. It is easier for larger schools to reap the benefits of common services since, by and large, they benefit from savings of cooperation, while some smaller schools find it difficult to meet a certain threshold level. The GTU schools are acutely aware of that reality and some of the larger schools have said that they would need to consider helping the smaller schools in an extreme crisis. That situation raises the question of whether a common fund could be created for addressing such crises. On the other hand, it is also clear that smaller schools need to work hard to create and fund budgets at levels that make them contributors to the common enterprise and that certain levels need to be maintained to be a school.

From the beginning GTU was meant to have jurisdiction for the doctoral program and to be a coordinating instrument. It would be logical then for it to promote and to be the vehicle for creating common systems. For some it seemed that moving in that direction made GTU a major school, competing with the others. That attitude was not alleviated as some in the GTU administration and board saw their role as creating and controlling such structures. It was easy to forget that such agencies were services, that the users of the services needed to be in the loop for both initial and subsequent developments, that the financial aspects needed to be open and above board, and that processes existed for dealing seriously with complaints and proposals for bettering the services. On the other hand, some schools entered into common services without really letting go, duplicating activities where the gain would have been in not doing so.

In effect, for various projects, schools with allied interests have set up cooperative patterns on their own, such as food services. At the same time, the GTU business office is doing the books, so to speak, for itself and some of the other schools, and there has been some cooperation on personnel policy issues. These developments make sense, but the full range of what could be done both with respect to better services and financial gain still lie ahead.

On the academic front, GTU's relation with the secular public University of California at Berkeley is unique. Essentially it is one of extensive cooperation with few formal documents, to the consternation of accrediting agencies. Educationally, it means dialogue between the secular and the theological, affinities that are not identities. GTU as a whole deals with faith communities, the university with communities of various stripes, including the religious. The result is a form of tension that is instructive to both. That creative tension is challenged on occasion by withdrawing from engagement with the university or by totally coalescing into the arts and sciences approach. Finally, it is important that the schools take their mandate seriously to provide sufficient faculty to teach at the doctoral level.

Fascinating and urgent issues on what comprises GTU lie ahead. The qualifications on criteria to be one of the member schools are clear enough. But to date, the schools, as contrasted to affiliates and program units, are Christian. One of the affiliates, the Institute of Buddhist Studies, is exploring becoming a full-fledged accredited school. Should that happen, the question is, "Could it become one of the member schools?" While I see no reason for that not happening, it is conceivable that rubrics need to be found that honor the Christian group while finding equality for schools from non-Christian traditions. At the same time, allied issues emerge regarding the current academic program units in GTU and the affiliates associated with GTU. Academic units are especially created bodies that focus attention in research, reflection, and policy with respect to specific areas where faculty interests emerge. The Center for Ethics and Social Policy, once popular and visible in the public arena, is such a unit. The Center for Women and Religion, also a program unit, has sometimes centered more on being a support group for women than on exploring feminist thought and its role in the curriculum. Academic program units are in the GTU budget, though they have been encouraged to raise funds on their own. Insofar as they raise funds, they tend to affirm independence in program, yet theoretically academic programs report to the dean. When monies are not raised and GTU judges it cannot provide the financial resources, the program units tend to atrophy. That is currently the case with the two centers mentioned above.

The Center for Jewish Studies, developed over time from a GTU faculty appointment into a three-person department, relies for more than half its funding on the regular GTU budget. Some of us had hoped that enough outside support could be found to make it an affiliate of GTU, affiliates being relatively autonomous groups whose programs provide facets of academic resources that would otherwise not be available and whose own work is enhanced through GTU associations. Affiliates raise their own funds, mainly from constituencies that would not be readily available to GTU and member schools.

The Institute for Buddhist Studies has already been mentioned as an affiliate seeking to become a school. The Patriarch Athenagoras Orthodox Institute, too small to become an accredited school in its own right, brings theological dimensions of immense importance and a common master's program. Crossing confessional lines and centering in specific academic subjects are the Center for Theology and the Natural Sciences and the Center for the Arts, Religion and Education, both of whom have national and international recognition.

In Jewish Studies, GTU faculty appointments were made with three criteria in mind, the first of which was competence in teaching at the doctoral level, the second was involvement in regular programs of the schools, and third, provision of programs that served the Jewish community. It was most successful in the first, which took on the form of joint programs with the university, and had the least success in relation to the Jewish community.

GTU has been mainly successful in adding religious traditions other than Protestant and Catholic when the respective bodies themselves provided the resources, such as in the Orthodox or Buddhist cases. It seems that faculty appointments in GTU are most successful when they strengthen areas of study, such as in areas of the sciences and the arts. An appointment in Islamic studies would be a significant addition but it would not address the religious dimensions that come with a group of scholars who themselves form a religious body. GTU at best consists of faith communities in common explorations with each other and the secular approaches of a university. It is obvious, I take it, that in this sense we are talking of the secular as contrasted with secularist or secularism.

In our consciousness about the broadening essential in relation to Islam, Buddhist, and Hindu groups, we need to be aware that these traditions, just as the Christian ones, are not monolithic. In early conversations with Hindu interests, proposals were sidetracked for they seemed too limited in representing Hinduism as a whole. In the GTU of today, various strands of Buddhism need to be taken into account. In the early days of GTU we used to say, with a bit of irony, that a by-product of the ecumenical aspects was introducing the Catholic bodies to each other. Such a strategy is necessary across the board.

In writing about institutional issues, I have given particular attention to GTU. Persons from the outside may well decide that this history is too complex and full of problems. On the contrary, I see it as a situation full of promising problems that are to be welcomed. It is not that current problems were there in the beginning and we should have seen them. When the rubrics of schools, affiliates, and academic program units were created, they made sense. But today orientations and existing categories may need to be modified. That is what institutions at their best can do.

One of the puzzling aspects about institutions is that creating a new reality is considered harder than modifying existing patterns. But my experience has been that working de novo is easier than making changes. For institutions to serve their missions, adaptations will need to be welcomed. In this sense, deans and presidents are not the custodians of the past, but the harbingers of change. To fulfill the dreams that created an institution, it may be necessary to institute changes that on the surface look as if they were the repudiation of the original dream. Yet, most of the time, changes are more prosaic, that is, when they are merely cumulative. Of course, there are two extremes, not changing enough or changing too much. It takes a discerning eye to combine stability and change. But that can also be the joy of administration.

13

A THEOLOGICAL PROFILE

"Science and theology meet, not in the understanding supplied by one or the other, but in the exercise of our imagination with respect to both."

Institutionally, my pilgrimage has been unusual in several respects. First, I have taught and /or been in administrative positions at nine institutions, which is more than is ordinarily the case. Second, I have worked in theological schools and university departments during most of my career and never felt pulled exclusively one way or another. In fact, they have reinforced each other. Third, the institutions I have served were mostly non-denominational. Drew and San Francisco Theological were under the jurisdiction of the Methodist and Presbyterian churches respectively, but at the time of my association were attracting other groups and encouraging wider horizons. This means that I have only minimally experienced the pulse of a denominational theology and ethos, so characteristic of theological schools as a whole.

What has bothered me most is the perceived gap between the theological world and individual parishes. While laypeople increasingly have major roles in church life, they are not brought sufficiently into the thinking modalities that are also at the basis of religious traditions. Experience and thought belong together. It seems as if the accent on the life of congregations is so anchored in experience that the wider aspects of wrestling with the understandings that theological knowledge and reflection bring are sidetracked.

For me personally, I have belonged to a church body that is open to all the wider sensibilities. In the tradition of the Evangelical and Reformed Church in which I grew up, theological exploration had a double characteristic; affirmation and exploration, faith and doubt. One lived with elements of certitude, permeated by critical scrutiny. Life and affirmations about life were equally vibrant. Theology was neither an abstraction, nor was it formless. Rather, it was always being formed.

In this respect that church stood in the reformation tradition, particularly formed by Luther and Calvin, who are in turn to be distinguished from Lutheranism and Calvinism. Luther and Calvin formed their thoughts out of living in the world of scripture, while the traditions that emerged from them formed theologies that became the key to the proper understanding of scripture. For example, Calvin wrote the *Institutes* as a helping hand in reading Scripture, but the orthodox Calvinist followers created systems of thought that organized thought as the one and true interpretation of Scripture. That was a major reversal, for the latter represented an orthodoxy whose claims were more rigid than those of the previous medieval world. While Luther and Calvin were different from each other, that difference was less than that between Luther and Lutheranism or between Calvin and Calvinism.

Starting in the eighteenth century, the reigning orthodox Protestantism was softened on the continent by pietism and in England by evangelical movements, the latter spawned by John Wesley. But intellectually and philosophically, orthodoxy was challenged by the Enlightenment, as personified in Immanuel Kant. Instead of a system of thought as the core of religion, Kant proclaimed two indubitable realities, the starry heavens above and the moral world within. In short, the Newtonian ordered world could be accepted. But so could the moral. For protestant liberalism, which was most ascendant in the late nineteenth through the early part of the twentieth century, Jesus was the personification of the moral. God, the created world, and the moral comprised a whole.

In revolt to that religious liberalism, the neo-orthodox movement accepted the methodological tenets of the Enlightenment, that is, a critical approach to tradition. But it affirmed a God whose life and relation to the world was marked by difference rather than continuity or direct affinity between the two. It was this latter outlook that marked my thoughts as I entered Union Theological Seminary and at some levels I have never left aspects of that tradition, particularly when I reflect on what might be called the God question. But beyond that, my initial and then graduate programs exposed me to philosophical questions, particularly the concept of being, so central to Heidegger and to Paul Tillich. In a nutshell, the question of being involves God as being or the power of being. So, it was natural that my doctoral dissertation was centered in the concept of *deus absconditus*, the hidden God, in Luther and in its subsequent interpretation.

The concept of God as hidden, and if revealed at all, still veiled or even particularly hidden was critical to my thinking. At the time, I was not deeply interested in the search for the historical Jesus, for the results of the quest for the historical Jesus seemed no more than a self-image, like looking into a well and seeing a reflection of one's self. At this point, Martin Kahler and Paul Tillich interested me, for the religion about Jesus was more interesting than the quest to understand the religion of Jesus. The Jesus Seminar has changed all that. We now see a picture of a person whose teachings are not platitudes but rather are transformative. Jesus' life and teachings coalesce in new paradigms, where instruction and mystery confront us, much as in the case of the God figure itself.

The notion of God as wholly other, so forcefully propounded by Karl Barth, or the idea of the holy as *sui generis* or the *mysterium tremendum* as formulated by Rudolf Otto, removed the God question from the problem of how to reconcile the world and God. Instead, it placed a mystery at the core of things, indeed a mystery so deep that it raised the question as to whether we could still talk of the existence of God in traditional terms. At best, the God concept was symbolic in nature, one in which the term "existence" was not appropriate.

When Claude Welch and I were writing the first edition of *Protestant Christianity*, I became increasingly interested in the intersection of theology with other disciplines, particularly astronomy and physics. Just as I had become interested in historical theology to understand Tillich's systematic theology, so I began addressing the history of theology and natural science in order to understand the contemporary currents of thought. Indeed, if there is a methodological motif in my work, it is that I study an issue historically in order to have a background that permits delineation of the current scene with its own options. For me writing is a discipline of sorting things out, as necessary for me as to speak in the classroom or in public. Early on writing was a way of addressing issues, as natural as speaking.

Returning to the cosmological aspect of science, I can remember as a boy lying on my back, watching the sky beyond the clouds, imagining worlds beyond worlds in an unending progression, while also imagining the opposite direction, the infinitely small with its expanding of worlds within worlds. What an illumination it was decades later to discover Pascal's ringing words: "What is man in nature? A mere nothing when compared with the infinite, all when compared with nothingness, a mean between all and nothing." Then when Pascal coordinated nature with human nature, it was for me as if a new theological agenda opened itself. He wrote "Our intellect holds the same position in the world of thought as does our body in the expanse of nature... We have an inability to prove, which cannot be surmounted by dogmatism. We have a notion of truth, which cannot be overcome by skepticism." Ethically speaking, "Man is neither angel nor brute and the unfortunate thing is that he who would act the angel acts the brute." (*Pensees* 390, 287, 275)

These passages illumine the nature of humanity. The human is a midpoint, a focusing that is an exercise in imagination, a work in process. Theology then is focused in anthropology, that is, theology is rigorously related to how we see ourselves and our actions. We have been thrown into being and becoming. Why there is something and not nothing is beyond our ken of comprehension.

What we know and what we do not know mingle in our very beings and, whatever the discipline by which we examine our world, we cannot escape that bipolar reality. In this sense, science and theology meet, not in the understanding supplied by one or the other, but in the exercise of our imagination with respect to both. Both the notion of conflict, even warfare as it has been called, and confluences in which positive relationships are spelled out, wrest and risk identifications that are not appropriate to either or both modalities. We no longer have the grip of certainty. This means that theism is no longer relevant, for theology as we knew it has come to an end, a suggestion I first made in *Contours of Faith* in 1969, though at the time I did not deal rigorously with what that implied.

The consequence is that our central concern is with the humanity that has emerged in the expanses of material nature, perhaps currently the only emergent species that can reflect on itself. Modern science tells us that we emerged over vast stretches of time, that the combinations that produced us are both legion and very concrete. So one can try, if one is so disposed, as the neo-Creationists are, to reconstitute the old argument from design, that the complexity and concrete circumstances that lie behind the emergence of life suggest the work of a designer. It is a circumstance in which the wish gives way to the thought. Rather, I think we stand again before a mystery and it is better not to extrapolate from what we think we know today and what may be different tomorrow.

While much of the theological enterprise is no longer directly relevant for us, we must still read the older thought, for hidden within it are perceptions that are relevant to our lives. There was considerable diversity of thought among the early church fathers, in the emergence of medieval theology, in the forces that forged renaissance and reformations. It was the late seventeenth century that codified and affirmed truth in propositional form, and the earlier period should not be read as if it were the seventeenth century. For example, in orthodox theology original sin was described in terms of our need to be reconciled to God in judicial form; so humans were involved in a series of transactions that brought them back to God. But insofar as sin is a category that describes our lack of mutual regard for each other, indeed our abuse of each other, whether personal or community based, the term may be anachronistic but the reality is not. We wrestle not just with flesh and blood but with principalities and powers, where good and evil seem intertwined, where doing good is not simple, for the alternatives are not that clear.

The older theology spoke of our need to be forgiven before God. More importantly, we have a hard time living without being forgiven or forgiving in relation to others. For Luther, if one cannot be forgiven and in turn forgive, the gospel is not good news but bad news, and the freedom to live and love is subverted. The choices are seldom between totally good and bad alternatives, but in a mixture. At best our decisions are relatively just, neither black nor white, through alternatives that require the best of us. Theologies born out of repression fight the good fight, but they tend to forget their own need for forgiveness.

In the last four decades, theological positions have emerged that are uninterested in the wider theological ranges. The first of these, the death of God theologies saw no way of affirming that God was an active agent in the dynamics of the world, whether for good or evil. For them, we now live in a post-Christian time, one in which the past no longer illumines the present.

A series of theologies emerged in which God and the needs of an age are commingled, ranging from metaphysical to social cultural groups that see their own spiritual and material needs intertwined. Within the first group is process theology, built on the ideas of the philosopher Alfred North Whitehead, which sees religion unfolding and identifies God as the concrete pivot, the agent through which the concrete emerges. Then there are theologies that are based on existential foundations, such as the New Hermeneutic, anchored in the transformations of the thought of Rudolf Bultmann. Central to its way of thinking is that faith is a speech event, one in which we are captured in the proclamation of the Word of God.

Characteristic of the abandonment of overriding theologies are movements in which the theological and social elements are combined, and that share in hopes of liberation. The first was black theology, which in turn was followed by feminist theology and theologies of liberation. In all three, the urgency and intensity of social issues are transfigured through the use of theological terms.

Riding a wave of ascendancy are the various forms of spirituality, which I would call an interest in sanctification, disclosing the effects and characteristics of faith in processes and disciplines of living. The accent falls, not on that faith makes a difference, but on the difference that faith makes. Spirituality is living in a state of being, lived out by disciplines and practices. I myself have used the category of perceptions of the spirit, though not as a state of existence but rather as representative of various forms of active imagination.

All of these groups assume the reality of God, though a doctrine of God is seldom developed. Occasionally, God is featured through a series of attributes that are projections of the human writ large. The issue is mainly sidetracked. My problem is not the existence or nonexistence of God. It is rather that the mystery of the universe and of life is so great in comparison to the theories of God that I find the God question too limiting. Gordon Kaufman has suggested that the God concept can be seen as serendipitous creativity, a concept rich in focusing on the unexpected turns life takes as one thinks of God, but limited in his case by restricting the serendipitous to creativity. Creativity, which is so absent in most thinking, in and of itself assumes too positive a picture of reality. Creativity embodies the uncertain, including demonic ingredients.

I am neither for nor against the God concept. If there is a God, that reality is greater than we know or can imagine. Our attention must be directed to the wide dimensions and possibilities we see buried in a world that is all too inhumane as it struggles for humanity. It is as if the riches of humanity do not come to be without diverting elements. That is one of the mysteries for which there is no convincing answer.

It was in that broader sense of what humanity is about that I entered the world of art. Through it, I learned that the other sensibilities, particularly seeing, were part of our humanity, however central speech had become. Seeing is a sensibility that tells us much about ourselves and our world in a way analogous to but not identical to the verbal. It fleshes out the range of our humanity, and, in order to do so, demands training and discipline, as do all the sensibilities we have. Without that we neglect too much of what comprises our humanity. However central the verbal may be, it does not stand by itself.

Many of the artists working from the forties to the end of the twentieth century frequently dealt with religious themes, taken from religious traditions. But the object was not the delineation of the religious subject matter as such, but the way in which such themes affirmed our humanity, both its grandeur and penchant for evil.

Such imagination transforms how we see things, that is, how we read in order to see. Surely it is not arbitrary that we can refer to the verbal as seeing. But the implications need to be taken seriously. Here I return again to Luther. His accent on hearing the text in proclamation is moving from the literal to the imaginative. Indeed, that is why he could be open to the visual arts. Imagination is the key to reading and seeing, and one might add, smelling and touching. However, imagination, articulated in allegorical terms, may have stretched texts to the point that it subverted them. But for Luther returning to the literal text was not a literal reading. Indeed, a literal reading was a misreading. That should be remembered as Protestants in particular read literature or understand movies in illustrative rather than imaginative ways. They forget that literature, while verbal, is not the same as declarative sentences, that instead something is communicated that is unique in its own way. It has troubled me to see some colleagues refer to Flannery O'Connor's writings, to Bergman's movies or to *Babette's Feast*, to name but a few, as literal analogues to biblical texts, leading to a misunderstanding of Scripture and literature.

Mystery and imagination belong together, providing insight with limits. I have said much about mystery. It is not to be worshipped; but it is to be acknowledged and respected. The boundary between essential mystery and mystery that exists only because we do not yet know is ever shifting. Drawing on the resources of various religious traditions and the secular disciplines, we find ourselves involved in the endless thinking and doing that comprises life on this planet. Just as humanity has come to be, so it may also come to end, through entropy or our own destructive propensities. We have no way of knowing whether there is life after death; so we also give thanks for death, our beginning and end being shrouded in mystery.

One consequence for our thinking is that this is not the time for overarching expanding theologies. In itself, the theological agenda will be more focused and limited, but more related to the wider dimensions of existence that make up our world, including both the arts and the sciences. We must learn from all of them, both the positive and the negative. We will move more from the many avenues of knowledge before us in order to understand humanity than from a single preordained view which orders or focuses the rest of what we know.

We must abandon the attempts to write "theologies of," that is, attempts to bring other disciplines under the sway of theology. More productive is to step into various disciplines and religious traditions, seeing what they bring to our understanding of humanity, to the making of life that is fruitful for the inhabited world. Rather than theologies of, we must write as if so-and-so were the case, and what would the consequences be.

It is surely obvious that the distinction between the secular and the religious, once so prominent, is hardly instructive for our time. The secular city has become the religious city. Today, the religious and secular are more intertwined than distinguished. Most of the conservative theologies are secular in their political agendas, while many of the secular claims are like a religion in their unbending assertions. We live in a religious age, where the bizarre and the profound instruct and confound us. Finding our way is an endless endeavor. It is much like the early church, where religions vied with each other while trying to live together. It, like ours, was a time when total dominance of a group was not possible. It took a long time for the church to become the dominant agency for religious and social life.

The future shape of religious institutions is hard to visualize. Services of worship may be less central inasmuch as accent on the direct transactions between God and humans is abating. More emphasis will be on the human services that religions provide, services that define our evolving relation to each other. Religious forms will be multiple, with variety and diversity taking the place of uniformity. In this they will reflect the societies in which we live. What is already true of the Bay Area — that there is no ethnic or religious majority, — will, in this decade, become characteristic of California as a whole.

Religiously, the world is a polyglot and even the dominant religions are more than we can comprehend or manage to deal with easily. Two extremes are tempting but not viable. A common denominator of convictions shared does not serve the diverse religious bodies in terms of how they see the whole. But emphasis on the uniqueness of each body does not adequately address what we must also become, a neighbor to one another. We must become neighbors in conversation and dialogue, appreciating the difference and challenging where a credo does not serve the neighbor, within and without each body. We are being given a new chance, though we need to face that so much of the conflict in the world stems from religious bodies. But then, so much that defines us as humane also comes from religious perceptions. Hence we must choose, within the confines of all religious traditions, that which enhances the possibilities for all of us, and reject that which pushes its own agenda at the expense of others.

14

A VISUAL PROFILE

"John, your eyes are the key to the expressiveness of your face.
The right one is the observing one, that takes in everything
around you. The left eye is active, and participates in what
is going on, even forms it at critical junctures."
— Reindert Falkenburg on the bust of John Dillenberger

While it was said that I flunked my first retirement in 1983, actual retirement, defined as my being free of delegated responsibilities, began to emerge in the summer of 2000.

First, we participated in the wedding ceremony and the attendant events of Jean's daughter Tsan. While she has positive memories of her deceased father, I soon noted, to my delight, that she was also referring to me as her father A graduate of Dartmouth, her first career was in the culinary arts, establishing a kosher restaurant for Alan Dershowitz et al in Cambridge, Ma., and then heading the culinary program at UCLA. After taking degrees in business administration and law, she specialized in intellectual property law. Her husband, Daniel Abrahamson, also an attorney, currently is the legal director for the Drug Policy Alliance, a section of the Soros Foundation dealing with drug law and policy. To our delight, they live, with their young son, Moses, just five minutes away. In addition we have become close friends of Dan's parents, Seymour and Shirley. We are glad too that our grandson Benjamin also lives in San Francisco, that our grand daughter Kate and great grand daughter Grace are a few hours away, that only Timothy and Michael are respectively in Minneapolis and New York City. Jean's step son, Lee Kresy, lives at Lake Tahoe.

After the wedding, Jean and I went off to Europe, just to enjoy familiar places we had come to love and not seen for some time. For the first five weeks we stayed in a London flat, secured for us by our friend, Tom Devonshire Jones. We spent our time in and out of London, with art and reading (mostly Ken Follett) our main preoccupations. Then we flew to Paris, where we joined our friends, Yodie and Marvin Adelson, for a month in Spain. We went by car, wanting to see the countryside as well as selected art and architectural places in major cities, and to do so at our own pace, though that pace was determined on occasion by the availability of hotels. Wherever possible we stayed in paradors, originally government-sponsored low budget accommodations, now upscale establishments.

Who could not be impressed and moved by Frank Gehry's museum in Bilbao; the pilgrim paths and cathedral in Santiago de Compostela; the Prado, the Thyssen Bornemisza collection, and Picasso's Guernica in Madrid; Toledo, a city that is a museum in and of itself; the remnants of Moorish and Jewish art and architecture in Cordoba and Granada, where one still encounters the destructive ethos of the Catholic Medieval Inquisition; the ancient and contemporary side by side in the thriving, expansive Barcelona, with its Gaudi cathedral and park.

After a leisurely return to Paris we left the Adelson's at the airport. A day later, having leased a seven-seat van, we picked up my two sons, Eric and Paul, and their spouses Tess and Suzanne, at the same airport. With baggage and six persons we had a snug fit and headed toward Germany, to places Eric and Paul had known over four decades before. We drove along the Mosel River Valley, with its endless grape orchards up and down the cliffs, driving toward its confluence with the Rhine. But some fifteen miles short of that juncture, we went diagonally over the hills toward St. Goarshausen, a little village on the Rhine just north of the Lorelei and about three miles from Nochern, the ancestral town from which my great-grandfather emigrated. While we visited little towns from which Dillenbergers had settled nearby Nochern and saw the many cemetery graves with Dillenberger names, our destination was the precise family house in Nochern and its inhabitants that I had visited frequently over the years. Adolf, about my age with a common great-great-grandfather, and his wife, and son-in-law greeted us with delight and immediately opened bottles of wine from their vineyard. Adolf remembered Eric and Paul as young boys, as well as my previous wives, and of course he welcomed Jean, whom he had now known for ten years. It was then, on their third day in Germany after all the intervening years, that I noticed that Eric and Paul were entering into the conversation in German, apparently not overly conscious that this was happening. As they translated for Jean, Tess and Suzanne, my translating task was short lived. So too was my and Jean's driving, since Eric and Paul loved driving in Europe.

We visited Dillenburg on a Monday when the castle and most of the cultural entities were closed. But we had a wonderful time walking the streets of the city center. All we knew was that this was the city our ancestors had left in the sixteenth century for the Rhineland area.

Next came Heidelberg, the city in which Eric, Paul, Hilde, and I had lived for fifteen months. We walked around the house, peeping at it from various angles not having the courage to ring the doorbell after forty years. The boys remembered the wonderful view of the castle and the center of the old city, with the same shops on many corners, and the cathedral, on whose walls was the same newsstand at which we used to purchase the *Herald Tribune*. Then, there was the university and the library in particular, just a block away from which was Paul's school, looking much as it had decades before. Eric's school building, located in what is known as Little America, was extant but now used for other purposes. Needless to say, we did a lot of walking in the old city.

Then on to Frutigen, a Swiss village some twenty miles southwest of Interlaken and the place from which one enters the higher mountain elevations. We had spent about ten days in a pensione in Frutigen during the Heidelberg year, and Eric and Paul recalled the walks in the mountain hillsides. We found the creek that flowed past the pensione, but no sign of the latter. But we found a hotel with an annex of three apartments and stayed for several days, exploring the town and the countryside for miles around. One excursion took us over the mountains to the Rhone, only to discover that the glacier could not be reached for the road was closed due to unexpected snow fall. The second was for Eric and Paul to go to the top of the Eiger, but there was blinding snow, restricting the views on which they had counted. But we spent a half day in Interlaken, a paradise for shopping and eating. Then to Freiburg and the surrounding hills that Suzanne had called to our attention; then to Paris where Paul and Suzanne caught a flight back to the States, while Eric and Tess still had a week with us.

Our next stop was Weimar, where cultural and political facets are intertwined and ever present. I had been there several times to see the extensive number of Cranach paintings in the castle museum and one of the major Cranach altarpieces in the Herder church. Already in his college days, Eric had become interested in the Bauhaus tradition. So the Bauhaus museum in Weimar was of special interest to him, as were the Bauhaus educational buildings in Dessau and the Klee and Kandinsky attached houses that had just been opened to the public after extensive renovation. Two wonderful, large photos of the Klee/Kandinsky interior, taken by Eric, now grace our dining room. Then we went to Wittenberg, covering the Reformation monuments: the castle church, site of the alleged posting of the *Ninety-Five Theses*; the city church, site of another Cranach altarpiece; Luther's house with a special museum; the Melanchthon house;

and the building in which Cranach lived. Wittenberg, on the flat land next to the Elbe, was considered a backwater town in the time of the reformation, and for all practical purposes, that can be said of the expanded town even today.

Next we headed for Dresden, where the Elbe is the geographical setting for the city. Dresden, like Weimar, is a monument just as a city, with its range of museums and concert facilities. It is also a city that was probably the target of saturation bombing in World War II at a time when it was probably no longer necessary to do the bombing. At an international conference a decade before this visit, I had been asked to give a lecture that was open for attendees from the city, and felt that I could not do so without referring to that event. So I sought the help of a German friend, Marburg professor Horst Schwebel, to make sure that my German sentences conveyed the nuances that I intended. In the city itself, there were differences as to whether the destroyed Frauenkirche should be rebuilt in its original style, the church authorities having said no, but the city authorities overruling the church. Today, the church is reemerging stone by stone from the rubble.

We had a wonderful trip, but I arrived back exhausted, only to discover a major vitamin B-12 deficiency, followed by some minor balance problems. In the meantime, Jean had developed back and walking problems involving pain in her legs A surgeon announced with confidence that back surgery would cure her leg pains, and that the back pains should be manageable. But the result of surgery was extensive nerve damage so that she has a dropped foot, limiting how far she can walk at one stretch. Soon thereafter I was told that I had symptoms of early Parkinson disease. Both of us have been busy in various physical therapy sessions, designed to minimize our loss of the natural functions we took for granted. We are making progress and have learned to avoid activities that create stress for us.

Two years ago, Reindert Falkenburg and his family arrived in the Bay Area from the Netherlands. Reindert had taken the position of professor of art history at GTU. Since they initially lived only half a mile away, we became friends in the enterprise of facilitating their entering into life here. So we have kept in close contact with all of them, Reindert, his wife Johanna Klein, and their three children.

I had noted that Johanna was a sculptor, with various objects of her work placed in their house. But about a year after their arrival I saw that she had done a ceramic portrait of her husband and of a university friend. It seemed that portraiture was her real métier. One evening at dinner, I noted particularly that she was visually focused on me as we were having a lively conversation around the table on various subjects. That was followed by her saying "I have been wanting to ask you, "Would you be willing to sit for me for a portrait head?" Without hesitation I responded affirmatively, being somewhat surprised by my rapid yes. But a reason lay behind it. In my art interests, I had heard and read about the special relation between artist and model, and I was ready to experience it firsthand.

A few days later began a series of three two-hour meetings, with my wife sitting in the corner observing the two of us while we ignored her. The first session was Johanna photographing my head from every conceivable angle, doing precise measurements, and intensely observing my face. A few weeks later, she asked me to come back to her studio garage. There was a clay bust. And I variously stood and sat beside the work, while Johanna looked at me intensely, moving and switching positions like a ballerina, while simultaneously using her hands and fingers to reshape parts of the bust. This happened again for a third session. All I can say is that the eye contact was intense, nothing special was said, but I felt that I was being exposed for whatever I was, and that at some levels Johanna knew me like no one else. I was pleased by the result, but how was I to know, though my wife Jean said it was very much "me." Johanna said she would give me a ceramic version, a very generous gesture. Then entered Doug Adams, who happened to visit her studio. His instinctive reaction was, "You have captured John. This is who he is." He immediately decided there should be a bronze version, which is now owned by the Center for Arts, Religion and Education. A second version is in our possession and Johanna has the ceramic one.

The Center (CARE) had a party for the unveiling, at which Johanna spoke and I responded. But Reindert probably said what Johanna the artist would not have said so directly. "John, your eyes are the key to the expressiveness of your face. The right one is the observing one, that takes in everything around you. The left eye is active, and participates in what is going on, even forms it at critical junctures." Johanna nodded; and I realized that was how I experience myself.

Jean and John on holiday in Santa Fe, New Mexico

Vita

1918, July 11, born in St. Louis, Missouri

1924–1932, Canniff Grade School, Fults, Illinois

1932–1936, Waterloo High School, Waterloo, Illinois

1936–1940, Elmhurst College, Elmhurst, Illinois, B.A.degree

1940–1943, Union Theological Seminary, New York City, B.D degree

1942, Married Hilde Lohans

1942, (May)–1946 (February), Navy Chaplain

1946 (February)–1948 (February), Student in Ph.D. program, Columbia
University and Union Theological Seminary.

1948 (Fall), Ph.D from Columbia University

1948 (February)–1949 (July 1), Instructor, Dept. of Religion, Princeton University

1949 –1954, Columbia University
Assistant Professor of Religion, 1949–1952
Associate Professor of Religion, 1952–1954
Chair, M.A. program in Religion, 1951–1954
Assistant Chair, Ph.D. Program in Religion, Graduate Faculties, 1951–1954

1954–1958, Harvard University
Associate professor of Theology, Divinity School, 1954–1957
Chair, Program in the History and Philosophy of Religion, Faculty of Arts
and Sciences, 1954–1958
Parkman Professor of Divinity, 1957–1958

1958–1962, Ellen S. James Professor of Systematic and Historical Theology,
Drew University

1962, Married Jane Daggett Karlin

1962–1964 San Francisco Theological Seminary
Dean of Faculty
Dean of Graduate Students
Professor of Historical Theology

1963–1978, Graduate Theological Union, Berkeley, California
Assistant Dean, January 1963–July 1963
Dean (chief officer until creation of office of President), 1963–1969
President, 1967–1971 (December)
Professor of Historical Theology, 1963–1978

1978 (January)–1983, Hartford Seminary President

1983 to present, Professor Emeritus, Graduate Theological Union

1992, Married Jean Poree Merritt Kresy

1997–1999, Acting Librarian, Graduate Theological Union

1999–2000, Sixth President, Graduate Theological Union

PUBLICATIONS

1938

"Britain in Palestine." *Elmhurst College Forum* 2, no. 1: 9–10.

"Which Way Christianity?" *Elmhurst College Forum* 1, no. 4: 9–11.

1939

"Majorities, Minorities and Christianity." *Elmhurst College Forum* 2, no. 4: 16–18.

1941

"Food and Freedom." *Union Review* 2, no. 2 (March): 5–6

"From a Persecuted Church," with Cedric Haggard. *Union Review* 2, no. 2 (March): 16–17, 26.

"Introduction to Vol. III." *Union Review* 3, no. 1 (December): 1.

"Barth's Letter in America." *Union Review* 3, no. 1 (December): 1–2.

1942

"From Vol. I to Vol. IV." *Union Review* 4, no.1 (December): 1–2.

1943

"Justification and Sanctification." *Union Review* 4, no. 3 (May): 15f.

1944

"I Go to War as a Christian." *The Messenger Official Journal of the Evangelical Reformed Church* (May 16): 17–23.

1945

"The Church and Society." *Christianity and Society* (winter): 26–32.

1946

"Reflections of a Protestant Chaplain." *Union Seminary Quarterly Review* 1, no. 4 (May): 14–17.

1949

"Christianity, Science and Truth." *Perspective: A Princeton Journal of Christian Opinion* 1, no. 2 (May).

1951

"Introduction to Tillich's Theology." *Drew Gateway* 22, no. 1 (autumn): 17–23.

1952

"God the Creator." *Counsel* (October): 1f.

1953

"Tillich's Use of the Concept 'Being.'" *Christianity and Crisis* 23, no. 4, (March 16): 30–31.

God Hidden and Revealed: The interpretation of Luther's deus absconditus and its significance for religious thought. Philadelphia : Muhlenberg Press.

1954

Protestant Christianity interpreted through its development (with Claude Welch). New York: Scribner.

"Christianity not the only option." Part 2 of symposium entitled "Can and should a college be Christian?" *The Christian Scholar* 37, no.1 (March): 19–22.
"History and the Kingdom of God." *Counsel* (January/March): 12f.
"Teaching Religion: Problems and Requirements." *Union Seminary Quarterly Review* 9, no. 3: 9–15.

1956
"Literature in Luther Studies (1950–1959)." *Church History* 25: 160–77.

1958
"Faith." In *A Handbook of Christian Theology.* New York: Meridian Books. Revised and enlarged in *A New Handbook of Christian Theology.* New York: Meridian Books.
"The Holy Spirit Outside the Church." *Bulletin of the Hartford Seminary Foundation* 24 (June): 15–23.

1959
"Nature versus Biblical Literalism." *Christian Century* (May 20): 609–11.
"Man and the World." *Christian Century* (June 3): 667–69.
"Science and Theology Today." *Christian Century* (June 17): 722–25.

1960
"Apologetik" and "Wissenschaft und Religion" in *Weltkirchen Lexikon.* Kreuz-Verlag.
Protestant Thought and Natural Science: A Historical Interpretation. Garden City, NY: Doubleday. Reprinted by Notre Dame: University of Notre Dame Press, 1980.
"The Reformation and its Transformation: A Spectrum of Systematic and Historical Problems." *Drew Gateway* 30, no. 2: 72–87.

1961
"Major Volumes and Selected Periodical Literature in Luther Studies for 1956–59." *Church History* 30, no. 1: 61–87.
"Protestantism in the United States: Its temper and main tendencies." Offprint from *Studium Generale* 14, no. 2.

1962
Martin Luther: Selections from his Writings. Edited with an introduction. Garden City, NY: Doubleday.

1963
"Revelational Discernment and the Problem of the Two Testaments." Pp. 159–73 in *The Old Testament and Christian Faith.* New York: Harper.
"Notes from a Theological Perspective." *Social Action* (November): 22–23.
"Theological-Cultural Factors Demanding Union of the Churches." *Mid-Stream* 2, no. 4: 8–68.

1964
"On Broadening the New Hermeneutic." Pp. 147–63 in *New Frontiers in Theology 2: The New Hermeneutic,* New York: Harper. Translation: Zur Ausweitung der neuen Hermeneutic, in *Neuland in der Theologie.* Zwingli Verlag, 1965.
"The Catholic Protestant Opening." *Season: A Quarterly on contemporary human problems* 2 , no. 4 (winter): 200–206.

1965
"GTU Aspirations as set forth by head of School." *Pacific Churchman* (January).

"The Graduate Theological Union in the San Francisco Bay Area." *The Journal of Bible and Religion* 33, no. 1 (January): 49–52.

"Theology in Conflict." Pp. 115–24 in *D-Days at Dayton*. Edited by Jerry Tompkins. Louisiana State Press.

1966

"Paul Tillich: Theologian of Culture." Pp. 31–41 in *Paul Tillich: Retrospect and Future*. Nashville: Abingdon Press.

"Judaism and Protestantism: Some Patterns of Understanding." Harvard Colloquium paper at Syracuse University Library Special Collections.

"What is Christian Art?" (with Jane Dillenberger). *Christianity Century* (April 20): 497–99.

1967

"Miracles in the Bible and Christianity." *Encyclopedia Britannica, Inc.*

"Theological Givens as Theological Orientations." *Mid-Stream* 6 , no. 4:42–52.

"Religious Stimulants and Constraints in the Development of Science." *Continuum* 5, no. 1: 6–11.

1969

Contours of Faith: Changing Forms of Christian Thought. Nashville: Abingdon Press.

"The Graduate Theological Union Seven Years Later." *Nexus* 12, no. 3 (spring): 21f.

"The Integration of Theological Faculties." *Concilium: Theology in the Age of Renewal* 44: 54–63.

"Traditional Library Functions and the Economic Factor." *Theological Education* 6, no. 1: 70–78.

1971

John Calvin: Selections from his writings, Edited with an introduction. Garden City, NY: Anchor Books. Currently Oxford University Press.

1972

"Picasso's Crucifixion Iconography." Pp. 160–84 in *Humanities, Religion and the Arts Tomorrow*. Edited by Howard Hunter. New York: Holt, Rinehart and Winston.

1977

Benjamin West: The Context of his life's work, with particular attention to paintings with religious subject matter. San Antonio: Trinity University Press.

Perceptions of the Spirit in Twentieth-century American Art (with Jane Dillenberger). Indianapolis: Indianapolis Museum of Art.

"The Seductive Power of the Visual Arts: Shall the Response be Iconoclasm or Baptism?" *Andover Newton Quarterly* 17, no. 4 (March): 303–7.

1978

"Faith and Sensibility." *Journal of Current Social Issue* (fall): 62–68.

"Grace and Works in Martin Luther and Joseph Smith." *Sunstone* 3, no. 4: 18f.

"Perceptions of the Spirit in 20th Century American Art." *American Art Review* (May): 62f.

"The Visual Arts in Worship." *Modern Liturgy* 5, no. 8 (1978): 34f.

1979

"Artists and Church Commissions: Rubin's 'The Church at Assy Revisited.'" *Art*

Criticism 1, no. 1 (spring): 72–82. Reprinted in *Art, Creativity and the Sacred*, ed.
Diane Apostolos-Cappadona. New York: Crossroad (1984), 193f.

1980

"Address, delivered at Creatio et Spiritus Award honoring Barnett Newman, St.
Peter's Church (February 15). Syracuse University Library Special Collections.
"Art and Architecture in the Religious Community." *Faith and Form* (fall): 30–34.
"The Diversity of Disciplines as a Theological Question: The Visual Arts as
Paradigm." *Journal of the American Academy of Religion* 48, no. 2: 233–43
"The Soverignty of God in John Calvin and Brigham Young." *Sunstone* 5, no. 5:
31f.
"Unraveling the Library Mystique." *Theological Education* 17, no 1 (autumn):
74–78.

1983

"Theology and Abstract Expressionism: Historical Notes and Test Cases."*Religion
and Intellectual life* 1, no. 1: 54f .

1984

"The Landmarking of Religious Institutions: A plea for vision with wider con-
texts." *Faith and Form* (Fall): 13–20.
The Visual Arts and Christianity: The Colonial Period through the Nineteenth Century.
Chico, CA: Scholars Press.

1985

"Contemporary Theologians and the Visual Arts." *Journal of the American Academy
of Religion* 53, no. 3: 599–615.

1986

A Theology of Artistic Sensibilities: The Visual Arts and the Church. New York:
Crossroad.
Reprinted in 2004 by Wipf & Stock Publishers, Eugene Oregon.

1987

On Art and Architecture by Paul Tillich. Edited and with an introduction by John
Dillenberger in collaboration with Jane Dillenberger. New York: Crossroad.

1988

Protestant Christianity: Interpreted through its Development (with Claude Welch). Second
edition revised and enlarged. Macmillan.
"The Society for the Arts, Religion and Contemporary Culture." *ARTS* 1, no. 1:
11.
The Visual Arts and Christianity in America from the Colonial Period to the Present.
Expanded edition. New York: Crossroad. Reprinted in 2004 by Wipf & Stock
Publishers, Eugene Oregon.
"To Clean or not to Clean: The Sistine Ceiling Restoration," (with Jane
Dillenberger). *Bible Review* 4, no. 4: 12–19.
"Visual Arts and Religion: Modern and Contemporary Contours." *Journal of the
American Academy of Religion* 56, no. 2: 199–212.

1990

"The Grandeur of Humanity: The Lure of Ideal Form in Classical Greece, the
Renaissance, and Abstraction." Pp. 178–82 in *Morphologies of Faith. Essays in*

Religion and Culture in Honor of Nathan A. Scott, Jr. Edited by Mary Gerhart and Anthony C. Yu. Atlanta, GA: Scholars Press.

"Barth, Tillich and Abstract Expressionism." *New Observations* 13: 14–15.

1991

"Visions for the Future: An Interview with Jane and John Dillenberger," by Doug Adams. *ARTS* 3, no. 3 (summer), 14–18

"Educating the Eye in Theological Education: An Interview with Jane and John Dillenberger," by Doug Adams. *ARTS* 4, no. 1 (fall): 11–17.

1992

"Theological Education and the Visual Arts: The situation and strategies for change." *ARTS* 5, no. 1 (fall): 3–6.

1993

"Paul Tillich: A Personal Perspective." *North American Paul Tillich Society Newsletter* 19, no. 1: 3–7.

1994

"A Review of Sacred Imagination: the Arts and Theological Education." *ARTS* 7, no. 1: 15–18.

1996

"Response to address by Hans Schwarz on 'The Americanization of Paul Tillich.'" *North American Paul Tillich Society Newsletter* 22, no. 4 (October): 3–5.

1997

"Paul Tillich (1886–1965) ." Pp. 420–26 in *Makers of Christian Theology in America*. Nashville: Abingdon Press.

1998

"Richard Meier's Church of the Year 2000." *Faith and Form* 31, no.2: 7f .

1999

Images and Relics: Theological Perceptions and Visual Images in Sixteenth-century Europe. New York: Oxford University Press.

2001

"Paul Tillich, The Union Years: Always in Transition." Pp. 173–81 in *Spurensuche Lebens-und Denkwege Paul Tillichs*. Band 5, Tillich-Studien. Münster: LIT Verlag.

Index